The Novels of
MULK RAJ ANAND

A Study of His Hero

Neena Arora

ATLANTIC®
PUBLISHERS & DISTRIBUTORS

Published by

ATLANTIC®

PUBLISHERS & DISTRIBUTORS

B-2, Vishal Enclave, Opp. Rajouri Garden,
New Delhi-110027
Phones : 25413460, 25429987, 25466842

Sales Office
7/22, Ansari Road, Darya Ganj,
New Delhi-110002
Phones : 23273880, 23275880, 23280451
Fax : 91-11-23285873
web : www.atlanticbooks.com
e-mail : info@atlanticbooks.com

ISBN 81-269-0458-5

Printed in India
at Nice Printing Press, Delhi

Dedicated To

Mr R.K. Arora

Eesha and Abhishek

ACKNOWLEDGEMENTS

I take pleasure in acknowledging my debt to all those who have helped me in my study. I am deeply beholden to Dr Tajindar Singh whose constant guidance, encouragement and affection enabled me to complete the present work. Words fail me to express my gratefulness adequately for his patient discussions and valuable counsel. His special support is implicit in every page of the book. I am grateful to Dr Mulk Raj Anand himself whose prompt response to my letters provided a number of clues to his fictional creed. I wish to express my thanks to Balarama Gupta, M.K. Naik and Hilda Sales Pontes who not only made available to me a lot of material on the works of Anand but also helped through valuable suggestions. I feel obliged to Late Shri Harindra Singh for his assistance. I record my sense of profound gratitude to my dear friends who readily extended their co-operation whenever there was a difficulty. Further, my thanks are due to the members of the library staff of G.N.D. University Regional Centre, Jalandhar; Punjab University, Chandigarh; Kurukshetra University, Kurukshetra; Dyal Singh College, Karnal; D.A.V. College, Jalandhar; Central Institute of English and Foreign Languages, Hyderabad and American Studies Research Centre, Hyderabad. I must express my thanks to Atlantic Publishers and

Distributors for their willingness to publish the book. I owe special obligation to my parents and my family, particularly Rakesh Arora, my husband, but for whose co-operation the work would have remained an unrealized dream.

Neena Arora

PREFACE

Anand's *Weltanschauung*—his humanistic philosophy—shapes his fiction. He terms his philosophy as "poetic realism," "comprehensive historical humanism," and "existential expressionism." All these terms, however, underline the fact that Anand's art, contrary to that of pure aesthetes, is in close relationship with life. He repeatedly confesses that art emerges out of the variegated experiences of the artist himself; and, because the artist is himself an everyman, a piece of art communicates the actions, reactions, thoughts, feelings, desires, hopes, despair and frustrations of a common man. Not only does a writing project the life of man in all its essential aspects, it tries to alleviate the suffering of mankind through an exposure of the negative aspects.

The present study presents a confrontation and interaction between Anand's métier as an artist and the compelling demands of his humanistic creed. Not that humanism is, in any way, contrary to art. It will not be far from truth to assert that all art is, at bottom, humanistic even though not expressly "a criticism of life." The greatness of an artist lies in synthesizing art and reality. When he handles reality imaginatively and presents it artistically, the result is great aesthetic delight both for the reader and the artist. But it is when humanism obsesses the mind of the artist so strongly that he is ready to make art subservient to his philosophy, that the artist's failure starts. The present study discusses the oscillation of Anand between his integrity as an artist and his enthusiasm as a reformist.

However, the greatness of Anand lies in his bold stride both in the choice and treatment of themes. He fearlessly chooses his protagonists from the "dregs of humanity" and tries to identify them with the so-called high-caste and high-class people. Anand's delineation and use of the sufferer and saviour characters is all his own, and, to me, it seems to be a very important feature of his fictional output, right from *Untouchable*. The present study proposes to analyse this essential component of Anand's fictional art and use it as a litmus test for evaluating the overall relative aesthetic merit of his various novels.

Neena Arora

CONTENTS

1
INTRODUCTION

Pace Aristotle, character in drama and fiction is now regarded as of primary significance as compared to plot and other elements. In recent criticism of the novel there has been a perceptible shift in favour of recognition of the importance of character *vis-a-vis* the other elements which make up a novel. The New Critics tended to pooh-pooh character, especially in isolation from the totality of a fictional work. These followers of the autonomy theory of criticism concentrated on the creative process and the created artefact. But after the wide following of "art for the sake of art" dictum for a period of time, recent critics such as W.J. Harvey, Wayne C. Booth, Iris Murdoch and Ortega have tried to correct the critical perspective by giving character its due. These modern fictional theorists are highly critical of "the retreat from the character"[1] as practised by the New Critics. Harvey, with his preference for mimetic theory, condemns, like Iris Murdoch, the dry novel which is "the hard, jewel-like object, immune from the viscous flux of existence"[2] and makes a plea for a novel "which dares to remain open to life, which dares to say, 'This is the world.'"[3] It is in such a novel that true to life, live, or memorable characters are found. Iris Murdoch, herself a practising novelist, finds characters to be more significant than form, style, or technique. She makes a statement which may be called daring: "When we think of the works of Tolstoy and George Eliot, we are not remembering Tolstoy and George Eliot, we are remembering Dolly, Kitty, Stira, Dorothea and Casaubon."[4] Although Iris Murdoch's statement cannot be approved of unconditionally, her emphasis on the importance of characters is not unreasonable. Even Virginia Woolf, who departs from the traditional character portrayal in her novels, remarks: "I believe that all novels...deal with character, and that it is to express character—not to preach doctrines, sing songs, or celebrate the glories of the British empire, that the form of the novel, so clumsy, verbose, and undramatic, so rich, elastic and alive, has been evolved." Virginia Woolf, however, modifies her statement: "To express character, I have said; but you will at once reflect that the very widest interpretation can be put upon these words...besides age and country there is the writer's temperament to be considered. You see one thing in character, and I another. You say it means this, and I that. And when it comes to writing, each makes a further selection on principles of his own."[5] The statement, however, is a comment on the large variety of characters found in fiction—both individuals and types. Mulk Raj Anand, the most prolific and the most widely criticized Indo-Anglian novelist, too, feels that characters in his novels have been the motivating force—rather the chief cause—behind the writing of his novels. About the genesis of his novels Anand makes an interesting confession. He observes: "...all my novels and short stories arose from a long confession of nearly two thousand pages, which I wrote from the compulsion of a morbid obsession with myself and the people who possessed me, deep in my conscience."[6] But the narrative being too long, no publisher was ready to accept it for publication. His girl-friend, Irene now inspired him to write about some "wonderful living characters"[7] and "I found that these characters began to compel me to write them out. In this way, through the next few years, several short and long stories were written."[8] So, in this case of Anand, it was not the action that decided the choice of characters in his novels. The action, instead, was chosen according to the characters he decided to write about. His characters are mostly people who once were "men and women."[9] Anand, in his childhood and youth, had been intimate with them. He had himself shared their feelings, thoughts, actions, reactions, troubles, and joys. And he had studied their emotions from such close quarters that he could easily identify himself with them. The autobiographical element in his novels is revealed by his remark: "Meanwhile through the many adversities, trials and errors, heart-rending experiences and several breakdowns, the characters from my long confession have become a miscellany of novels and short stories. The passions which have occupied them were perhaps my own dominant moods, and, therefore, all those characters may be said to be part of the same autobiography of the torments, ecstasies and passions of the last two generations."[10] Anand's complete identification with his characters accounts for the remarkable authenticity in their portrayal.

The choice of characters in a novel is determined, to a large extent, by the exigencies of the period in which the novel is written and by the writer's own interests, whims, and idiosyncracies. That is why there is a noticeable change in the concept of hero from time to time. Tom Jones, Moll Flanders, and Huckleberry Finn of the early and middle eighteenth century with its love for travelling and adventures gave place to Emma, Elizabeth, and Mr. Bingley enjoying the unperturbed, easy, and comfortable life of upper middle class society of the last decade of the same century. They, in their own turn, were replaced by David Copperfield, Oliver Twist, Nicholas Nickleby fighting the naked and hard facts of life in the nineteenth century. In the modern age, with its complexities and interest in psychology, Virginia Woolf and James Joyce rang the knell of the traditional hero and introduced heroes sans heroic qualities. "Perhaps when James Joyce made Ulysses into a mean sensual man," remarks H.M. Williams, "wandering round a distinctly unheroic Dublin town in 1904, he signalled the end of that old type of hero and ushered in the new, a kind of shuffling Chaplin figure in baggy pants."[11] About Indo-Anglian fiction, Williams aptly remarks that "it too seems to have begun with the unheroic."[12] In fact, Indian literature in English came to be written when India was engulfed by innumerable and enormous social, political, and religious evils. The nation was writhing under the suppressing yoke of foreign rule. The British rulers subjected the poor Indians to slavish, subhuman existence. The rigid class and caste structure of India itself caused intolerable sufferings to people. The exigencies of the situation demanded an exposure of these evils and agitation against them.

Mulk Raj Anand, at this period, took a bold and fearless plunge by going to the lowest stratum of life to pick his heroes from the soil and dirt. He decided to paint real India in stark colours and not as an abode of oriental philosophy, mysticism, and magic as many of his predecessors had done. Real India, he felt, could be found amidst untouchables, coolies, landless labourers, exploited wives, and ousted princes. He introduced these victims of society as protagonists in his novels because, as Walter Allen rightly observes, "It is only, through his characters that the novelist can succeed in what is his main social—as opposed to aesthetic—function, which is to awaken...'sympathetic comprehension in our readers.'"[13] And Anand's aim is to prepare people through this "sympathetic comprehension" for a revolution against oppression, exploitation, and injustice. Hence the introduction of hero-anti hero or what Anand himself calls "negative heroes"[14] in the novels of Mulk Raj Anand.

But the fact that strikes our curiosity is not so much the presence of the suffering heroes as that of those who, with their sympathy and love for the suffering humanity, fight for the cause of the former and who may be justly termed as saviour characters. Most probably, while dealing with the fate of suffering characters, Anand is conscious enough not to present their world as unrealistically and hopelessly dismal. To relieve the gloom, he provides a ray of hope in the form of these selfless, benevolent, and benign saviour characters. The presence of the saviour heroes in his novels, according to Anand, is not intentional, but is a concession to life. About the saviour figures he observes: "Actually, the saving graces were not created in the novels with the intention to show everytime that there is one character who may retrieve the situation. In life there are always such people. And in the presentation of contraries of good and evil, one leaves hope against despair."[15] Despite Anand's assertion that the people like his saviour characters are found in life, the fact remains that in the fictional world of Anand, many times these saviour characters appear unwelcome intruders. Very often they appear to have been forced in the novels with the purpose to preach. They are often used as lifeless instruments to voice Anand's message. And often they preach the message so overtly that the authorial presence is all too palpable. Unable to conceal his purpose in the veil of art, he tries to "put his thumb in the scale,"[16] which, according to Lawrence, is immoral on the part of a novelist. It is in such novels that Anand fails to strike a proportionate blend of art and purpose. His reformative zeal erupts here and there, which offends the aesthetic sense. But it is only in the case of those novels in which the sufferers are too passive to raise a voice against injustice. Otherwise there are novels in which the sufferers themselves undertake the job of their amelioration. Here the author is able to acquire the required objectivity in the treatment of suffering humanity. He still protests against cruelty, but the protest is well veiled. Still there is another category of novels in which Anand's sympathetic vision of suffering never degenerates into unaesthetic propagandistic sermonizing. There is another category of his novels in which Anand maintains artistic integrity and does not force a saviour hero on the novel.

Anand's choice of characters—both sufferers and saviours—is consistent with his theory of literature and life. Anand has not given a well-organised theory of literature; nor does he feel the need of formulating one for writing literature. As Anand observes: "Those people who say I have no theory of fiction are more or less correct. And yet one does not need to formulate a systematic theory to write fiction or react to its various expressions, to enjoy its flavours and even to write some criticism of one's own. I have certain hunches about the novel, but I have not put these down in any book or formal essay yet. I have jotted down several reflections."[17] These reflections are scattered in his essays, letters to critics, prefaces to his books, articles in books and journals, some reflective books like *Apology for Heroism, Lines Written to an Indian Air, Is there a Contemporary Indian Civilization*? and *Hindu view of Art*. But the thoughts are very ofen contradictory and casual. Anand himself warns that "these stray notes may be offered tentatively instead of a professional thesis."[18] His views on art and literature, if reduced to a summary leaving aside contradictions, may be regarded as largely mimetic as against the autonomy theory of the pure aesthetes. He is poles apart from the New Critics who regard aesthetic delight of the readers as the sole function of literature. He disapproves of the dictum of irrelevance of life to art. According to him, such a stance has no meaning in the Indian tradition in which "they never adopted the theory that they painted pictures just to satisfy one person [Rather], the whole of art was a communication.... of a very high level of sensitiveness."[19] Not only does he refute the principle of art for aesthetic delight on the basis of history of Indian art, but he also feels that in the present situation in India art must reform through communication and exposure.

Anand realizes that the social context of the Indian novelists is different from that of the European writers. He warns that "We have, however, in our newly emergent societies, to understand that we are not the middle classes of Europe and America. We must see ourselves as we are, we are struggling out of the days of contempt of the caste orders, emancipating our minds from the submission to one man rule, we are dimly becoming aware of the nature of our hopeless resignation in the past to the unknown fate, the Supreme God Vishnu, who will not wake up to help us, because the Kali Yug is not yet over."[20] In such a period of transition Anand felt that "The old world was dead and gone and only lingered in the minds of the sentimentalists who always dote on the past. And the old humanism, of which this old world was the product was a spent force,"[21] but people were still groping for moorings in the changed world because the "individual was disrupted by the commercialism which resulted through the industrial revolution that science had helped to perfect. And the ordinary human values, love, justice, beauty were consequently perverted and destroyed."[22] Like Matthew Arnold, Anand felt torn between two worlds—"one dead and the other powerless to be born." In this period of confusion, Anand felt that one could depend more on art and literature for solace than on religion and philosophy. According to him, "Literature, music and art are better able to fulfil the needs of our time than religion, and beauty is better worth worshipping than God or a Deity for whom the sanctions lie in the intuitions of a few mystics."[23] Anand, therefore, feels that the function of literature, particularly the novel, in India is certainly different from its function in Europe which is much ahead of India in scientific and technological progress. He observes: "We cannot, therefore, accept the novel of the western bourgeois, in its totality, even though we accept the form of the novel, evolved by the middle classes in the heyday of the industrial revolution. We have to reveal the new consciousness of our old-new people, in all the miscellaneousness, through the imaginative portrayal of human life that is the novel."[24] He, therefore, wants to be judged not with European canons but with exigencies of contemporary Indian situation in mind: "I wish to be judged as a writer, who has tried to tell the truth of life. And some compassion. I am not subject to western categories. The question is how far do my novels recreate life."[25] He reiterates the need of a different perspective of criticism for the novels of Indian writers: "I believe criticism of Indian novels in the languages in Indian English, must depart from European categories of realism, naturalism, idealism and the rest. Interpretation must emerge from the collective unconscious of the characters. For instance, how can an Indian critic treat the 'permanent stress' behind the consciousness of the new young of my time, who saw General Dyer's brutality? The Indian monkeys use the terminology they learn from the West. The truth is thus misinterpreted. My characters demand human sympathy from the critics as well in response to my own."[26] Anand, in this way, does not pretend to be an objective writer; instead, he clearly confesses commitment in his writings.

The fact that Anand uses literature as a means to modify society has led critics to dub him as a propagandist despite his repeated emphasis on the fact that Indian context demands art with purpose. He boldly accepts the negative appellation. As he observes: "All art is propaganda. The art of Ajanta is propaganda for Buddhism. The art of Ellora is propaganda for Hinduism. The art of western novel is propaganda for humanity against bourgeois. Gorky as a humanist dared to speak of man, man's condition, not only to say how awful it is, but he also suggested what man could be. And thus he did propaganda for man."[27] Anand, a great admirer of Gorky's fiction about squalor and dirt, regards him "the prophet of new literature."[28] And he tries to do in India what Gorky and Dostoyevsky had done in Russia. "Literature is the heart of the world," said Gorky to which Anand adds, "And the writer is the heart beat...There can be no life without a live heart."[29] Really, Anand's heart pulsates with the realities of the world and his novels are replete with "wisdom of the heart."[30] This wisdom is brought forth in his novels through the treatment of "the deep, complex and vital experiences of my [Anand's] characters who are mainly creatures that once were men and women"[31] and they are actually the experiences of Anand himself.

Anand chose fiction in preference to poetry because he found the novel to be the "most human of European forms, of creative literature."[32] For Anand who feels that "one writes perhaps because one loves, and wants to make contacts with other human beings,"[33] the novel was the most appropriate mode of writing because, as Anand himself writes: "I felt that, only in fiction, which is the transformation, through the imagination, of the concrete life, in words, sounds and vibrations, one may probe into the many layers of human consciousness in its various phases."[34] The novel being somewhat amorphous provides a chance for truthful presentation of human life. Not only does a novelist present life realistically, he also tries for the improvement of reality. About the function of literature he writes: "As an art work results from the reflection, in the mind of the artist of all the aspects of his experience, it is fundamentally related to life, only, improving on it, or rather intensifying it through the 'creative myth' so as to change life in the deeper centres of other people's experience and thus present an integral vision of what life could be like."[35] He regards an artist and writer to be the philosopher, saint, guide, and mentor of modern life.

About the role of a writer, Anand had the notion that the test of a writer lies in the transformation of words into prophecy. Because what is a writer if he is not the fiery voice of the people, who, through his own torments, urges and exaltations, by realizing the pains, frustrations and inspirations of others, and by cultivating his incipient powers of expression, transmutes in art all feeling, all thought, all experience—thus becoming the seer of a new vision in any given situation.[36] So confirmed is Anand's concept of the novel as representation of life that according to him, "any writer who said that he was not interested in *la condition humane* was either posing or yielding to a fanatical love of isolation—a perverse and clever defence of the adolescent desire to be indifferent.[37]" He regards those artists who believe in escapist literature as "whores of literature."[38] Such artists, according to Anand, fail to perform their function, namely, to reform society through revolution. He very vehemently discusses the responsibilities of an artist:

> So that whether we take the task of destroying the spurious elements of contemporary civilization or of reconstructing the future society, the creative artist occupies an important role in both spheres. And any attempt on his part to shirk responsibility is a betrayal of his own powers and the acceptance of mental and spiritual death. Above all, it is a betrayal of the common humanity to which he is committed as an individual born to live in community with other individuals, a denial of all human relations, a secession from society.[39]

Anand's dictum, in this way, approximates to Shelley's oft-quoted notion that the poet is the unacknowledged legislator of the world. He is gifted with talents with which he can help in the development of mankind. About a writer's capability to uplift society, Anand avers that "the creative writer or the poet is in a position to expose the perverters of words, aspire to truth, to take a whole view of the world, a view which is both extensive and intensive. And he is possessed of the necessary apparatus to help to exalt men to the full heights of their dignity, to equip them with the necessary spirit to tackle the tasks before them."[40] And a writer can do so if he dedicates himself to "the discovery, at the deepest levels of truth."[41] Anand, in this way, differs largely from I.A. Richards, W.K. Wimsatt, Jr., Monroe C. Beardsley, Virginia Woolf, Henry James, and all those literary theorists who support the dictum that a writing has no other significance than the pleasure one derives from words on a page. Regarding the relationship between a writing and its critic, Anand remarks: "The alliance of the critic with a novel can only come from a creative criticism which allies itself with the intention of the author and not from external obiter-dicta, enunciated either by Henry James, Percy Lubbock or E.M. Forster—though the last mentioned critic was far more tentative in putting forward his thesis and called himself a pseudo-scholar."[42] Not only does Anand regard authorial intention as significant in appreciation of a writing, he also attaches importance to the effect of the work on the readers and ultimately on society. A book, says Anand, "should create a convulsion, a stir and if the book does not stir us, by its own momentum, or have 'bounce' as Morgan Forster calls it, or the 'spark' as I would like to call it—does not ignite the reader, then I feel the novel in question is as dead as dodo."[43] The ignition that a novel causes is to arouse the dormant sensibility. This notion is made clear in his inaugural lecture as the Tagore Professor at Punjab University: "All that a work of art can do is to stimulate the manifold world of faculty and experience, arouse the slumbering sensibility or consciousness and open up ever deeper areas of awareness."[44] The intentional and affective fallacies of the New Critics, in this way, are of no significance in Anand's concept of fiction and fictional criticism.

A novel, says Anand, can cause wider consciousness of the readers by arousing compassion. Although a novelist does not suggest solutions, he moves the readers through the cathartic effect of the novel. About the catharsis of emotions through a novel, Anand observes: "The novel is not quite meant to offer solutions: creative works offer appeasement or catharsis through one of the moods of *Navrasa*. In the case of most of the stories and novels of mine, it is *Karuna Rasa*.

This may have some affiliation with the compassion implicit in the Jataka stories of the Buddha."[45] According to Anand, a novel should make a reader feel one with the characters by enabling him to understand man's fate. He observes: "Both the sufferer and the saviour may be saved by the understanding of the reader of man's fate—when the reader says 'oh! I felt like that Bakha or Munoo, Lal Singh or the tragic prince of *Private Life.*'"[46] Anand traces the concept of *Karuna* in remote history—much earlier than Aristotle's incorporation of it is his *Poetics*: "This concept of *Karuna* or compassion came to men and women in travail as the first enunciation of expiation through art, centuries before Aristotle's famous *Katharasis.*"[47] However, Anand's idea of catharsis differs from that of Aristotle. Aristotle writes about the feelings of pity and fear aroused by the suffering of the protagonist because of a tragic flaw whereas Anand's concept implies sympathy for those who suffer for no fault of their own. Their destiny is largely controlled by social forces beyond their control.

Although Anand emphasizes the close affinity between life and literature, he does not believe in a photographic projection of reality as do the followers of Naturalistic theory of literature. He does not undermine the role of imagination in art. An artist's own vision of things is significant in the creative process. About the artist's original view of things, Anand avers: "He discovers, new, ever new shapes from his deepest experience. And thus rejects the dead forms of tradition. He learns from the impulses which inspired the past, also from old techniques but with new tools, new materials, new insights, he ever renews his own sensibility and that of others, by the most challenging truths based on the various planes, by organising his creative work into the expression of his new integral vision."[48] A writer, says Anand, has to sift the universal from the individual, the essential from the accidental, and present it imaginatively and aesthetically because "art, though like life and reflecting it, is not life. Literature and life are parallel developments."[49] He observes that although a writer is a committed artist, his commitment must not make writing a vehicle of his own thoughts only; his thoughts should be moulded with the universal perspective in mind. About the creative process of universalising the personal experiences, Anand writes: "The significant novelist broods upon human existence, feels himself at one with its sources, becomes obsessed in his soul with a theme, interprets experience, arranges and disarranges, recalls the rhythmic life, even as he controls and constrains the flow of harmony and disharmony, and produces a pattern which may accord with the universal urges of man.... This may require a certain detachment in attachment, disarrangement even in arrangement because what is part of the novelist is also part of the other people."[50] For achieving the universal element in a novel a distancing of the author from the created work is necessary. Anand holds that just as a painter corrects his perspective standing at a distance from the canvas, so the author looks at his composition standing afar. An artist, he remarks, is like God who observes from a distance the universe that he has created. In a letter to Cowasjee, Anand writes: "The novelist should try to become the great god, Brahma, who creates mankind, but is not responsible for it, that is to say does not determine their destiny."[51] This is what Wayne C. Booth calls the maintenance of "aesthetic distance."[52] About characterization in a novel, Anand remarks: "Actually, even in any single character other humans, who are similar, become mingled."[53] About the imaginative handling of characters in his novels, he remarks: "The characters are taken from my intimate experience, but are transformed creatively from within...often a lamb becomes a lion and a dove becomes a jackal. I rely on my sub-conscious life a good deal in my creative work, and allow my fantasy to play havoc with facts."[54] He moulds real people according to the requirements of the story.

Although a supporter of art with commitment, Anand does not rule out the role of unconscious mind in the treatment of both the action and characters in a novel. Although he repeatedly emphasizes that all the characters of his novels are from his real life, he does believe that many times the character gets out of control of the novelist. He also argues that a writer should give maximum freedom to the characters to express themselves to make his writing both a convincing portrayal of reality and aesthetically satisfying. Like T.S. Eliot, he believes that a writer has to efface his personality to achieve spontaneity and artistic appeal though, he admits, it is difficult to set aside one's own feelings and ideals while writing. As a novelist tries to keep outside his writing, he exercises no control on his characters. He lets them feel, think, and act independently without any check imposed by the author. In his Preface to *Morning Face,* Anand intimates how the hero of the novel emerged automatically in the novel: "Dear Krishan: I am offering this novel to you, because though I was to be your creator, you took control of the book, almost from the beginning, and wrote yourself out, almost as if you were the author. So it is really your book and I am only the catalyst of the words in which your body-soul burns and melts."[55] Here Anand comes close to critics like Lawrence, Rene Wellek, I.A. Richards etc. who believe that the story runs out of the author's control reducing the artist's intention to irrelevance. He seems to contradict his own dictum that all art is written with a purpose and is intended to arouse compassion among the readers.

Anand's concept of literature as closely related to life is a by-product of his humanistic ideas. It is his own ardent love for human beings and his pity for the suffering, wretched, down-trodden humanity that lead him to believe that all writers write for the sake of man and the function of literature is to enable man recognize his dignity. Anand calls his humanism "comprehensive historical humanism"[56] and discusses it in detail in his *Is There a Contemporary Indian Civilization? Apology for Heroism, Hindu View of Art,* and "Prolegomena to a New Humanism" incorporated in *Lines Written to an Indian Air* with many scattered remarks in his articles, essays, and letters. His humanistic faith has been discussed with minute observation by Margaret Berry in her *Mulk Raj Anand: The Man and the Novelist* and Balarama Gupta in his famous *Mulk Raj Anand: A Study of His Novels in Humanist Perspective.* There have also appeared a large number of articles by various critics concentrating on this aspect of Anand's novels. All these reveal that Anand's concept of humanism is not original.

It has its sources in Indian tradition, western scientific theories and a number of systems prevalent both in India and abroad in the modern times. Anand's originality lies in synthesizing these heterogeneous ideologies to evolve a fairly systematic theory of his own.

Anand's is a "comprehensive historical humanism" because he derives much from the history of Indian religious and philosophical thought and blends it with modern scientific ideas so that his theory achieves universal significance and comprehends the whole of mankind. The traditional values which Anand wants to be operative in modern times are universalism, "intolerant-tolerance," and compassion. Universalism has been inherent in Indian tradition since very remote periods of history. Anand traces this element in the Vedic hymns in the "simple universal values of mankind, in their worship of nature and their bold speculative outlook about the meaning of creation. It is almost as though men discovered not one part of the world but the whole cosmos for the first time."[57] The idea was confirmed by Buddhism and Jainism. The fact that Indians have tolerated foreigners for a long time reveals their tolerance because of the belief that all people are alike. About the second virtue, that is "intolerant-tolerance," Anand observes that it "means to me non-acceptance of fanatical, partisan assertions, with a kind of good humour, without fighting back with one's own assertions."[58] This, according to him, was necessitated by the infiltration of aliens in India. The Indians, after a few encounters with the foreigners, accepted them and started tolerating their religions, customs, and traditions. The third virtue, "compassion" was an outcome of the first two qualities. These virtues, according to Anand, should be operative along with the rational, scientific ideas of the modern age. Anand is intolerant of orthodoxy and irrational taboos of Indian religious thought, but he is full of admiration for the human values which have percolated through traditional history to modern periods.

Anand is an admirer of humanistic philosophies of Mahatma Gandhi, Rabindranath Tagore, and Jawahar Lal Nehru.

But he does not accept the ideology of any one of them unconditionally. He owes much of his love for the downtrodden humanity to Mahatma Gandhi and his synthetic approach towards the ideologies of East and West to Rabindranath Tagore. He is full of praise for the socialistic pattern of society as preached by Jawahar Lal Nehru and stands for his humanism laced with a scientific approach. But he differs from Mahatama Gandhi's capitalistic ideas and from the spiritual sanctions which Tagore and Gandhi find for their philosophies. He wants to strike a combination of Gandhian love for humanity and Marxian gospel of classless and casteless society. He admires the ethics of Tagore based on a deep study of eastern and western cultures but he does not approve of spiritual sanctions in his philosophy.

Anand's humanism is "ethics without God."[59] Like existentialists, he denies the existence of God. His faith in God was shattered by the death of his cousin Kaushalya at the very young age of nine years. He started questioning God for the justification of the death of an innocent young girl. Having got no response to his queries, he started challenging God, spitting on his name and violating religious injunctions. About this loss of faith in the Almighty, Anand writes: "So I have tended to regard him, since then, as the enemy of mankind. In fact, from that time my belief in the man with the big beard sitting on top of the sky, determining the fate of everyone, has been shaken more or less completely. And unless I am in the dark, and frightened of ghosts, or in some other danger, or using proverbial speech like 'Oh, God' I have never invoked the giant Patriarch."[60] So he does not treat man's relation to God or supernatural forces in novels; instead, he is concerned with man's relation to man and society. Discussing his theory of humanism, Anand points out that his "humanism believes, in opposition to all theories of fatalistic acceptance of God, predestination and determinism, that human beings, conditioned by man's history, possess genuine freedom of creative choice and action. And, within certain limits, set by subjective circumstances, every man is master of his own destiny."[61] Anand, in this way, admits the role of chance in the life of man. Otherwise he believes that man himself is responsible for his pleasures and pains and those of other men in society.

Anand's humanism, we find, differs from Vedantic philosophy of omniscience and omni presence of God. He, unlike Vedantists, does not accept God as the ultimate reality. He, on the contrary, like Protagoras, believes that "Man is the measure of all things."[62] He implies that all actions and values of life are to be evaluated by the extent to which they better human life. He recognizes the dignity of man even in his weaknesses. He argues that all policies of the state and all endeavours of public and private institutions should be directed to one destination—the happiness of human beings. Anand does not connive at the vices of human beings—their selfishness, cruelty and greed. He holds these vices to be responsible for the prevalence of social evils. The removal of these social evils which hamper all round development of man, according to Anand, should be the chief aim of all writers and artists. The highest human ethic is the conquest of pain and the realization of social and economic freedom, the mental and emotional awareness in order to gain wholeness. His belief in the endeavours to fight against suppressive elements is revealed in his confession of his aim as a writer: "[I] began to write about the suffering men and women I had known to find out the reasons for their heart-rending failure to live happy lives, and to learn for myself what were the things and ideals I could honestly believe in, and to help to remould the tragic world in which I had grown up into a less harassed world."[63] And that is what he wants all novelists to do—to understand the fate of suffering human beings and strike at the causes of the suffering by their exposure through writings.

Anand's notion of the function of literature is based on his idea that man has the potential to improve himself. He can achieve perfection through the integration of body and soul. His emphasis is on the whole man and he advocates the development of all facets of his personality. Explaining his philosophy of the whole man, Anand remarks: "This humanism believes that the individual attains full manhood by integrating his personal satisfactions and continuous creative self-development through significant creative work with the hand, the heart and the brain, such as may contribute to man's renewal, to the welfare of the community and express the love of life, the awareness of death, and thus balance the essentially unstable and maladjusted human personality, involved in the inevitable conflicts of existence in this universe."[64] Thus, his, philosophy takes into consideration the whole man—the body, the heart, and the mind. And in his writings he tries to treat man as an integrated, whole being. As he writes: "...as my media as a writer were the memory and imagination, and the substance of my work the whole of my varied experience, the theme of my work became the whole man and the whole gamut of human relationship, rather than one single part of it."[65] In the present confused world, he regrets, there is often lack of "a balanced view of man, a view which embraces reason, emotion and imagination as well as knowledge of the facts—a view of the whole man."[66] And the world can improve if men are given full freedom for their development. It is for the freedom of men, rather so many freedoms of humanity, that he is fighting with the weapon of his writing. Art, according to him, can be the saviour of humanity in the present hour of crisis when religion has degenerated into the hands of mean, selfish priests.

Anand also pins his hope for amelioration of mankind on *Karma* and *Bhakti Yoga*. Dead against fatalism of orthodox Indians, he wants men to organize themselves and dedicate themselves to the cause of mankind. It can be possible if there is a feeling of brotherhood among men and if they selflessly fling themselves in the arena to fight against all those forces which condemn them and their brethren to sub-human life. This feeling of brotherhood, again, can be furthered by art and literature. Anand's faith as a humanist and his faith as a writer are well revealed in his speech delivered at the Second Afro-Asian Writers' Conference held at Cairo:

> Our literatures and arts are thus the weapons of a new concept of man—that the suppressed, the disinherited and the insulted of Asia and Africa can rise to live, in

> brotherhood with other men, but in the enjoyment of freedom and equality and justice, as more truly human beings, individuals, entering from object history, into the—great history when there will be no war, but when love will rule the world, enabling man to bring the whole of nature under self-conscious control for the uses of happiness, as against despair.[67]

And he dedicated the gathering of the conference "to the task of healing the wounds of the insulted and the injured, through full engagement in the widest areas of knowledge and action, so that all the tears of all the children can be wiped and in the words of the Spanish poet Garcia Lorca: 'The black boy come announce to whole of the world the beginning of the reign of an ear of corn.'"[68] He reiterates his faith in the capability of artists to liberate mankind from the shackles of pain: "This, then, seems to me the mission of the writer today. To act as the conscience of the people aware of their pain. To have a creative vision of all that affords joy in life, to release the vital rhythms in the personality, to make man more human, to seek apperceptions of freedom from all forms of slavery and to give this freedom to other people throughout the world—in fact to awaken men to the love of liberty, which brings life and more life."[69] And that is what Anand himself is doing vigorously even at the risk of being called a writer with propagandistic leanings. However, the Jewish writers of America have evolved almost a similar theory of literature because they are fighting for their freedom as the Indians were doing before independence. Amiri Baraka, one of the chief supporters of Black Aesthetic Theory declares: "...my conception of art, Black art, is that it is collective, it has to be functional, it has to be committed and actually if it isn't stemming from conscious nationalism, then at this time, it isn't valid. When I say collective, then it comes from the collective experience of Black people, when I say committed, it has to be committed to change, revolutionary change. When I say functional it has to have a function to the lives of Black People." Baraka sounds very much like Anand only speaking from a different dais.

Anand's humanistic philosophy is sufficient explanation for his choice of characters—the sufferers and the saviours. The sufferers reveal the real plight of contemporary India and the saviours provide hope against despair. They reveal Anand's existentialism combined with a streak of an optimistic attitude towards life. The relation between the two heroes, however, differs in various novels. The present study categorises novels on the basis of the relationship between the sufferer and the saviour. The relationship depends on the suffering hero's own personality. When he is too passive and weak to fight, a saviour figure is introduced from a higher stratum of society. When the sufferer attains maturity of sensibility and strength of mind, he himself fights for the liberty of all those who suffer like him. And when the plight of the sufferer is beyond redemption, and when he is a man of high social profile, no saviour character is brought in. In other words, no saviour characters are introduced when either the suffering protagonist himself is strong and combative enough to throw a challenge to the iniquitous and suppressive forces of society or when the conditions are so terrible as to be irremediable. In addition there are also some novels in the Anand canon which are fairly free from the shadow of suffering syndrome and therefore have a more disinterested aesthetic dynamic of their own. This study intends to trace the effect of the introduction of the saviour characters on the overall aesthetic appeal of Anand's novels.

NOTES

1. A phrase used by W.J. Harvey, "Appendix I," *Character and the Novel* (New York: Cornell Uni. Press, 1965), 191.
2. *Ibid.*, 183.
3. *Ibid.*, 196.
4. Iris Murdoch, "The Sublime and the Beautiful Revisited," *Yale Review*, Vol. 49 (1959), 226.
5. Virginia Woolf, "All Novels Deal with Character" in *Novelists on the Novel*, ed. Mirriam Allott (London: Routledge and Kegan Paul, 1959), 290.
6. Mulk Raj Anand, "The Story of My Experiment with a White Lie,"

in *Critical Essays on Indian Writing in English,* ed. M.K. Naik *et al.* (Dharwar: Karnatak University, 1968), 17.

7. Mulk Raj Anand, "How I Became a Writer," *Contemporary Indian Literature,* Vol. V, No. 11-12 (Nov.-Dec., 1965), 15.
8. M.R. Anand, "The Story of My Experiment with a White Lie." *op. cit.,* 17.
9. M.R. Anand, personal letter to me dated Oct.18, 1985.
10. M.R. Anand, "How I Became a Writer," *op. cit.,* 15.
11. H.M. Williams, "The Doomed Hero," in *Three Contemporary Novelists,* ed. R.K. Dhawan (Delhi: Classical Publishing Company, 1985), 97.
12. *Ibid.*
13. Walter Allen, *The English Novel* (Harmondsworth: Penguin Books Ltd., 1954), 17.
14. S.C. Harrex, *The Fire and the offering: The English Language Novel of India* (1935-1970) (Calcutta: Writers Workshop, 1977), 82.
15. M.R. Anand, personal letter to me dated Dec. 27, 1989.
16. A phrase used by D.H. Lawrence, "Morality and the Novel," in *Twentieth Century Litrary Criticism,* ed. David Lodge (London: Longman Group (FE) Ltd., 1971), 131.
17. M.R. Anand, "Reflections on the Novel," in *Commonwealth Literature: Problems of Response,* ed. C.D. Narsimhaiah (Madras: Macmillan India Ltd., 1981), 49.
18. *Ibid.*
19. See Marlene Fisher, *Wisdom of the Heart: A Study on the Novels of Mulk Raj Anand* (New Delhi: Sterling Publishers, 1981), 174.
20. Mulk Raj Anand, "A Note on Henry James and the Art of Fiction in India," *Commonwealth Quarterly,* Vol. 2, No. 7 (June, 1978), 6-7.
21. Mulk Raj Anand, "Prolegomena to a New Humanism," *Lines Written to an Indian Air* (Bombay: Nalanda Publications, 1949), 4-5.
22. *Ibid.*
23. *Ibid.*
24. Mulk Raj Anand, "A Note on Henry James and the Art of Fiction in India," *loc. cit.*
25. Mulk Raj Anand, personal letter to me dated Oct.18, 1985.
26. *Ibid.*
27. Mulk Raj Anand, "Speech," *Soviet Review,* Vol. V, No. 21 (Nov., 1968), 92.

28. Mulk Raj Anand, "Gorky's Contribution to the Contemporary World Literature," *Contemporary Indian Literature*, Vol. VIII, No. 2 (May, 1968), 7.
29. *Ibid.*
30. A phrase used repeatedly by Anand in his letters, articles, and autobiographical novels. To Saros Cowasjee he once wrote: "Against the obstructing mind of Anglo-Saxon, their science and their reason, I put the wisdom of the heart of my mother."
31. M.R. Anand, personal letter to me dated Oct.18, 1985.
32. M.R. Anand, "Why I Write?" in *Perspectives on Mulk Raj Anand*, ed. K.K. Sharma (Ghaziabad: Vimal Prakashan, 1978), 2.
33. *Ibid.*
34. *Ibid.*, 5.
35. M.R. Anand, *Apology for Heroism* (New Delhi: Arnold Heinemann, 1986), 89.
36. M.R. Anand, "Pigeon-Indian: Some Notes on Indian-English Writing," in *Aspects of Indian Writing in English*, ed. M.K. Naik (Delhi: Macmillian Co. of India Ltd., 1979), 41.
37. *Apology* for *Heroism*, 123.
38. A phrase used by Dr Havre, one of the characters in *Two Leaves and a Bud*, 127 to describe the writers who believe in ornamentation against an austere expression of reality.
39. *Apology for Heroism*, 136.
40. *Ibid.*, 135.
41. *Ibid.*, 203.
42. Mulk Raj Anand, "Reflections on the Novel," *op. cit.*, 52.
43. *Ibid.*
44. Mulk Raj Anand, "The Third Eye: A Lecture on the Appreciation of Art," *Research Bulletin (Arts) of the University of Punjab*, Fine Art Series No. 1 (1965), 31.
45. Mulk Raj Anand, personal letter to me dated June 2, 1992.
46. *Ibid.*
47. Quoted by Dr Shyam M. Asnani, "A Critique of Mulk Raj Anand's Literary Creed," *Commonwealth Quarterly*, Vol. 4, No. 13 (Dec, 1979), 71.
48. Mulk Raj Anand, "The Third Eye," *op. cit.*, 5.
49. Mulk Raj Anand, "Art is not Life," in *Critical Thought*, ed. S.K. Desai and G.N. Devi (New Delhi: Sterling Publishers Pvt. Ltd., 1987), 238.

50. Mulk Raj Anand, "A Note on Modern Indian Fiction," *Indian Literature,* Vol. VIII, No. 1 (1965), 45.
51. Mulk Raj Anand, *From Author to Critic: The Letters of Mulk Raj Anand to Saros Cowasjee* (Calcutta: Writers Workshop, 1973), 14.
52. Wayne C. Booth, *The Rhetoric of Fiction* (University of Chicago Press, 1961), 122.
53. Mulk Raj Anand, personal letter to me dated June 12, 1992.
54. Mulk Raj Anand, *From Author to Critic: The Letters of Mulk Raj Anand to Saros Cowasjee,* 14-15.
55. Mulk Raj Anand, "Preface," *Morning Face* (New Delhi: Arnold Heinemann Publishers Pvt. Ltd., 1968), 5.
56. Mulk Raj Anand, *Is There a Contemporary Indian Civilization*? (Bombay: Asia Publishing House, 1962), 15.
57. *Ibid.*, 83.
58. Quoted by Balarama Gupta, *Mulk Raj Anand: A Study of His Novels in Humanist Perspective* (Bareilly: Prakash Book Depot, 1974), 14.
59. Mulk Raj Anand, personal letter to me dated May 9, 1990.
60. Mulk Raj Anand, "Why I Write," *op. cit.*, 1.
61. *Is There a Contemporary Indian Civilization*? 159.
62. *Apology for Heroism*, 140.
63. Mulk Raj Anand, "Prolegomena to a New Humanism," *op. cit.*, 4.
64. *Is There a Contemporary Indian Civilization*? 160.
65. *Apology for Heroism*, 78.
66. Mulk Raj Anand, "Task Before the Writers," *Contemporary Indian Literature,* Vol. II, No. 9, 16.
67. *Ibid.*, 38.
68. *Ibid.*, 17.
69. Quoted by S. Krishnamoorthy Aithal, "Black Aesthetic Theory: An Anti-Formalist Jihad," *Indian Journal of American Studies* (Special issue on Survey of Theory) Vol. 18, No. 1, Winter (1988), 37.

2

PROTAGONISTS FROM THE DIRT AND THE DUST

We first take up the novels in which the protagonists are too meek to retort against the evil forces which tend to suppress them and their like. These hero-anti heroes, no doubt, are endowed with certain admirable qualities of the head and the heart; but the cruel, irrational social forces hamper the proper development of these qualities. The diligence, intelligence, and sensitiveness of these characters are so awfully suppressed that they can never gain confidence to wage a fight for their cause. They, however, do sensitively feel the torture of the unjust practices, but the reaction is limited merely to their acknowledgement of the social status which they are doomed to accept without a hope for emancipation. The knowledge of their helplessness against the established social set-up, traditions, taboos, and customs makes them writhe with acute mental agony. They can do nothing but accept their fate. The suppression of their desire to retort results in frustration which obstructs a complete realization of their potentialities. But the author, however, wants to present not only the dismal realities, he wants to project the desire image—the life as it should have been. One of the tools for creating the desire image is the introduction of the saviour characters who fight for the cause of these spineless, gutless sufferers.

Almost all the saviour characters belong to a completely separate world from that of the suffering heroes; they enjoy higher status because of their birth in a higher caste and class of society. Their condescension to fight for these slavish, groveling, and servile people many times seems contrived with a purpose. Their appearance seems forced to articulate a thesis. Their feelings, thoughts and actions seem to be schematized to fit in with a pre-conceived plan to propagate a particular point of view. Very often these saviour characters appear as lifeless puppets dancing to the tune of the author's inclination. It is in such novels that the authorial intrusion is clearly felt. Anand seems to be actually treading the pages of the novel. He fails to strike an aesthetic blend of detachment and attachment, which he advocates to be a requirement of art. In these novels, we, like Margaret Berry, feel that Anand's commitment as an artist overpowers his objectivity. Margaret Berry regrets the lack of detachment in Anand's novels: "In his theory of the novel Anand demanded of the writer simultaneous detachment and engagement. Engagement Anand had, in high degree. Unfortunately for his novels, he did not achieve the detachment, disinterestedness, freedom from commitment to causes which might have enabled him to create 'centres of consciousness' more authentic, penetrating, and finely responsive to the nuances of human behaviour and the complexities and depth of human affairs."[1] Although Margaret Berry's remark is not applicable to all the novels by Anand, it is certainly true about those novels in which the saviour characters overtly preach in favour of or against a specific cause. But despite this limitation, these novels cannot be dismissed outrightly as mere pieces of propaganda. Despite the eruption of the authorial intention here and there, the novels reveal the novelist's extraordinary insight into the psyche of the poorest poor, his ability to balance art with humanism, and his great success in employing a European genre to Indian reality.

The novels in this category are *Untouchable, The Road, Coolie, Two Leaves and a Bud, The Old Woman and the Cow,* and *Lament on the Death of a Master of Arts* (*The Old Woman and the Cow* and *Lament on the Death of a Master of Arts* have been treated in a separate chapter because the protagonists in these novels are victims of a different problem—the problem of domination.). R.S. Singh's remark about Anand's protagonists does not apply completely to characters in these novels. Dr Singh observes that they "are alone, weak and helpless, and dynamic because they try to understand the causes of their plight and in their own ways wage battle against the social and economic forces that deny them their human rights."[2] Their effort to understand the causes of their plight, no doubt, is genuine but their waging a battle against the social and economic forces that "deny them their human rights" applies only to the last part of *The Old Woman* and *The Cow.* Even there a change is wrought in the otherwise tradition-ridden attitude of Gauri by the repeated advice of the saviour hero, Dr Mahindra. Otherwise, in all these novels it is not the sufferers but some characters outside the class of the sufferers who try to wage a fight against the inequitable practices prevalent in society. Hence the presence of the saviour figures mars the aesthetic appeal of otherwise well-planned, technically admirable, and stylistically valuable novels. Here we find a conflict between an artist and a reformist which Eliseo Vivas explains: "The matter of experience attempts to reveal itself in the creative act, but the non-aesthetic demands of the artist predominate or at least are strong enough to present fully adequate aesthetic transmutation of matter into informed substance.... In a genuine artist the clash is never radical; it is never a question of unconditional surrender."[3] But in these novels by Anand, the artist, though at his best in technically handling the action, ultimately does surrender to the propagandist. He fails to resist his temptation for direct statement of his ideology.

This propagandistic element in Anand's novels has earned him severe criticism at the hands of his critics. Margaret Berry accuses Anand of failure to cope with the demands of art in so far as his socialistic leanings restrict the scope and range of his writings. She observes: "Anand is technically unable to cope with the dangers to art of 'writing for a cause.'"[4]

R.K. Kaushik is severer in his criticism of Anand's social concerns. He indicts Anand's choice of characters from the low strata and his introduction of saviour characters or "wisdom figures"[5] as Margaret Berry calls them. He remarks in rather harsh words: "Anand often seems to use the novel for the distillation of his social and political ideas; and his characters mostly work out to be little more than elucidators and amplifiers. It is argued, and sometimes justifiably so, that the actions, sayings and thoughts of characters in a novel should be regarded as strictly their own attributes and not reflecting the private convictions of their creator. But such a vindication, in Anand's case, cannot bear too close a scrutiny."[6] Although it is not true of all his characters, particularly his suffering heroes, it is certainly an appropriate judgement of the saviour heroes. Kaushik continues his criticism of the introduction of some specific characters for propagation of his philosophy: "The vein of systematic and manifest radicalism, for example, running through his characters—Dr Shankar, Ananta, Dhooli Singh, Lal Singh, Dr de la Havre, Colonel Mahindra, Sarshar, Sauda Sahib and others, copiously demonstrates the nature and pitch of the novelist's personal philosophy and bias."[7] Although we cannot agree with this criticism without certain provisions and conditions, it is also difficult to agree to the remark by Harish Raizada: "Though a writer with a purpose like the famous dramatist, George Bernard Shaw, he maintains a judicious balance between art and social concerns in his novels."[8] Though in some novels Anand has been able to maintain a "judicious balance between art and social concerns," the fact remains that there are some other novels of his in which the reformist zeal of Anand supercedes his artistic integrity. It is particularly so in the novels in which the sufferer and the saviour characters come from different worlds. Let us scrutinize those novels in which the aesthetic charm of the novel is spoilt, to some extent, by the intrusion of the novilist in the guise of a saviour character.

The suffering heroes in these novels are, no doubt, delineated with rare psychological insight and great sympathy. Having imbibed the faith from many humanists, particularly

Mahatma Gandhi, Anand had come to realize that "the least little untouchable, the darkest dark villager and the most exploited coolie, will come into his own."[9] These suppressed people of society are treated in Anand's novels as equal to all other members of society belonging to any caste, class, or designation. Anand probes into the basic human qualities of those characters who have been treated as dirt by the interpreters—rather the misinterpreters—of Indian traditional thought. What Anand writes about the protagonists of his *Untouchable* and Raja Rao's *Kanthapura* is, in fact, true of many of his protagonists, particularly of the novels in which the suffering heroes hail from the lowest classes of society. Anand posits:

> The human beings rooted in the soil of India are thus recreated, until they flower, not as the expressions of maya of the past, or as lifeless average men and women of the naturalistic European novel of Zola, but into individuals who are coming up for air from the labyrinthine depths of despair, with all their psychological, social and moral motivations, on the plane of the inauguration of man into the various freedoms...the same roots which had remained stunted in the barren earth are transplanted into the new landscape of the novel. And they seem to open up from the mud, like many petalled lotuses, extending in all directions of the universe.[10]

And really Anand deserves credit for his courage in deviation from tradition in choosing his protagonists from among the dregs of humanity and treating them with rare authenticity trying to "seek awareness of every feeling, every dim thought, every possible action, of human beings, as indissoluble parts of the struggle of the peoples for emergence."[11] But the objectionable feature of his novels is the clear peep which his novels provide into the author's inclination to propagate for the uplift of these men of the soil through direct statement by the saviour characters. Their harangues against the social and economic evils offend the aesthetic sense of the readers.

Anand's maiden venture *Untouchable* (1935) is a fine example of great technical skill and artistic handling of a plot spoilt somewhat by the propagandistic element. It is here that the sufferer and the saviour belong to widely divergent worlds—one belonging to the dirt and the excreta and the other no less than the father of the nation. Anand created a furore in literary world by treating an untouchable as the protagonist of his novel. He, however, achieved grand success in dealing with unconventional theme. The novel, though rejected by nineteen publishers in England in the beginning, proved to be a big success. But Anand could not control his propagandistic zeal completely. Although he again and again remarks that the function of an author is to reveal the facts, not suggest the solutions, he cannot leave his protagonist in utter depression and confusion. He must show a path out of the murky world. And the torch to provide the light is given to the saviour characters, Mahatama Gandhi and the poet Iqbal Nath Sarshar. Although there is also the Christian missionary, Colonel Hutchinson, Anand dismisses his proposal with his usual sneer for the missionaries.

The urge for writing a novel about an untouchable was the result of his deep attachment with a scavenger, Bakha during his childhood. Anand "developed a guilt about him which compelled appeasement"[12] because he acutely felt the tragedy of one whose inborn talents had not been allowed to bloom because of certain irrational taboos. He felt pain at the thought that "this otherwise near-perfect human being was a sweeper who was always being humiliated by most of our elders on account of his low caste, was not allowed to go to school even if his father had sent him (which he would not have), flawed his excellence for no fault of his. And though patronised because he was a good worker and obedient, he was suspected of leading all the young people astray and therefore vigilantly watched and kept at bay.[13]" The desire to give the exploited untouchable his due became his passion and he found fiction the most appropriate weapon to fight for his cause. Anand, after reading Russian writers like Gogol, Tolstoy, and Gorky, had already come to know that "even the so-called lowest dregs of humanity, living in utmost poverty, squalor and degradation, could become heroes of fiction."[14] Anand's close observation of the predicament of the untouchables was further sharpened by his own agony when once on board a ship to India, he himself, alongwith other Indians, was treated like an untouchable by English passengers. The first hand knowledge of the feelings of an outcaste provided authenticity to the projection of the plight of his protagonist. Anand's own experience of latrine-cleaning in the Ashram of Mahatama Gandhi was also of great help in measuring the thoughts of untouchables about their job.

Anand was conscious enough to present his untouchable protagonist as any other human being with dignity of his own and at the same time not to idealize him unauthentically. He confesses his problem: "I would have to do a tight-rope walk, to maintain the beauty of the rough diamond without making him into Koh-i-Noor.... I could overcome the temptation to make rounded philosophical judgements, from any predetermined categories. I must be one with the hero and create him, spontaneously from within the hell, in all the truth of his subhuman life, in the concrete situations of a day in his life."[15] Though Anand has not actually been able to curb the temptation to make "rounded philosophical judgements," there is no denying the fact that his hero does emerge as an admirable but true to life character. Anand has successfully brought him forth as an individual as well as a type. He does not present the physical world of untouchables; he, on the other hand, dissects and lays bare the very mind and soul of Bakha. The tussel between orthodox taboos on one hand and advanced attitudes on the other takes place in the arena of Bakha's mind. Because Anand's concentration is on the feelings and thoughts of his protagonist, he has chosen the Joycean stream of consciousness technique. Anand had actually been inspired to write a novel after he had read Joyce's *A Portrait of the Artist as a Young Man.* He too, like Joyce, strictly observes the unities of time and place. Narrating the incidents of only one day in the life of only one scavenger, he has given realistic vignettes which very lucidly demonstrate the complete life of the whole class of untouchables. The result is a very compact, well-knit plot of the novel. Cowasjee applauds the compactness of the novel: "*Untouchable* opens quietly on an autumn morning, and by the time the evening approaches, the author has been able to build round his hero Bakha a spiritual crisis of such magnitude that it seems to embrace the whole of India."[16] The "spiritual crisis" is in fact, the tension in the mind of the protagonist. He is oscillating between passive submission to a conservative, rigid caste-system on one hand and a keen desire to assert his human identity and fight for his amelioration on the other.

Anand develops the plot towards the conflict by revealing the feelings, thoughts, and emotions of Bakha from the moment he gets up on this specific day. Anand very sensitively feels the pulse of his hero and shows the latter's reaction both to humiliations and sympathy. Bakha's retaliation is that of any other human being under similar circumstances. But the reaction fails to find expression in the form of his annoyance at his exploitation or his pleasure at the benignity shown towards him. The centuries-old barriers obstruct the spontaneous expression of feelings. Whenever he tries to assert himself, the effort is suppressed by a deep-seated knowledge of his helplessness against social barriers. The result is that he can only writhe with the pain of the knowledge of his actual position. The suppression of spontaneous urge thwarts the natural growth of the mind of the protagonist. This conflict between "rage and despair"[17] forms the basic tension of the novel. The defeat of the rebellious spirit and the resulting agony of the sensitive mind retard the development of the talents of the negative hero. Anand himself remarks about the predicament of the untouchable: "The tragedy of my hero lay in the fact that he was never allowed to attain anything near the potentialities of his qualities of manhood."[18] Each incident of the novel either adds to the bitterness in the mind of Bakha or is vitiated by the reminiscences of the bitter moments. Whenever Bakha feels a little happy, there follows something to spoil the happiness. As the plot develops, the realization of Bakha regarding his low social status is confirmed. After the climactic slapping scene, Bakha realizes his place in society: "I am a sweeper, sweeper—untouchable! I am an Untouchable!"[19] The realization is so complete that it permeates all his senses and leaves nothing vague or unclear. Anand shows how fully the fact of the fate dawns upon him: "A shock had passed through his perceptions, previously numb and torpid, and had sent a quiver into his being, stirred his nerves of sight, hearing, smell, touch and taste, all into a quickening" (59). And whatever follows is a confirmation of the feeling that he is a polluting agent. A person can never hope to attain the full development of his capabilities who is continuously abused at home and whose touch is shunned by everybody outside. After hard toil of removing the dung, his fatigue is not to be relieved by a kind word or a noble gesture. If a word of sympathy is said sometime, there follows something so venomous that the feeling of happiness is completely lost.

Anand's portrayal of his hero is marked by sympathetic attitude combined with rare detachment. He keenly feels the pains and pleasures of the untouchables. He is full of compassion for these outcastes and indignation against those who victimize them. But his sympathy and indignation do not result in exaggeration or diminishing of the virtues and vices of these intimidated castaways. He individuates Bakha, imbues his personality with certain admirable qualities but at the same time he has something negative and ironical to bestow on his hero just as he has some incidents to devote to the credit of those high-born Hindus who rise above petty caste prejudices and treat the untouchables with kindness and human feelings. This is what Narsimhaiah terms as "ambivalence in attitude."[20] This mingling of positive and negative attitudes towards his protagonist and those who torture him enables Anand to preserve detachment despite his obvious intention to uphold the cause of the untouchables. Narsimhaiah commends his objectivity in the treatment of his characters, particularly his hero. He observes that Anand "preserves his detachment and there is a continuous mingling of approval and disapproval. Actually it is this tension which has redeemed a novel which otherwise may justly be accused of being a propaganda piece."[21] Most probably Narsimhaiah accuses the novel of being a propaganda piece (but for the novelist's dual attitude) because of Anand's choice of the theme of untouchability, a theme very likely to tempt an author to indulge in direct protest against it. But the achievement of the artist lies in the fact that he has been able to keep the flow of emotions under control. Whenever he tends to idealize his protagonist or exaggerate his sufferings, he puts in some incident to check exaggeration. So does he moderate his disapproval of the high-born Hindus.

In the very beginning of the novel Anand establishes the superiority of Bakha over other untouchables by referring to his disdain for the dirty atmosphere of his congested house, his efficiency at his job, his love for fashion, particularly his fondness for English style of living though Anand's tone in presenting the last trait is that of ridicule. Anand, however, individuates him by revealing how Bakha acutely feels the tragedy of being born in a family of untouchables whereas his father and brother seem to accept their lot without a thought of the need of improvement. Bakha's love for learning, skill at games, and talent of singing too make him prominent among other boys of his caste. Unlike his father and brother, Bakha feels the uncongeniality of his home. Anand attributes this feeling of Bakha to a kind, human treatment that the latter has received at the hands of the British people and to his observation of the life-style of the British. Such has been his admiration of the British way of life that "he tried to copy them in everything, to copy them as well as he could in the exigencies of his peculiarly Indian circumstances" (13). Anand has been able to project this love of Bakha for the English way of life because he himself had once taken a fancy to English life and dress. His friends nicknamed him "Pilpali Sahib" and so do Bakha's friends call him. But Anand scoffs at Bakha's exaggerated fondness for English life. Bakha foregoes the warmth of a quilt and sleeps with a blanket on even in the cold nights of autumn. Anand seems to frown at Bakha's obsession with fashionable life when Bakha wants to forget his dead mother because she was not of the modern world.

The satire, however, becomes very acute in Anand's remark about his protagonist: "He [Bakha] didn't feel sad, however, to think that she was dead. He couldn't summon sorrow to the world he lived in, the world of his English clothes and 'Red-Lamp' cigarettes, because it seemed she was not of that world, had no connection with it" (16-17). After such mockery of Bakha's love for "fashun," Anand pays a glowing compliment to him for his deftness at his work: "He worked away earnestly, quickly, without loss of effort. Brisk, yet steady, his capacity for active application to the task he had in hand seemed to flow like constant water in a spring. Each muscle of his body, hard as a rock when it came into play, seemed to shine forth like glass" (18). By bestowing such dignity and grace on his protagonist, Anand is able to present him as different from Lakha, Rakha, and other scavengers. Bakha's cleanliness leaves the high-caste Hindu Charat Singh spell-bound. The latter's amazement spurts out in his thought: "Here was a low-caste man who seemed clean!" (19). Bakha's clean ways of work and his exotic dress win him an offer of a hockey-stick from Charat Singh.

Bakha's superiority is further revealed in his sensitiveness to injustice meted out to him and his kind. Unlike his father, he is not complacent with what he has. He does not accept his fate passively. No doubt, he cannot rebel openly against the centuries-old taboos, but at least he wants to retort. The spark of wrath remains unignited, but it reveals that a revolution against the inhuman practices is in the offing. Every humiliation inflicted on Bakha leaves a deep impression on his sensitive mind; his realization of his position is keener but at the same time the desire to liberate himself from the disgraceful position is stronger. When the touched and polluted Hindu Bania slaps him in the face, he wants to take revenge. There is a mingling of the feelings of rage and revenge in him. The novelist sums up the mental state of Bakha in these words: "...his whole countenance lit with fire and his hands were no more joined. Tears welled up in his eyes and rolled down his cheeks. The cumulated strength of his giant body glistened in him with the desire for revenge, while horror, rage, indignation swept over his frame. In a moment he had lost all his humility, and he would have lost his temper too, but the man who had struck him the blow had slipped beyond reach into the street" (57).

There is a "smouldering rage" in his soul and he repents his failure to hit back: "Why was all this?... Why was all this fun? Why was I so humble? I could have struck him" (58). His retaliation is much stronger in the next humiliating scene when the temple priest tries to molest Sohini and then shouts "Polluted! Polluted!" (69). His desire is nothing less than to kill the hypocrite: "He felt he could kill them all. He looked ruthless, deadly pale and livid with anger and rage" (70). When he comes to know what the priest actually did, he exclaims: "I will go and kill him!" (71). He rushes to the courtyard. Only Sohini prevents him from doing so. Bakha's reaction is extremely different from that of his father who, on hearing about the priest's filthy attempt, simply asks: "You didn't abuse or hit back, did you?" (89). When Bakha goes to collect food from the people in the lanes, he feels much hurt when the lady throws a pancake from the upper storey for him to catch. Picking up the pancake from the ground leaves him so deeply hurt that he goes away without cleaning the drain and decides never to go to the lanes again.

Despite Bakha's resentment against the unfair treatment he receives at the hands of the high-born Hindus, he fails to rebel openly against them. Whenever he is ready to hit back, the inhibitions and humility which he has inherited and acquired from the surrounding atmosphere, obstruct his attempt to strike. He has to resign himself to his fate and accept passively the pangs of failure to take revenge. Though unlike his father and brother in his thoughts and feelings, he is quite like them in actual action. In the slap scene, when Bakha is surrounded by a crowd, he wants to run away. But he is reminded that he is a polluting agent. His passive acceptance of the traditional attitude is evident in these lines: "His first impulse was to run, just to shoot across the throng, away, far away from the torment. But then he realized that he was surrounded by a barrier, not a physical barrier, because one push from his hefty shoulders would have been enough to unbalance the skeleton-like bodies of the onlookers, but a moral one. He knew that contact with him, if he pushed through, would defile a great many more of these men" (54). He can only brood over his low position in society and start again the warning against his touch: "Posh, posh, sweeper coming!" (59). Again when the priest makes indecent suggestions to his sister, Bakha feels "a wild desire to retaliate, retaliation meaning to him just doing anything, from belabouring him with blows to killing him if need be" (73). But even this powerful urge for of retaliation ultimately gives way to his conformity to tradition. He has to put up with the torture he undergoes at his passivity and helplessness. Anand beautifully presents the conflict between a revolutionary spirit and a submission to customary taboos. He remarks about the mental state of his hero: "A superb specimen of humanity he seemed whenever he made the high resolve to say something, to go and do something, his fine form rising like a tiger at bay. And yet there was a futility written on his face. He could not overstep the barriers which the conventions of his superiors had built up to protect their weakness against him. He could not invade the magic circle which protects a priest from attack by anybody, especially a low-caste man" (73). He can only hope for a change to be wrought in the attitude of people towards untouchables, or for the flush system to be introduced. Critics like Riemenschneider and P.K. Rajan condemn Anand for making his protagonist too passive and unable to make any conscious effort for his liberation from brutal subjugation. Riemenschneider finds Bakha to be a mere passive listener. Rajan criticises Anand for his failure to handle the character of the protagonist appropriately: "The external reality under the pressure of which Anand wrote the novel had in it the stirrings of an awakening of the socially deprived sections; and in depicting this reality as it operates through Bakha, the novelist should have laid emphasis on the conscious factor in Bakha's upheaval. That he did not do this is a pointer to a contradiction within himself between what the theme demanded of him and his own class limitations."[22] But Rajan's view that Bakha's conscious action against untouchability would have been more convincing seems wrong. In 1920 when Anand wrote this novel, the untouchables had, no doubt, started feeling the inhumanity and injustice of casteism, but it would have been too much to expect an open rebellion by them. Perhaps, if Anand had done so, the novel would have lost much of its authenticity in the presentation of both character and situation. Saros Cowasjee's remark sounds appropriate: "... it is in his failure to act that the fidelity—if not the strength—of the novel lies."[23]

Equally realistic is Bakha's response to the feelings of love shown towards him by a few high-born Hindus. He responds with great modesty and humility whenever some generous Hindu treats him with love. When Charat Singh promises to give him a hockey stick, his gratitude and humility are the only expected response from a young boy who has been utterly deprived of love and admiration. Anand presents Bakha's gratefulness quite effectively: "Charat Singh's generous promise had called forth that trait of servility in Bakha which he had inherited from his forefathers: the weakness of the down-trodden, the helplessness of the poor and the indigent suddenly receiving help, the passive contentment of the bottom dog suddenly illuminated by the prospect of fulfilment of a secret and long-cherished desire" (20). Again, when Bakha goes to collect the hockey stick and Charat Singh warmly welcomes him, Bakha is full of admiration for the liberal Havildar. How grateful he feels for Charat Singh's kindness is well revealed in his one thought: "For this man, I wouldn't mind being a sweeper all my life. I would do anything for him" (118). When Bakha actually gets a hockey stick, Anand tells us: "He [Bakha] was grateful, grateful, haltingly grateful, falteringly grateful, stumblingly grateful, so grateful that he didn't know how he could walk the ten yards to the corner to be out of the sight of his benevolent and generous host" (122). Such humility is further revealed when Mahatma Gandhi speaks for the untouchables. When the Mahatma says that he will like to be born as a scavenger if he should be born again, Bakha is full of admiration for him. He is ready to sacrifice anything for him: "He adored the man. He felt he could put his life in his hands and ask him to do what he liked with it.

For him he would do anything. He would like to go and be a scavenger at his Ashram" (165). All these incidents reveal that Bakha is one with his father, brother and other untouchables though with a difference. But he could not be condemned for such servility because heredity and centuries of passive acceptance of tradition and taboos by his race have left very deep marks on Bakha's consciousness. It would rather seem unrealistic if Anand made Bakha utterly different from his father and brother. Anand has struck a beautiful blend of revolutionary feelings and traditional passivity in the character of his protagonist. Otherwise, too, the response of Bakha to even the least kindness shown to him is quite authentic. One can hardly expect anything different from a young boy who has always been deprived of any love or kindness.

Bakha's acute sensitiveness is further revealed in his attitude towards nature. His pleasure in natural surroundings is sensuous which ultimately assumes spiritual hues though he is unconscious of the spiritual experience he undergoes. After cleaning the latrines, when Bakha goes out to sweep the streets, he enjoys the heat of the sun in the open *maidan*. He wants the heat of the sun to reach each part of his body. His sensuous delight in the sun is acute and profound. Anand reveals how Bakha wants to capture the heat in his corporeal frame: "He wanted to warm his flesh; he wanted the warmth to get behind the scales of the dry, powdry surface that had formed on his fingers; he wanted the blood in the veins that stood out on the back of his hand to melt. He turned his hands to show them to the sun, open-eyed for a moment, then with the pupils of his eyes half-closed, half-open. And he lifted his chin upright" (38). While profoundly engrossed in his enjoyment of the physical sensation the heat of the sun causes to him, he undergoes a spiritual pleasure though he is unaware of the spiritual aspect of the happiness: "He caught the full force of its glare, and was dazed. He stood lost for a moment, confused in the shimmering rays, feeling as though there was nothing but the sun, the sun, the sun, everywhere, in him, on him, before him, and behind him. it was a pleasant sensation inspite of the disconcerting suddenness with which it had engulfed him. He felt suspended, as it were, in a region of buoyant tenseness..." (38-39). Again Bakha has a similar experience while gazing at the pool on the slope of Bulandshahar hills. Significantly, he is again facing the sun which now is being "reflected from the sheen of the rippling water with a restlessness like the pain in Bakha's soul" (106). Anand, in a very subtle manner, uses pathetic fallacy revealing the mood of nature demonstrated in the heat of the sun, in congruity with Bakha's own tormented mind. As he leans back with his eyes towards the sun, his experience is that of a mystic in a trance: "in a moment or two his frame seemed to have sunk into insignificance, drowned as it were in a pit of silence, while the things on the sunny bank began to take life, each little stem of plant becoming a big leaf, distinct and important. The whole valley seemed to him suddenly aglow with life" (106). The experience is reminiscent of some Laurentian characters and even of Wordsworth's ecstatic experience in "Tintern Abbey": "We are laid asleep in body and become a living soul."[24] The scene is rich in philosophical profundity. Therefore S.C. Harrex's criticism of the scene seems a bit too severe: "E.M. Forster's point in the preface that 'the fact that he [Anand] has come to fiction through philosophy has given him depth' seems to break down at this stage."[25] Such harsh criticism seems to be baseless because the scene is replete with deep mystical and philosophical overtones. Bakha has a somewhat similar experience again, and again it is in the light of the sun. Bakha is walking through the *maidan* again and as he looks at the rubbish heaps, he has a strange feeling: "So lofty did he feel in his mood of righteous indignation that he had the strange sensation of being a giant, commanding a full view of everything in the hollows and hills" (133). All these experiences reveal his inner ability to feel keenly the deeper pleasures of nature. But the cruel social forces have rendered him unable to develop this dormant quality.

In Bakha, Anand presents the conflict between potentialities and circumstances. He himself clearly reveals the predicament of his protagonist: "It was a discord between person and circumstance by which a lion like him lay enmeshed in a net, while many a common criminal wore a rajah's crown. His wealth of inner experience, however, was extraordinary... But it wanted the force and vivacity of thought to transmute his vague sense into the superior instinct of the self-conscious man" (105-06). Such conflict between person and circumstance has been emphasized in the novel a number of times both on the physical and the spiritual level. On the physical level we again and again find that he is rebel in mind but a victim in reality. On the spiritual level, his inner experience remains crude and unsophisticated because of his birth in a low caste. The conflict on the spiritual level is vividly presented in the scene in the temple. Bakha, out of sheer curiosity, dares to cross the steps to the temple and peep into the inner sanctum. The hymns sung in the temple have a deep effect on his mind and soul. He reaches that level of ecstasy which few among the shallow-minded worshippers can. The novelist presents the deeply felt response of Bakha to the hymns chanted in the temple in these words: "Bakha was profoundly moved. He was affected by the rhythm of the song. His blood had coursed along the balanced melodic line to the final note of strength with such sheer vigour that his hands joined unconsciously, and his head hung in the worship of the unknown god" (68). But this delight is cruelly suppressed by the hypocritical words of the priest: "Polluted! Polluted!" He loses all strength in a moment and feels as if he were dead. He is kicked away from the house of God because the holy books ordain that a temple gets pulluted by a low-caste man coming within sixty-nine yards of it. Anand lashes at the people who blindly agree that the temple can be purified again by the sacrificial fire. The religious instinct in Bakha is, thus, suppressed before it can bloom properly. Christianity offers a shelter to such low-caste men. Bakha is presented with a chance to adopt the Christian religion. Colonel Hutchinson who does his duty of proselytizing rather too vigorously, tries to allure Bakha towards Christianity. But whatever he sings in praise of Jesus is beyond the understanding of Bakha. The latter finds the Colonel's words confusing and muffled. Such confused talk fails to tempt Bakha although he is curious to know everything about Jesus Christ and God. His flight from the Colonel's house is further encouraged by the dominating wife of the Colonel who takes offence at her husband's contact with the untouchables. His curiosity again remains unsatisfied but it is a good riddance from the tenacious hold of the Colonel. Anand obviously mocks at the clumsy efforts of the Colonel to convert untouchables to Christianity. The satire is apparent in the statement that Hutchinson has succeeded in effecting only five conversions in twenty-five years. The rebukes by his dominating wife further add to the discomfiture of the Colonel. But the scene enables Bakha to rise higher in our estimation. That he does not yield to the allurements offered by the Colonel proves his mettle. He is no push-over.

The authenticity of the novel is further heightened by Anand's treatment of other characters. Again we find in his delineation a combination of the positive and negative attitudes. Lakha, though a cruel, dominating, abusive father, is capable of love and sympathy too. Like any loving father, he at once feels that Bakha is in low spirits and insists to know the reason. When he comes to know about the insults that Bakha and Sohini have suffered, Lakha too is annoyed. Anand reveals the reaction of Lakha to such disgrace: "Lakha was touched. A queer self-conscious smile hovered on the edges of his moustache, a smile of impotent rage" (89). The "impotent rage" of Lakha is quite like the "smouldering rage" of Bakha. Centuries of passive suffering have led him to compromise with any humiliation. His helplessness against the rigid taboos makes him fear that Bakha might have tried to retaliate. His question "You didn't abuse or hit back, did you?" not only shows his inability to hit back but also the helplessness of a human being who is in rigid shackles of casteism. Again, Anand presents Charat Singh as a very liberal, kind-hearted man but in the beginning we are told that he too has the typical prejudice of a twice-born Hindu against stink. When he pays compliments to Bakha, Anand modifies his kind words with the remark that he "did not relax the grin which symbolised two thousand years of racial and caste superiority"

(19). The high-born Hindus in the novel are not invariably cruel nor are the untouchables unrealistically pitiable and submissive. When one woman rebukes Bakha for having defiled her house by sitting on the wooden platform, there is another to console him: "My child, you shouldn't sit on people's doorsteps like this" (81). This dexterously struck blend of appreciation and condemnation, sympathy and criticism makes the novel an authentic presentation of life. This skilful mingling of attitudes is well exemplified in the revelation that even untouchables, who are shunned and despised by the so-considered pure Hindus, have their own hierarchy of castes and they too suffer from caste complexes. Gulabo the washerwoman looks down upon Sohini because she claims a higher place in the hierarchy. Bakha too realizes that "there were degrees of caste among the low-castes, and that he was the lowest" (100). Thus, with subtle irony, Anand mocks at those people who themselves are victims of rigid casteism but do not spare others from a similar treatment whenever offered a chance.

Anand is able to conceal his purpose in the veil of art so far as the presentation of the life of untouchables is concerned. He has also treated the mentality of the caste-conscious Hindus with great insight. But the reformer in him is not content with mere presentation of the situation. He must suggest the solution to the problem. Towards the end of the novel he fails to maintain the artistic integrity and the intention of the author erupts when he introduces saviour figures. He brings Mahatma Gandhi *in propria persona* to preach against the inhuman practice of untouchability. No doubt, the Mahatma is able to provide a ray of hope in the otherwise dismal world of the untouchables, but his long speech stands out separately from the framework of the novel. No doubt, Gandhi's campaign against untouchability was one of the chief social phenomena in the nineteen thirties. The excitement among people to listen to the Mahatma, the appeal of his speech to the hearts of the people, and even the physical appearance of the Mahatma are quite authentically presented but the incorporation of the speech in the novel mars the aesthetic appeal of the novel which is otherwise very successful both in form and content and the fusion of the two. The propagandist in Anand seems to assert himself a bit too clearly and strongly. After the long speech by Mahatma Gandhi, there follows an equally long harangue by the poet Sarshar who finds flush system to be the best way to free the sweepers from their dirty job and also from untouchability. Bakha is attracted by the humanism of Mahatma Gandhi but he is more impressed by the talk about the machine which can clear the dirt away. He has rejected Christianity as a way out of his predicament. But when he proceeds homewards, he has both the speech of the Mahatma and the proposal of the poet in his mind. Paul Verghese condemns the propagandistic effort of Anand to preach against untouchability and to suggest the solutions. "The English missionary, Gandhi and the poet," says Verghese, "are brought in towards the end of the novel for the specific purpose of suggesting a solution to the problem of untouchability. This is as a result of Anand's desire to play the part of the social reformer at the expense of the novelist, as in almost every other novel of his.... Anand, it may be said, plays the role of the propagandist a little too obviously."[26] Narsimhaiah's admiration of the novel and the novelist, though applicable to the major part of the novel, sounds a bit exaggerated keeping the last part in mind: "Anand does not, of course, employ the tone of attack—that would go against the grain of the artist—but makes an excellent use of the tone of subtle irony unsuspected in Anand because of the popular assumption that he is a propagandist who hammers his point home."[27]

No doubt, Anand has successfully used irony to expose the social evil of untouchability, but Gandhi's speech and the poet's commentary are examples of direct propagation of ideology. H.M. Williams gives a fair judgement of the novelist's triumph and failure: "*Untouchable* suggests both the strength and the weakness of Anand as a novelist: fine sympathetic portrayal of Indian reality in terms of the lives of the dispossessed, to some degree marred by glib 'socialistic' answers to imponderable questions bound up with religious traditions and deep-seated social customs."[28]

The novel, in this way, reveals the author's zeal for protest against the inhuman evil of untouchability a little too clearly. The contrivance of making a saviour character speak against the evil goes against the grain of art. Art which, according to Anand himself, demands detachment despite commitment of the author, here seems to have become a cry against the social exploitation of those born in the so-called low families. Anand reveals an admirable restraint against exaggeration, distortion, and personal commentary. But he cannot remain distant from the novel for long. His own thoughts creep in through the speeches by the saviour characters. Such direct statement certainly brings discredit to the artist despite his otherwise rare success in handling a new theme and a new kind of protagonist.

Although Anand had fairly exhausted his subject in *Untouchable,* he came out with the same theme after twenty-five years in *The Road* (1963). The novel again presents an untouchable as a victim of agonizing mental torture because of rigidity of caste considerations in Hindu society. The protagonist now is a leather worker, a *Chamar*—a step higher than Bakha in the hierarchy of outcastes. He, therefore, is presented to be more active than the introspective but passive Bakha. Still he is not strong enough to be able to fight alone against the established social norms. He wants the support of somebody, somebody stronger than him to violate the traditional taboos. Anand, therefore, presents a saviour character, Dhooli Singh, who is kindness incarnate. The saviour character now is more active in the novel than the saviour heroes in *Untouchable.* He sacrifices a lot and actually throws himself in the fray against those who victimize the poor untouchables. But now Anand is guilty of exaggeration; he presents Dhooli Singh as a symbol of sympathy, selflessness, and sacrifice. The latter, therefore, does not appear as a real man—a combination of virtues and weaknesses. He seems to have been devised by the author to fit in with the plan of the action and fails to be a lifelike and convincing character.

The Road was, in fact, written with a specific purpose—to prove to the then Prime Minister that despite legislation against untouchability, the evil existed and had a strong hold on the minds of people. Once in a village near Gurgaon in Haryana, Anand found that caste prejudices prevailed in a shocking degree despite the legislative attempts to remove untouchability. He found something "tragi-comic" in the fact that the caste Hindus were not ready to touch the stones quarried by the untouchables to make the road. They found the stones defiled by the touch of the untouchables. Anand mentioned it to Pt. Nehru who refused to believe it. The novelist decided to prove it to the Prime Minister in the "enchanted mirror."[29]

This time Anand did not depend only on the conflict in the mind of the hero; he presented a direct fight between the untouchables and their supporters on one hand and the rigid caste-Hindus on the other. Instead of realism, he chose the technique of allegory and symbolism. The road is symbolic of the emancipation and liberty of the untouchables; the construction of the road symbolises the rebellion against caste-taboos. But towards the end of the novel, the road serves only to take Bhikhu out of the village to Delhi, the capital of Hindustan where he hopes to lose himself in the crowd. He hopes that in the capital he will be able to identify himself with others because there will be no castes and no outcastes.

The Road has earned Anand very harsh and severe criticism at the hands of critics like Saros Cowasjee, M.K. Naik, Paul Verghese, and R.S. Singh. Most critics find the novel lacking in intensity, authenticity, and novelty. While comparing the novel with *Untouchable*, they exaggerate their admiration of the latter and adjudge the farmer rather severely. Saros Cowasjee rejects the novel outrightly with this harsh opinion: "*The Road* is a timid work, and one cannot help suspecting that Anand's concern for the outcastes is somewhat eclipsed by his fear or embarrassment in what he calls 'the human empire of Jawaharlal Nehru.'"[30] R.S. Singh rejects it as an artistic failure. Paul Verghese finds the propagandistic effort a bit too obvious. Jack Lindsay, however, admires the novelist's deft handling of the technique of symbolism. "There is no intellectual imposition of symbol on material that in itself lacks all significance," says Lindsay, "Instead we get a natural dynamic relation between an actual situation and its total meaning, all canalised in the image of the road."[31] K.N. Sinha too appreciates the novel for "greater stylistic maturity and finesse,"[32] as compared with *Untouchable*. But Sinha's appreciation of the novel is somewhat self-contradictory. Unlike Jack Lindsay, Sinha finds the symbolism interfering with the material, particularly character delineation. According to him, "Artistically speaking, the symbolic design of the novel interferes with the reality of characterization. The core of the novel lies elsewhere—in the dramatization of the social conflict."[33] But again he concludes with a compliment: "*The Road*, then, is a brilliant piece of symbolic construction. It stands out as a fresh landmark in the art of Mulk Raj Anand...especially with respect to its artistry and symbolism."[34]

However, the fact remains that; the novelette is not a mere replica of *Untouchable* nor is Bhikhu a pale imitation of Bakha. Bhikhu belongs to a higher rank in the hierarchy of untouchables—he is a leather worker. But he stands for the whole hierarchy. Like Bakha, Bhikhu too is ambitious, but he has been able to achieve many things which remain only a dream with Bakha. Bhikhu can read, write and sing. Whereas Bakha, after feeling a desire to retaliate against any injustice meted out to him, reconciles with his fate passively, Bhikhu actually rebels. He fights against the twice-born Hindus so that he can lead his mother to the temple. Instead of feeling contented with the realization of his social position—"I am an untouchable! Untouchable! Untouchable"—he fights for his rights and declares his lack of faith in casteism: "One is a leather worker by profession and not by birth!"[35] He feels disgusted with his mother's acceptance of fate that we are chamars.... And they are twice-born" (66). When the twice-born Hindus try to bar their way to the temple, he takes the direct path to the temple instead or turning back. Whereas Bakha can only hope for his amelioration by the introduction of flush system or the change in the mentality of people, Bhikhu actually works for his salvation. He actively helps in the building of the road which ultimately takes him out of the village towards the capital of India. No doubt, his hopes may be frustrated, but at least he tries to convert his dream of equal status with others into reality. The pains inflicted on untouchables are greater than those in *Untouchable*. In the latter, the biggest atrocity against an untouchable is a slap on the face for polluting a caste-Hindu as Bakha unconsciously touches him. In *The Road*, on the other hand, the huts of untouchables are burnt down; these poor outcastes are left homeless. But Anand has failed to arouse pity here as he does in his first novel. The feelings of Bakha after each humiliation are much more intense than those of Bhikhu and his friends in *The Road*. Like Bakha, Bhikhu is also slapped towards the end of the novel, his crime being soiling a brass tumbler by drinking water which Rukmani has given him. But Bhikhu's reaction to the slap, unlike that of Bakha, is not a mere brooding over his lot passively. No doubt, he too feels the restraint of the caste taboos but he is afraid that he may not resist an urge to hit back. "Bhikhu stretched out to his full height again, till the landlord's son cowered back. Then he felt he must withdraw before either hand should strike" (96).

Bhikhu, we find, is not the one to suffer only but he can strike as well. Only he wants to avoid a clash and find a permanent solution to prejudices against him. He, unlike Bakha, does not go back accepting the blow as his lot but leaves the village for good with the hope of getting rid of the inhuman practice of casteism.

Like Bakha, Bhikhu too believes in the dignity of work. Bakha is unconsciously a disciple of Gandhi insofar as his devotion to work is concerned. Bhikhu too is dedicated to duty. He gets his inspiration from another leader: "Take the name of Jawaharlal and carry on!" (92). He derives his strength from the preachings of Kabir too. While wielding a hammer he finds himself to be very powerful and proclaims his strength: "Call me, if you need two strong arms!" (19). Dhooli Singh calls him "demon of work" (73). Bhikhu's notion of work and his achievements are quite authentically delineated but the novelist seems to be consciously trying to add another feather in his protagonist's cap in the scene where Bhikhu goes in the burning hut to bring the goat out. The scene seems to be forced in the novel to emphasize the admirable courage of the hero.

In *The Road*, the sufferer, we find, is more active and courageous than his counterpart in *Untouchable* and so is the saviour figure. Dhooli Singh, unlike Gandhi and the poet in *Untouchable*, does not merely preach against the evil practice of untouchability, he actually fights for its removal. The dumpling nose readily snaps all connections with the caste-Hindus and sides with the untouchables. He is ready to suffer excommunication; even the matrimonial prospects of his son and daughter are at stake, but he unflinchingly persists in his efforts for building the road which stands for the riddance of people from a number of inconveniences. The construction of the road also stands for a demand for justice and equal status for the untouchables because he insists on the need of the quarrying of stones by the untouchables. He gives shelter to the untouchables both in his fields and his home. When his wife, daughter, and son leave him, he calls the homeless untouchable men and women to his house and distributes clothes among them: "'Come then,' he said, suddenly, impetuously. 'Come into the house.... Come.... The woman of God is gone to her proper place, the temple!... And that rascal Lachman will not be my son again! And I shall be an outcaste forever.... So the house is yours.... Come, my sons and daughters....'" (48). No doubt, the action is "impetuous" but it is very much congruous with his actions in the rest of the novel. The appearance of the saviour figure, unlike that of Gandhi and the poet in *Untouchable*, is not abrupt and so unconvincing. He, on the other hand, occupies the stage from the beginning till the end. Nor does he indulge in long harangues against untouchability. He, instead, actually works with the untouchables for their good. Only he seems to be unrealistically good—a man with all virtues and no vice. Anand makes only one negative remark about him—that physically he is not appealing. But physical appearance has no significance in a man who has such lofty notions as he actually practises.

The villain Thakur Singh, his son Sajnu, and his daughter Rukmani are quite convincingly portrayed. The prejudices of Thakur Singh, the fluctuating alliances of Sajnu and Lachman, and Rukmani's suffocation in her rigid father's house are quite realistic. As in *Untouchable*, here too Anand mocks at the hypocrisy of the priest. Pt. Suraj Mani is more or less an imitation of Pt. Kali Nath. The satire in both the novels is subtle but acute. No doubt, the symbolic names that the novelist bestows on his characters like the "Dumpling-Nose Dhooli Singh," "Tomato-Face Thakur Singh," "Fox-Face Daya Ram," "Cowherd Mahesh," and "Cock-Eyed Ram Nivas" are jarring and irritating but it seems unfair to agree with Saros Cowasjee who very severely remarks: "*Untouchable* owed its success to Anand's sharp insight into the character of Bakha, as well as secondary characters like his sister Sohini, and his father, Lakha. In *The Road*, however, there are no characters—only people into whom Anand tries to infuse life by impressionistic techniques."[36] Saros Cowasjee overlooks the fact that almost all the characters in the fiction of Anand are common "people" and there is no difference between the characters of *Untouchable* and the "people" of *The Road*. They have been realistically presented in both the novels. We cannot think that Sohini is more suitable a character than Mala or Rukmani or Lakha is more authentically presented than Laxmi. If Bakha's feelings are more intense than those of Bhikhu, it is because Bakha is more introspective. In *The Road* the emphasis is more on action than on introspection and psychological analysis.

The objectionable feature of the novel, however, is the unauthentic presentation of the saviour hero, Dhooli Singh and his foil Thakur Singh—the former being an embodiment of virtue and the latter an incarnation of rigid and narrow caste considerations. If Thakur Singh is nothing but a villain. Dhooli Singh too seems to be a bit idealized. He fails to emerge as a living, lifelike character. Both of them seem to be instruments in the hands of their creator performing exactly the contrasted roles allotted to them. The relationship between the sufferer and the saviour, however, differs somewhat from that in *Untouchable.* The sufferer is not the lowest in the hierarchy of untouchables nor is the saviour a man of national and international repute. The sufferer, therefore, is not so much ridden with caste complex as is his counterpart in *Untouchable.* The saviour too is not an unapproachable, distant figure speaking from a platform to the audience. The awe-inspiring personality of Mahatma Gandhi and the profound talk of the poet make them saintly, adorable figures to Bakha whom he cannot hope to approach. Bhikhu, on the other hand, works vigorously with Dhooli Singh for the betterment of men of his caste.

Anand's love for the underdog also informs and shapes *Coolie* (1936). His sympathy for the downtrodden and venom against the ruthless oppressors again result in a novel which marks both his achievement and failure as an artist. As in *Untouchable,* here too he has failed to conceal his intention in the garb of art completely. An urge to protest against the cruel social set up and propagate for the suffering humanity is a bit too strong for the novelist to put down. The contemporary capitalistic system with its gaping disparity between the haves and have-nots is the target of Anand's bitterness in *Coolie.* Anand particularly lashes at the role of the British and their Indian sycophants in creating a gulf between the rich and the poor. Like a true Marxist, Anand cries for justice and fairplay for the exploited labourers. He introduces some saviour characters to bring home his ideology.

Untouchable and *Coolie* are alike so far as their themes are concerned. The former portrays an untouchable in his true colours and the latter lays bare the life of a coolie, a victim of capitalistic economy. *Untouchable* attacks the social set up; *Coolie* concentrates on social evils which issue from an inequitable economic system. The protagonists in both the novels are passive, intimidated victims though Munoo is an iota ahead of Bakha as he, at least, takes the initiative to escape from the causes of his suffering. But though thematically akin, the two novels are widely divergent regarding the treatment of the themes in the two. "In treatment, two novels could hardly be more dissimilar,"[37] remarks Saros Cowasjee.

Untouchable is celebrated for its well-knit, concentrated plot and meticulously observed unities of time and place; *Coolie*, on the other hand, has a very wide canvas with a large variety of people painted in various hues. Anand adopted the stream of consciousness technique to reveal the thoughts and emotions of his scavenger protagonist and through him present the plight of those who have fallen victims to the cruel casteism; in *Coolie* he chooses expansion and variety in preference to economy and compactness to bring to light not only the intensity of the tyrannical class consciousness but also the universality of the problem. Anand wants to reveal that no part of the country is free from the shackles of caste prejudices. Every village, town, and metropolitan city is a prey to the evil of class disparities. Anand traces, in particular, the strains and stresses which are a result of the growing economic structure and expanding commerce. Because of the change in the economic pattern of society, people have thrown their spiritual heritage and idealism overboard; the monetary considerations are so predominant in society that almost every economically sound person wants to exploit and fleece the weaker. In this world of monetary considerations, the Darwinian "survival of the fittest" is the predominant rule though it is not the physical fitness nor is the survival physical. And, according to Narsimhaiah, "In the circumstances, sheer survival must be looked upon as a triumph of the spirit, the very will to live must be reckoned a strength."[38] The curse of poverty renders a person absolutely misfit among those who enjoy a sound economic position. Whatever potential is left in a poverty-stricken coolie goes waste because he develops an inferiority complex which cripples his mind terribly.

With the intention to expose the evil of class disparities, Anand chooses Munoo, a coolie whom he personally knew and who worked in a pickle-and-jam factory in Anand's neighbourhood in Amritsar, to serve as the protagonist of his prose epic. The concentration of *Untouchable* gives place to comprehensiveness because Anand wants to show how widespread the evil is. The novel has been cast, to, a large extent, in the mould of the picaresque although it differs considerably from picaresque novels like *Joseph Andrews, Tom Jones,* and *Huckleberry Finn*. The hero is not a picaro, a rogue, or a ruffian; he does not indulge in any anti-social activity; he, on the other hand, is a victim of the rogueries of society which seem to be bent upon squeezing him to the last drop of blood. Anand has struck a very dexterous balance between the picaresque and the *Bildungsroman*. The novel shares the vastness of *Huckleberry Finn* and the development of thought of *A Portrait of the Artist as a Young Man*. Munoo has the ambitions and desires of Stephen Dedalus but he is thrown from pillar to post like any hero of a picaresque novel. Destiny plays a significant role in determining the actions of the hero but, unlike Bakha, he himself too tries to escape to a new world when the circumstances at one place become too oppressive. His life, like that of anybody in the actual world, is a blend of conscious efforts on one hand and destined results on the other. Munoo shuttles from one place to another and wherever he goes, he finds the plight of the coolies to be the same. They are exploited and maltreated. Munoo suffers economic exploitation at Sham Nagar, Daulatpur, and Bombay; at Simla, he is victim to the sexual exploitation of a Eurasian lady. The change of place in no way means the change of fate for the coolies. Only the exploiters and their modes of exploitation change.

Whenever the scene shifts, we find new exploiters and so do the saviour figures change. Wherever Munoo goes, he not only finds his cruel masters but also some people who come to his rescue. The place of action in the novel being very vast, we find a large number of saviour figures, some of them fitting well into the main framework of the novel and others sticking out of the chief plot and serving as only the mouthpieces of the novelist. Dr. Prem at Sham Nagar, Prabha Dyal at Daulatpur and Ratan at Bombay are quite convincingly introduced into the novel whereas Gokal Nath and Sauda at Bombay and Mohan at Simla have been forced into the novel only to vociferate the intentions of Anand. The trade-unionists are as clumsy and inefficient as the revolutionaries in *The Sword and the Sickle*; the actions of both the groups are unorganised and unplanned. Mohan, on the other hand, is unrealistically virtuous and modest like Dr de la Havre in *Two Leaves and a Bud*; the sacrifices of the two for the sake of coolies are a bit too improvised to be authentic. They offend the credulity of a person. The advice of Mohan to Munoo and other coolies gives an unaesthetically didactic tone to the last part of the novel as Dr Havre's harangues mar much of the aesthetic appeal of *Two Leaves and a Bud*.

The troubles of Munoo begin in his very early childhood. A parentless child, he is the subject of his aunt's very frequent abuse and physical torture. The very first speech of the aunt is, in a way, a premonition of what is in store for the young five-year-old Munoo: "Munoo Ohe Munooa oh Mundu! Where have you died? Where have you drifted, you of the evil star?"[39] And Munoo himself considers himself to be "of the evil star" after he has undergone a lot a suffering at different places. While at Bombay, he broods over his lot: "Am I really ominous?... My father died when I was born, and then my mother, and I brought misfortune to Prabha, and, it seems I've brought misfortune to Hari now. If I am ominous, why don't I die? My death would rid the world of an unlucky person. I would like to die. It were better to be dead" (217). The events that take place between the aunt's call and Munoo's musing are pressing enough to justify such distress and self-accusation in the hero's mind. He has to accompany his bullying uncle to the town of Sham Nagar to serve as a servant in the house of Babu Nathoo Ram. His fascination for the city life enables him to leave his village without any regret. The curiosity about the life-style in towns fills him with excitement and hope. But his dream receives a sudden jolt at the cruel reception that he is given in the household of the bank employee. The filthy abuse and tyrannical behaviour at the hands of the dominating Bibi Uttam Kaur make him feel nostalgic for his life in his village where his aunt beat him "more than he beat his cattle" (11). Munoo's relieving himself outside the kitchen of the house and his breaking of the china tea-set in the presence of Mr England add to his misery. But the cruelty of Babu Nathoo Ram and his wife becomes intolerable when in a playful mood Munoo forgets his status and bites Sheila on the cheek. The innocent action of Munoo is associated with all the perverted ambitions and urges of man; it is regarded as an assault on the honour of the girl. The ruthless beating he receives at the hands of his employer compels him to leave the house and go somewhere, anywhere. Otherwise, while in the household of Babu Nathoo Ram, Munoo tries to reconcile with his fate. He is able to keep up his zest for life. The warmth of Dr Prem's humour, his occasional kind words to Munoo and Sheila's innocent kindness keep him in high spirits. The fashionable life-style of the Chota Babu inspires ambitions in Munoo's mind to grow up and possess the things which the Chota Babu has—things like a tea-set, a stethoscope, an electric razor, and a silken suit. First he had been fascinated by the black boots of Babu Nathoo Ram. He really wanted to possess a pair of such shiny boots himself. His desire is quite like Stephen Dedalus' ambition: "When would he be like the fellows in poetry and rhetoric? They had big voices and big boots and they studied trigonometry."[40] But the irony, in Munoo's case, is that he is beaten with the same boots by Nathoo Ram for biting Sheila on the cheek.

No doubt, Munoo's father had died because of poverty and so had his mother. But it is at Sham Nagar that he first realizes the importance of money in the world. Now he is able to recognize the difference between the rich and the poor; in this world of monetary values, even a high caste is of no significance; the possession of riches only is required to enjoy dignity and status in society. Munoo's observation is, in fact, the conclusion of a mind matured by various experiences: "I am a Kshatriya and I am poor, and Verma, a Brahmin, is a servant boy, a menial, because he is poor. No, caste does not matter. The babus are like the sahib-logs, and all servants look alike. There must only be two kinds of people in the world: the rich and poor" (69). It is this gap between the haves and the have-nots which Anand wants to expose and preach against. As if not satisfied with the exposure of the evil through the musings of his protagonist, he later on makes the trade unionist, Sauda, one of the saviour characters in Bombay section articulate his intention in a vociferous oration: "There are only two kinds of people in the world: the rich and the poor and between the two there is no connection" (266). The repetition of not only the thought but even the words, no doubt, reveals the obsession of the author about the adequate presentation of life of the poor in contrast to that of the rich who thrive on the labour of the former. Munoo, we find, having undergone some bitter experiences has matured enough to observe how partial the world is towards the rich. Equally mature are his questions regarding his identity: "What am I—Munoo?... Why am I here in this house?" (46). Like Bakha in *Untouchable* realizing that he is only an untouchable, Munoo too realizes his identity: "I am Munoo, Babu Nathoo Ram's servant" (46). He accepts his lot as a servant as something pre-destined which nobody can alter. Anand remarks about Munoo's passive acceptance of his fate: "It did not occur to him to ask himself what he was apart from being a servant. His identity he took for granted, and the relationship of Nathoo Ram, who wore black boots, with himself, Munoo, who went about barefoot, was to him like sunshine and sunset, inevitable" (46). He reckons the superiority of the rich people like Babu Nathoo Ram as an unchangeable decree of fate. The notion of his own inferiority is so deeply ingrained in his mind that he decides to be a good servant, "a perfect model of a servant" (48). But his cruel master and mistress do not let him be even a very good servant. Their ruthlessness only awakens a spirit of rebellion in Munoo. Like Gauri, who gives up her docility at the repeated beating at the hands of Panchi, Munoo too revolts against the cruel treatment meted out to him: "The boy's soul surged up in rebellion and hate, in a hate of which he had not thought himself capable. He was startled..." (73). The rebellion in the case of Munoo, as in the case of Gauri and Bakha, is only to leave the home and find haven somewhere. Gauri has, of course, a destination before her; Munoo, like Bhikhu, wants to lose himself in the crowd where nobody should recognize him. "A whipped dog hides in a corner; a whipped human seeks escape" (73), remarks Anand. Such an escape is very frequent in his novels. Lalu in *The village* leaves his town and gets recruited in the army. Anand himself had taken shelter across the black waters when his father's cruel beating of Anand himself and his mother became intolerable. Destiny directs Munoo towards the railway station where he boards a train, any train at random. The scale of destiny tilts in Munoo's favour who meets Prabha Dyal, a childless pickle-and-jam factory owner at Daulatpur. Prabha Dyal takes him home and employs him in his factory where Munoo enjoys superiority over the other employees because of his master's affection. The master and his wife shower parental love on him. The wife of Prabha Dyal, in contrast to Bibi Uttam Kaur of Sham Nagar, is all love and sympathy for Munoo. Their kindness and affection towards the poor orphan do not appear to be forced on the novel with a purpose. Their behaviour is convincing and believable because Anand, very discreetly attributes it to the fact that the couple is childless. Their affection towards a young child, therefore, seems to be the result of a strong desire for a son. Anand further relates the kindness of Prabha Dyal to all coolies in general and Munoo in particular to the fact that he himself has tasted the bitterness of poverty. He himself was a coolie once and, therefore, can well understand their feelings and thoughts. Unlike Mohan in the last section of the novel, Prabha Dyal is not an outsider purposely brought in the novel to propagate for the cause of coolies. Nor is his sacrifice incredibly great as is that of Mohan and of Dr Havre in *Two Leaves and a Bud*. He, like Dr Prem at Sham Nagar, is imbued with human kindness which he must show towards all human beings, even poor coolies. Unlike Sauda in the Bombay scene of the novel and Dr Malhotra in *Gauri*, Prabha Dyal does not overtly preach the novelist's desire for equality and brotherhood. Nor does he stand on a platform like Mahatma Gandhi in *Untouchable* for inspiring the audience for humane treatment of the down-trodden. Prabha Dyal's ultimate impoverishment makes him more identical with the poor coolies. That Tulsi and Munoo undergo bitter experiences to earn money for their master reveals that their love is reciprocal—not the condescension of one much higher in status towards those who are much weaker.

But the moments of pleasure, in the case of Munoo, are always transient and tinged with suffering. Prabha Dyal's affection for Munoo is offset by Ganpat's cruelty. At last Prabha Dyal, a coolie risen to prosperity, is impoverished again by the intrigues of his partner. The fraud of Ganpat renders Prabha a bankrupt with a number of creditors claiming their dues. One of the creditors, Sir Todar Mal, through the influence of an English health officer, Marjoribanks, has Prabha Dyal beaten mercilessly in the prison. All these calamities not only leave Prabha Dyal a demoralized, weak coolie, but his employees, including Munoo, too are on the road to face a cut-throat competition even for the humble job of carrying a sack of grain in the market or vegetables of rich ladies in the vegetable market. The coolies are treated as beasts of burden by the shopkeepers in the grain market. To the great regret of Munoo, he is too young to carry a sack of grain. His inability to earn by carrying heavy load makes him look at the other stronger coolies like Tulsi with envy; his desire to grow up and be strong like Tulsi indirectly reveals the plight of a coolie for whom to earn a meagre amount by carrying loads is a cherished dream. His helplessness is evident: "Lucky Tulsi, he will earn four annas today, and I shall have nothing to take home to Prabha.... I wish I had been strong enough to bear the sack of grain.' He was angry with himself and impatient. 'Oh,' he rebuked himself, 'when will I grow up and be a strong man?'" (145). The lines are packed with the pathos of the life of coolies. But in this world of monetary values, the poor still retain human sympathy and kindness. The employees of Prabha Dyal are ready to do any difficult job to save their master from the crisis. When Munoo fails to find any employment, his greatest regret is that he will not be able to help Prabha Dyal.

While working at Daulatpur vegetable market, Munoo, with his curiosity for experience, had developed a fascination for Bombay. A fellow coolie had told him that Bombay was a "wonder city" where there was plenty of work and a coolie could earn fifteen to thirty rupees a month. A stroke of destiny mixed with Munoo's own initiative puts him on the road to the ambrosial isle of palm and coconut trees. His chance meeting with the elephant driver in the circus show and the latter's appreciation of Munoo's bravery and curiosity land him in the world of variegated colours and shades. But as soon as he steps on to the land of his dreams, the elephant driver warns him: "The bigger a city is, the more cruel it is to the sons of Adam. You have to pay even for the breath that you breathe" (177). The warning is demoralising enough for a young boy who has stepped for the first time on a land of confusingly large variety of races, dresses, colours, shapes, sounds, and tongues—a land of large buildings whose grandeur impels him to believe that he is "completely insignificant and small" (178). His fascination for this civilized world receives a sudden jolt as he finds a coolie on the footpath who "lay huddled, pillowing his head on his arm, shrinking into himself as if he were afraid to occupy too much space" (179). The few words "afraid to occupy too much space" adequately reveal the poignancy of the whole life of coolies. "So even here the coolies sleep in the street!" (179) is the reaction of Munoo who has dreamt of streets strewn with money. Immediately after the thought, the realization of the plight of the poor becomes more acute when he enters a restaurant to quench his thirst with soda water. The nasty behaviour of the waiter is reminiscent of the confectioner throwing the paper with jalebis at Bakha, but now the reason is not the fear of contamination by touch, but a general contempt for the poor. The larger the city, the larger is the scale of miseries of the poor. The coolies in Bombay vie with one another for the space where they should be able to extend their sickly limbs for the night. The sight of coolies on the pavements of Bombay is only an enlarged picture of the scene of Daulatpur grain market: "The bodies of numberless coolies lay strewn in tattered garbs. Some were curled up in knots, others lay face downwards on folded arms, others were flat on their chests, pillowing their hands on their bundles or boxes, others still huddled together at the doorsteps of closed shops, or lay on the boards in a sleep which looked like death, but that it was broken by deep sighs" (180). The word "death" in this context loses much of its horror because it is a kind of release from the sufferings of life. Noticing some empty space to rest their limbs, Hari is about to occupy it when he is warned by a sobbing woman: "My husband died there last night!" (191). The answer of Hari—"He has attained the release...we will rest in his place" (190)—seems quite appropriate from the mouth of one who has survived prolonged starvation. The life of coolies in Sir George White Cotton Mills surpasses any comparison. Anand has to use a number of adjectives to give a true colour to the picture of coolies employed in the mill: "Shivering, weak, bleary, with twisted, ugly faces, black, filthy, gutless, spineless, they stole along with unconscious vacant look" (247). The infernal life in the mill and starvation at home, have weighed down the coolies who now find themselves incapable of even the semblance of a revolt. They accept long working hours and cut down wages without a thought of protest. They passively put up with all cruelty meted out to them by the foreman and the money-lender. Continuously in debt to the Chimta Sahib and Nadir Khan, they fail to raise their voice against injustice. Moreover, any attempt at rebellion is certainly to be crushed with a strong hand by the mill owners and the foreman. When Ratan protests against the cruelty of Jimmie Thomas, he is sacked from the mill. Anand's words "... the smile on the wrestler's face faded one morning" (268), amply bring out the ruthlessness of the foreman towards the employees. The words are reminiscent of Browning's "My last Duchess": "And all smiles stopped at once."[41] In Ratan's case the end of smiles does not stand for physical death; it indicates a life of unemployment which is life in death for the penniless coolies. In this world of monetary gains, it is only among the poor that the feeling of human kindness has retained itself. Ratan, Hari, and Munoo share the sufferings of one another. Munoo feels sympathy for Hari and admiration for Ratan. Ratan is a model for him to emulate: "I want to live, I want to know, I want to work, to work this machine. I shall grow up and be a man, a strong man like that wrestler" (218). Ratan comes to the rescue of Munoo and Hari's family when their hut is washed down by heavy downpour. Hari treats Munoo as his brother and Lakshmi shares his suffering by providing him the pleasures of flesh when he terribly needs this satisfaction. Lakshmi's words—"We belong to suffering! We belong to suffering! My love!" (247)—reveal that poverty is the uniting force among the coolies. Narsimhaiah, Saros Cowasjee, and M.K. Naik feel that Lakshmi's words form the climax of the novel and the novel should have ended here. But it would have been too abrupt an ending and a bit too tragic.

Upto this part of the novel Anand has been able to balance art with commitment very successfully. He has demonstrated the plight of poor coolies without indulging in direct statement. His treatment of both the characters and the episodes is highly artistic. The saviour characters so far seem to be an indistinguishable part of the novel. Like Dr Prem and Prabha Dyal, Ratan too is an authentically presented kind fellow. He, like Ananta in *The Big Heart,* is both the sufferer and the saviour. He is one with the coolies, still stronger than them. As in the case of Ananta, Ratan too has attained maturity and broad mentality because of experiences in big cities like Jamshedpur and Bombay. He has observed the activities of trade unions and has become aware of human rights. He, therefore, dares to protest against the cruelty of the owners of the mill. When he is sacked, he does not grovel before the masters begging for pity and kindness. He, on the other hand, knocks at the door of the trade unionists so that he may fight for his rights. In Ratan, as in Ananta, Anand has presented an admirable blend of kindness, benevolence, love for pleasure, and strength for struggle. But the attempts of the trade unionists to provoke the coolies for a fight for their rights reveal Anand's aim at propaganda quite clearly. Sauda's reading out the charter of demands of the coolies gives an unaesthetic touch to the novel. The rally of the coolies ends in a fiasco like the rally of poor farmers at Kisan Nagar in *The Sword and the Sickle.* The trade unionists themselves are divided and their attempts are as clumsy as those of the seditionists in *The Sword and the Sickle.* The scene ends in a communal riot between Hindus and Muhammadans. In such an atmosphere, Munoo is run over by the car of a Eurasian lady, Mrs Mainwaring. She carries him home as she finds in him a boy who will serve as a good servant.

Anand has received severe criticism for the shifting of the scene from Bombay to Simla. The critics find the last part of the novel as an unnecessary appendix. According to Paul Verghese, it reveals Anand's "predilection for propaganda."[42] Jack Lindsay too speaks against the addition of this scene to the novel: "The episode does not have the organic quality of the previous phases of Munoo's development, and could have been omitted with gain to the book."[43] Naik too is very severe in his judgement: "As in *The Road*, a hoary romantic device is suddenly employed to suit the author's purposes. Having shown Munoo in a middle-class and a low-class world, his entry into the world of aristocracy must somehow be effected, in order that the social panorama is complete. The extremely cheap expedient of a motor car accident is therefore used."[44] No doubt, the Simla section of the novel forms an anti-climax after the Bombay scene, but it is not unrealistic. The author, no doubt, here gives up his sense of proportion as he devotes an illogically large space to discuss the case history of the Eurasian lady, but his probe into the psyche of the race of the Anglo-Indian is quite authentic. Mrs Mainwaring's indulgence with Munoo seems credible when we know about her past marital life. Munoo's reaction to his mistress' affection and sex-indulgence is compatible with his behaviour after his visit to the brothel of Piari Jan at Bombay and his Oedipal intercourse with Lakshami after his return home. But, though over-indulged, he is still an overworked coolie who must run all errands that his mistress's caprices dictate him. Now he has turned a domestic servant-cum-rickshaw puller. The over exertion causes him the fatal disease of consumption. Here Anand not only takes the opportunity of having a dig at the shallow lives of the fashionable society, the scene also "provides Anand with ammunition for his bitterest diatribe against man—the exploiter,"[45] remarks H.M. Williams. But "the bitterest diatribe" proves very harmful to the aesthetic appeal of the novel. Anand chooses Mohan to serve as his mouthpiece. That Mohan has given up his comfortable life to penetrate into the plight of coolies and instruct them for their emancipation seems unbelievable. His occasional advice to the coolies overtly reveals the novelist's intention to preach.

Munoo, for all his zest for life, his desire to grow, his ambition to emulate people like Dr Prem, the circus artist, Tulsi, Ratan, and Mohan remains only a coolie, a servant; in the Sham Nagar scene he had accepted his identity as a servant of Babu Nathoo Ram and in the Simla episode too he is content with his position as the servant of Mrs Mainwaring: "It is nothing to me, what she does. I am only her servant" (315). His "absurd existence" ends with him serving as a coolie only. The last sentence of the novel is very significant as it reveals that Munoo is thrown from pillar to post without his having attained any development even at the end of his life. Anand remarks about the passing away of Munoo: "But in the early hours of one unreal white night he passed away—the tide of his life having reached back to the deeps" (318). The sentence, says Cowasjee, "is a tribute to Anand's unconscious spiritual predisposition for all the conscious protests he makes to the contrary. It sums up the tide that was tumbling Munoo from episode to episode without a conscious vertical development."[46] Rajan finds Anand's ambivalence in his failure to raise Munoo above the level of a mere coolie: "Munoo remains a victim of the society evoking our sympathy; he does not become a symbol of the rising force of working class in India. The suggestion here is not that he failed to elevate Munoo as a hero, but that, himself a tool of history, he could not have done it; to picture Munoo as a victim was true to the main revolutionary stream of the times."[47] According to him, there is a combat between Anand's conscious understanding of the situation and his unconscious role as a tool of history resulting into "thematic ambivalence" in the novel. According to him, this ambivalence results in Anand's failure in presenting the revolutionary working class authentically. He quotes the Russian critic Y. Tupikova that in *Coolie* Anand "underrates the conscious factor in the workers' movement in 1928-29, often does not see where the struggle must lead, and presents his revolutionary characters in rather a sketchy manner...."[48]

These critics are justified in their opinion about Anand's treatment of the revolutionary class. His saviour figures like

Sauda and Mohan are not artistically realised. They, like Dr de la Havre of *Two Leaves and a Bud* remain shadowy abstractions. They seem to be employed only to voice the writer's intentions. The novel in which Anand has dexterously managed to control a vast canvas providing unity to the action through comparison, contrast, and parallel situations loses much of its artistic appeal because of the introduction of these saviour graces. His treatment of these two characters differs largely from his delineation of Dr Prem, Prabha Dyal, and Ratan who are convincingly portrayed. Like Mahatma Gandhi in *Untouchable,* Sauda directly protests against cruel forces in society. Mohan, with his sacrifice, seems to be a symbol of virtue like Dr Malhotra in *Gauri* and Dhooli Singh in *The Road.* He does not appear to be a realistic, lifelike character.

Anand's anguished cry in *Coolie* gives place to an outrageous protest in *Two Leaves and a Bud.* Anand continues his theme of glaring disparities between the rich capitalists and the poor labourers in this novel too. The action in this novel is concentrated in the tea plantation of Assam. The British masters of the tea plantations become a target of Anand's furious attack—the fury sometimes harming the aesthetic appeal of the novel which otherwise presents the lives of both the planters and the labourers with naturalistic accuracy. In *Two Leaves and a Bud* Anand does not narrate the odyssey of an individual but presents the class-conflict between the two groups: the British masters and their Indian sycophants on one hand and the poor, exploited coolies on the other. The protagonist Gangu and the exploiter Reggie Hunt are only the representatives of their respective classes. So vigorously does Anand proceed to present the helplessness and miseries of the former and the cruelty and roguery of the latter that he unconsciously converts them into mere symbols of humility and vice. To provide his attitude a touch of objectivity, Anand chooses Dr de la Havre, an English man to fight for the cause of the down-trodden labouring class. But the effect becomes the reverse with Anand's failure to canceal his penchant for protest against the atrocities inflicted on the poor coolies. In an effort to idealize an English character for attaining an effect of objectivity, he loses whatever objectivity he had been able to bring in his handling of the subject because the authorial intrusion becomes all the clearer through Dr Havre's occasional indulgence in long harangues against the plight of the coolies. The sacrifices of Dr Havre, like those of Mohan in *Coolie*, are incredibly great, the speeches of the two fit ill in the framework of the novel.

Critics join hands in criticizing the propagandistic efforts of the novelist, which have a direct bearing on his character delineation. "*Two Leaves and a Bud* fails to integrate philosophy and drama in an artistically satisfying way,"[49] remarks S.C. Harrex. Saros Cowasjee who otherwise goes a long way to prove that Anand's presentation of life in the tea plantations is based on facts and that he does not exaggerate the cruelties meted out to the labourers in the tea plantations comes out with a general remark that "in fiction, straight facts in themselves mean little, and they must always be subordinate to the main interests—character and the story."[50] Anand has not been able to make his facts subservient to an artistic handling of his characters and the story. The result is that "*Two Leaves and a Bud* whittles down to propaganda,"[51] remarks Cowasjee. Marlene Fisher too adjudges the novel with an almost similar conclusion: "Although there are good moments in it, *Two Leaves and a Bud* is largely an unsuccessful work, and one of the reasons for this is the propagandistic use to which Anand has put his material. Another is the novelist's failure adequately to control content through form."[52] Fisher's opinion that Anand has failed "to control content through form" implies Anand's tendency to tell what he should have shown through artistically convincing situations and characters. The commentary of these critics, though harsh, is justifiable, as Anand has really failed to strike a balance between art and intention. "It was a real story which I was writing in thinly veiled fiction,"[53] affirms Mulk Raj Anand. But the veil is a bit too thin and so transparent; the intention of the author seems to peep through the covering of fiction. His Marxist leanings become unaesthetically obvious.

The novel narrates the journey of Gangu—"A journey into the unknown."[54] The novel opens with the end of Gangu's journey from the district of Hoshiarpur to the hills of Assam and his cliche about life: "Life is like a journey," and it ends with the end of the journey of his life and transportation into the other world—a world unknown. Between his journey to Assam and the metaphorical journey to the other world, Gangu's life if full of unbearable pains. He has been deprived of his land in his native town; the enticing promises of Buta, the intriguing Sardar of Macpherson Tea Estates, allure him to the distant Assam tea plantations. The promise of a piece of land is enough to ensnare the impoverished Gangu who has been deprived of his possession of the ancestral land in his native town. His innocent faith in Buta's cunning words proves fatal for him and his family. Like innumerable other coolies from all over India, he gets entrapped in the prison-like tea-plantation. The words of Narain—"This prison has no bars but nevertheless it is a prison"—give a jolt to his dream and bring him back to stark realities. He and his family are offered a hut which has been constructed without any attention to the hygienic requirements of the occupants. The insanitary conditions cause epidemics. The planters show inhuman indifference when Dr de la Havre suggests precautionary measures to avoid devastating epidemics. There are polo matches and hunting expeditions to occupy their attention in the time they spare from a vigilant supervision of the work of coolies. Their purpose during the strict supervision seems to be to squeeze the coolies to the last drop of blood. Sajni, the wife of Gangu, falls a victim to malaria which is mistaken for cholera. The loss of his wife leaves Gangu a completely shattered man; to add to his misery, he is refused any monetary help by the manager Croft-Cooke and the contriving Buta Singh for her funeral. Croft-Cooke kicks him away afraid that he may spread the contagion.

The fate of Gangu is, in fact, the fate of every indentured labourer. Long hours of continuous work under rigorous supervision of the British planters and the Indian sardars, very frequent abuses and even beating at the hands of the owners, deducted wages leading to starvation, and cruelty of money-lenders are all that their life consists of. Continuous and complete dedication to their job of plucking "two leaves and a bud" makes the refrain get into the very souls of the labourers. The planters adopt the attitude of nonchalance towards the coolies. Not only nonchalance (which would perhaps have been easily tolerable to the labourers) but atrocities and frequent beatings are the reward the labourers earn for their sincere efforts.

All kinds of humiliations are inflicted on the poverty-stricken coolies. The British, with their various complexes, regard the Indians, particularly labourers, with contempt and scorn. For them the labourers are subhuman creatures who will survive even if their barest necessities are not satisfied. At Dr Havre's insistence on the need of the provision of certain precautions against epidemics, the manager, Croft-Cooke (who himself has had an attack of malaria and really dreads the disease) remarks: "You know as I do.... These coolies are sub-human, and do not altogether value the benefits of hygiene..." (29). After Dr Havre's presentation of the memorandum on cholera, we are told that Croft-Cooke "repaired to his miniature office...And, being a man of business, with a certain amount of whisky in his head, he forgot all about de la Havre's memorandum on cholera, attending to the hard facts of s.d." (33). Anand's contempt for such an indifferent and inhuman attitude of the employer towards the labourers is reminiscent of Dickens' disapproval of Gradgrind's concern only with solid facts in *Hard Times.*[55] The indifference of Croft-Cooke "a man of business," is as inhuman as Mrs Croft-Cooke's return to Margaret Peterson's amorous novel *Love in the Sahara* after all the discussion of the fear of the epidemic to which the coolies are exposed. Tweetie too, though one of the most intelligent British in the plantation, has complex-ridden attitude which dehumanizes his feelings about the Indian coolies. Unable to feel the plight of coolies, he condemns Dr Havre's concern for the latter as exaggerated and proceeds to remark: "...the coolie is favoured here to some extent. We respect his customs, and conventions.

He is housed and fed. He can keep goats and fowls. His tastes are simple, and he is probably not unhappy. His ideas are few, his vocabulary small and limited. He may be oppressed, no one, in truth, could deny that, I suppose, but he doesn't feel it as we should" (32). Such prejudiced notions keep the British in their cocoons of complacency and they fail to realize what the coolies actually require and how they feel their oppression. With a complacent mind, Tweetie, like Croft-Cooke losing himself in the hard facts, "fumbled for his tobacco pouch" (32). So aloof are the British from the Indian coolies that they have their bungalows well guarded against any interference by the Indian coolies. Anand's irony touches almost Swiftian heights when he remarks about the location of the club: "Situated in the pit of the valley, its wide veranda overlooked a vast polo ground, tennis-courts, croquet-courts, and gardens, all duly protected against the intrusion of black men, wild animals, hungry goats and cows, by thick hedges and shady trees" (91-92). The statement is well substantiated when Reggie Hunt does not approve of Dr Chuni Lal's entrance into the club. The few words of Reggie—"I am afraid niggers are not allowed in this club" (104)—contain all the venom of complex-ridden attitude of the British towards the Indians. Through Reggie's order to the servant 'Turn the Babu out' (105), Anand has been able to reveal all the cruelty of the unfeeling British towards even the educated Indians.

In the world of tea plantations, women and children too have to druge for long hours for a pittance a major part of which is very frequently deducted on the pretext of bad plucking. Gangu is scarcely able to save a penny despite the involvement of his wife, daughter and children in the work. Such is the plight of Gangu that he has to run from pillar to post to borrow money for the funeral of his wife. Anand presents a pathetic but authentic picture of the infants who suffer negligence because of their mothers' working whole day in the plantations: "And they were really no trouble because they did not have to be left at home. No sooner were they born than they could come with their mothers to the bushes and sleep on the wayside. A whole gang of suckling humanity lay there under the torrid sun upon the Mother Earth" (188-89). Anand's words "they were really no trouble" are not to be taken literally. They actually present the helplessness of both the mothers and the children. "Mother Earth" too fails to provide the necessary protection to these angelic creatures. Narain's wife, we are told, found her child "lying face downwards in a drain," and still worse, another child had been discovered "lying dead at the foot of a precipice on the south side of the garden" (189). Narain's wife is chased back to work even when she is breast-feeding the child. The women, moreover, are perilously exposed to any sexual assault by some lustful British people, particularly by Reggie Hunt. Any kind of resentment by a woman or her husband is likely to be put down with a heavy hand. The wife of Neogi is a victim to the carnal desires of Reggie who is lust incarnate. Leila escapes an attack on her chastity with great difficulty. But her escape in her hut results in the death of Gangu. There is a foreboding of the incident at a very early stage in the novel. Leila, a very young child, runs away innocently at the sight of Reggie Hunt as she is afraid of the white man. Narain's remark introduces the character in the novel who, through his deeds, confirms the remark: "He is a very budmash sahib. He is always drunk. And he has no consideration for anyone's mother or sister" (42). Gangu's reply, "why, but my daughter is a child.... He could not have said anything to her," seems ironical when Reggie actually tries to molest her. Narain's warning—"Nobody knows what may or may not happen here...Nobody's mother or sister is safe in this place" (42)—comes true. Leila's fight for life against the python, as many critics observe, is an appropriate prelude to the incident of an effort of Reggie to attack the girl. "The python," asserts Harrex, "is a manifestation of the powers of anti-human darkness.... The girl, by contrast, is identified with natural goodness, beauty, purity, and innocence through her association with flowers which she picks...."[56] Premila Paul too calls Reggie "the human python."[57] The phrase explains the basic character of Reggie adequately. To associate Reggie with a venomous animal is not inappropriate because Reggie scarcely has any human consideration left in him.

Anand is conscious enough not to paint the Indians as invariably good and the British unrealistically evil. Moreover, the subject of the novel is the evil of capitalism, and not the east-west encounter as in E.M. Forster's *A Passage to India* or Kamala Markandaya's novels. No doubt, the novelist touches upon the theme of racial conflict but it is in the context of the capitalist-labourer relations. He, therefore, presents many of the Indian characters who too are the cause of trouble to the coolies. The greed of the grocer and moneylenders, the selfish motives of people like Buta and Neogi, and the money-mindedness of Shashi Bhushan and others like him make the life of coolies still worse and more unbearable. They are all bent upon fleecing the innocent and helpless coolies. The world of the tea plantation, therefore, is a veritable inferno. Anand, quite dexterously, sets the tone of the novel in the very beginning. Gangu, on reaching Assam, finds the forests to be like the kingdom of Yama, "the God of Death, towering supreme, a skull in his left hand and a sword in his right" (3). Life, in this hell is so painful that death seems to be a welcome escape to another world. Finding a pregnant coolie woman collapse and die, Gangu remarks at once: "Happy death, with a soul which had tired of pining in its sorrow." The words of Gangu are as full of pathos as those of Hari in *Coolie* who occupies the vacant space for the night despite a warning by a woman that her husband had died on that spot. Hari's answer—"He has attained release, we shall rest in his place" (225)—amply reveals his sickness with life. Gangu has such a mental state again after the suppression of the riot. He, very often, looks at the river flowing there as a symbol of annihilation. He is afraid that some day the river will cause the doom of many people by turning its side all of a sudden. But then, remarks Anand: "He himself had suffered so many ups and downs in his life, however, and the dull pain of a constant anxiety had so seeped into the cells of his body that the torment of this fear did not become violent. He even looked forward to it as a kind of relief from the continual nervous agitation of days of waiting for the storm to come. And Gangu does attain relief from the painful world only a few days later."

The British planters and their Indian officials demand complete passive resignation from the coolies. The British masters, though insensitive to the physical and emotional needs of the coolies, are sensitive enough to feel at once the revolutionary thoughts of the coolies. And they are prompt enough to make arrangements for the suppression of any agitation. When the coolies, under the direction of Dr de la Havre, go to put forward their complaints against the unjust cruelty of Reggie Hunt, the British masters mistake their mission for a rebellion. They at once call in the army to suppress any such attempt. The coolies have never heard of trade unions in the tea plantations. Anand tries to set aside his prejudices against the British by making Dr Havre, himself a Briton, a supporter of the poor Indian coolies. But Dr Havre fails to realize his plans as he too has to depend on the permission and approval by the planters. He has also to suffer a lot for only supporting the cause of the Indians. He is excommunicated, he is deprived of the love of his beloved, and he has to face ostracization from his own countrymen. He feels ill at ease among the unfeeling, and cruel British owners. Barbara, too, who once had admired his human feelings and undaunted courage, rejects him in a cold manner. The coolies, therefore, can never hope for justice. Gangu, along with Narain and Bhutia, is fined for having gathered the coolies to express their demands. Anand, very skillfully, employs a paradoxical statement—"he [Gangu] was allowed to enjoy the liberty of being a slave" (246)—to present the abjectness to which the coolies are forced. The satire reaches a climax when Gangu is killed by Reggie Hunt and the magistrate, alongwith the jury, acquits Reggie of the charge with the judgement: "An impartial jury has found you 'not guilty' on the charge of murder or culpable homicide.... You are discharged" (276). "The impartial jury," we are told, was very partially proportioned with seven European and two Indian members. There could scarcely be any episode more ironical. A dexterous stroke of irony adequately brings out all the pathos of the lives of coolies who are denied justice and fairplay. K.N. Sinha seems to overlook this concluding chapter of the novel when he remarks: "*Two Leaves and a Bud* may be regarded as a brilliant piece of naturalistic fiction. It has little or no use of irony, which alone could encompass the whole range of feeling from the sublime to the ridiculous. It leans rather on pathos, making it do the work of irony...it succeeds in transmitting an overwhelming sense of passion which gives it its telling dramatic force." That the novel has a "telling dramatic force" nobody can deny. But the remark that it makes "no use of irony," implies going against the textual facts. Anand makes a successful use of irony, both of episode and statement. The novel, no doubt, is "a brilliant piece of naturalistic fiction," as it presents the life of coolies in stark colours. That the pains of coolies and the atrocities of the masters are not exaggerated with a propagandist aim is well revealed by Saros Cowasjee. Cowasjee compares the plight of coolies in *Two Leaves and a Bud* with the facts in the report of the Royal Commission on Labour known as the Whitley Report from which Anand drew much of his material. The comparison drives the critic to the conclusion that "far from exaggerating he [Anand] has minimized the brutalities of the English planters and the hardships inflicted on the coolies."[58] Anand himself, in a letter to J.F. Brown remarks: "I admit that it is the most bitter of my novels, but it is poetic. Were it a literary reportage, it would be hundred times more bitter."[59] That it could be more bitter, critics do agree. Cowasjee, for instance, agrees with the reviewer of the *New Statesman* that "the book is a plain indictment of the Assam labour system. That being so, the documentary basis could have been made stronger."[60] Sinha, however, does not agree with Anand's own evaluation of his novel that "it is poetic." Sinha's criticism, however, does not seem very acceptable when he asserts that "*Two leaves and a Bud* is neither authentic reportage nor a poem in suffering. Its sensitized and to some extent truthful delineation of experience is much too peripheral and casual to be truly poetic, it is flashy and episodic in the extreme, whereas true poetic rendition implies an integrated and functional view of life."[61] It seems hard to agree with the view that Anand's delineation of experience is "peripheral and casual." Anand, on the other hand, seems to feel the pulse of his protagonist and reveals a rare insight into the heart and mind of coolies in general. His observation of life of coolies, no doubt, is "integrated." His portrayal of the character of Gangu is as true to life as that of Bakha or Munoo. The nostalgic reminiscences of his life in his village, the acute pains of his existence in the tea plantations, his reaction to various situations make his portrait lifelike and authentic. Saros Cowasjee, however, finds his indulgence in introspection to be unrealistic in a peasant. M.K. Naik too criticises the character delineation for the same reason. They quote different passages to show that such intellectual reasoning is unrealistic in a simple peasant. Saros Cowasjee, who otherwise praises the character portrayal, remarks: "The only flaw in this excellent portrayal is that Gangu is occasionally given a kind of introspection which does not seem true to his character. It is unlikely that the simple peasant would ask himself the following questions, and that even if he were to do so, he would frame them in these words." And he proceeds to quote the following questions: "Did all the Sahibs who came to own this land get their labourers by letting lies pass for truth, did they make deceit a virtue and exalt the virtue and exalt the worst to the best, make very pushful duffer like Buta into a sardar, and liberate all the selfishness that any charlatan could use for his own purpose? Do all good men die here, and others live on?" But we must not forget that pain may have either of the two reverse effects on the mind of a person: it may make a person dull-witted and blank; it may also, which is more likely, sharpen his wit. The reasoning, like that of Gangu, is a deduction of conclusion after observation, rather first hand experience, of highly pathetic situations. Moreover, his intellectualization of things is compatible with the thoughts in his mind about life in general when the train reaches the tea plantation: "Life is like a journey—a journey into the unknown" (1).

Anand's weakness lies in his inability in "integrating his humanistic philosophy and drama in an artistically satisfying way."[62] He fails to resist the passion to moralise. His Marxist tendency becomes obvious when he overtly protests against the atrocities of the capitalists, particularly the British. He again introduces an altruistic Dr Havre to support the cause of the labourers against their suppression by the employers. Anand, no doubt, chooses an English character to speak for the Indian coolies and he has tried to conceal his prejudices against the English colonialists; the fault, however, lies in making the saviour figure unconvincingly virtuous and making him indulge in direct propaganda for the suppressed coolies against the thriving British owners. Sometimes his harangues propagate against capitalism so overtly that he seems to be merely a device to articulate Anand's outraged feelings. The interference of the author is clearly felt in most of the episodes in which Dr Havre figures predominantly. Like Mohan in *Coolie,* Dr Havre not only articulates Anand's overtly Marxist thinking but also demonstrates it. Mohan gives up highly stationed family and chooses to live among the coolies. So does Dr Havre sacrifice the luxurious life of his compatriots to choose a comparatively austere life full of hard work. He dedicates himself to a consideration of the plight of the poor coolies although he fails to effect any change in the inequitable social order of the plantations. He only observes, prepares reports and gives impartial comments regarding the living conditions of the coolies. These documents do not fit into the framework of the novel. The reports read out by Barbara clearly reveal Anand's message for the coolies and the planters alike. The following statements about the labour conditions in India hardly seem to be a part of a work of fiction:

> The present system of plantation labour is a curse and a crime. It is a monstrous crime against humanity. All that was said generations ago by the Wilberforces and Cannings and Garrisons and Lincolns against the hideous shame of slavery, could be repeated and added to, in respect of what is transpiring today in the tea, coffee, rubber and other plantations In India.
>
> 75% of the coolies of Assam plantations suffer from caratomalaisia (bad eyesight) for lack of proper nourishment, fats and greases.
>
> 50% of the population of India suffers from dental diseases for lack of any milk in the diet. *Two million*

> *women* die in childbirth in India as a result of malnutrition.
>
> 20% Anglo-Indians and members of the upper classes of India die of gluttony, overeating—another form of malnutrition.
>
> ...Wages of coolies on the Indian plantations have not changed for the last seventy years. The wages of a coolie in 1870, were five rupees per month. In 1922, the maximum wages of a coolie of the Assam plantations did not exceed seven rupees per month... (126-127).

These facts are followed by a long quotation from Dr V.H. Rutherford about the sufferings of coolies. The pages with such comments seem to have been culled from some economic document instead of forming an integral part of a novel. Having devoted four pages to such remarks, Anand abruptly shifts from facts to poetry. What Barbara reads next is so different from what she has read first:

> 'Love has no wings
> To soar upto men's thoughts,
> Thought has no line
> To plumb the immensities of love.
> And all our pretence of virtue...' (127).

Anand seems to have been conscious that the economic facts may sound unaesthetic in a novel. He tries to relieve such effect of the economic facts by putting in a few lines of poetry and about the art of poetry. But these lines seem a bit too abrupt after a discussion of hard, prosaic facts.

Dr Havre's failure to actually effect a rebellion by the coolies against their masters makes him all the more an unauthentic character. He has dedicated himself to the cause of coolies, he has incurred the wrath of his compatriots, but when the coolies actually want to go to Mr Croft-Cooke to complain against the atrocities meted out to them, he can do nothing except tell them to go "to the Burra Sahib and report to him" (200). When the coolies want him to go with them to the *Burra Sahib*, he, instead of doing so, prefers to stay back and attend to the injured coolies. At such a moment of excitement, he feels no sentiments: "De la Havre stood for a moment to ask himself what he could do, what he really felt. But he could find no answer. He was only aware that he must go to the surgery. He tried to force himself to feel something, some pity, some remorse or tenderness. But all his blood seemed to have dried up. And he stared before him, still, detached, apart. Even in his brain he could not see the crowd except as a solid mass" (202). At such a critical moment, a "tremor of weakness travelled down his spine" (202). And when he actually wants to go with the rebellious crowd against the cruel masters, he is sacked. He is no more successful in effecting a revolution against the cruel capitalists than Kanwar Rampal Singh in *The Sword and the Sickle* against the feudal lords.

Dr Havre again fails to change the orthodox thinking of Indian people. His visit to the house of Shashi Bhushan to attend to his wife who is in labour makes him appear as an ineffective fellow in his practical life. The wife of Shashi Bhushan refuses to be attended to by a male doctor. Dr Havre can do nothing against such rigid orthodoxy. He has to come back without ever seeing the patient. Anand remarks that Dr Havre was "angry with himself for having intruded, and still angrier with the stupid conventions of these people" (153). But he feels helpless against these conventions and comes out only to brood over some of Indian superstitions.

Dr Havre's relations with Barbara too seem unconvincing because of their too flimsy basis. Dr Havre is excommunicated because he sides with the coolies. Barbara, who has revealed great admiration for Dr Havre's sobre and profound thoughts against the shallow thinking of her parents, Macaras, and Reggie Hunt, ultimately chooses English life of merry-making in preference to the austere and thought-oriented life of Dr Havre. Unlike Maya in *The Sword and the Sickle*, Barbara gives in to the ways of her parents and snaps all relations with Dr Havre with unconvincing abruptness. Dr Havre, in this way, appears to be a clumsy figure—an "ineffectual angel beating in the void his luminous wings in vain."[63] Almost all the critics on Anand, with varying degree, have severely criticized Anand's failure to make Dr Havre a lively, dynamic, and convincing character. Harrex comments on the lifelessness of the saviour fagure: "...the combination of tendentiousness and moral passion in de la Havre's character comes directly from Anand. The main danger of this mind transplant is that 'life' tends to be lost in the process."[64] H.M. Williams who adjudges the novel a bit too harshly, finds Dr Havre to be merely "a card-board figure cut out on the pattern of English 'liberalism' and parlour-room Marxism."[65] Though we cannot completely agree with his appreciation of the novel in general, his appreciation of the character of Dr Havre is just. Dr Havre really seems to be only a spokesman of Anand.

Anand's sympathy for the poor coolies is again unaesthetically apparent in his prejudiced treatment of the British tea planters and their Indian sycophants. His contempt for the British is as obvious as is his love for the coolies. Reggie Hunt is lust incarnate. Riding, playing polo, drinking and womanizing are the chief characteristics of his personality. His sexual instincts have overpowered his rational and moral self. No beautiful coolie woman may avoid an assault on her chastity once Reggie takes a fancy to her. Any defeat or unhappy experience of Reggie must end in his forgetting the incident through a rape. His rough treatment of Neogi's wife reveals the beast in him who is unable to suppress his lust. Again it is in a frenzy of lust that he chases Leila and the chase ends in the cruel murder of Gangu. Anand caricatures Reggie through incidents like his being helplessly caught in heavy rain, his defeat at polo, and his failure to face these difficult situations in a manly manner make him a ridiculous figure. The other English characters like Croft-Cooke, Hutchinson, Macara, and Tweetie do not indulge in immoral practices but they too are to blame for imposing no check on the open, lustful activities of Reggie. These English characters, as Premila Paul rightly remarks, "with their slimy ways have become parties to the dastardly acts of Reggie Hunt."[66] These English planters are inhumanly indifferent to the feelings and thoughts of the coolies. Among themselves too, they are not bound by any bondage of mutual affection or even a feeling of patriotism.

They are bound by drawing room conventions and club etiquette whereas the coolies have instinctive affection and sensitive consideration for one another. Gangu and Narain, for instance, feel a kind of comradeship though they were complete strangers before they came to Assam. Even when commenting on the importance of gold in an ironical style, Narain does not forget the significance of love. "For it would be difficult," remarks Narain, "to keep afloat in the ocean of gold, unless we rescue from its beautiful but bitter waters a little fragment of love" (264). Such affection is hard to expect from the aloof, complacent, and self-centred British. The shallowness of their lives is clearly presented through the tiger-hunt scene. A number of coolies have to work day and night to prepare for the hunt which is only a way to satisfy the false ego of some of the Englishmen. Anand, with subtle irony, mocks at the English when a professional hunter kills the tiger and Croft-Cooke applauds the Governor of Assam, Geoffery Boyd: "Excellency! That was a good shot! Excellency!" (258). His Excellency is photographed with one of his feet on the tiger. The scene is also an instance of the British cruelty towards the coolies. The tiger assaults a coolie and the British ladies in the distance shout: "A rabbit! A rabbit!" (258). Anand, with skilful and subtle satire, lashes at the inhuman pretentiousness of the lives of the British. That Anand has consciously tried to paint the British in dark colours is clear in his own confession: "As I got into the book, I was biased in favour of my Indian characters and tended to caricature the Englishmen and Englishwomen who play such a vital part in this book."[C7]

Despite Anand's confession of his bias in favour of the Indian characters, the latter do not escape unlashed with their own weaknesses. The piercing eye of the novelist probes into the weak spots of the coolies which are responsible for much of their trouble. Anand criticises them for their unhygienic ways of work, their habits of deceiving, their undue servility, and their inferiority complex. They are taken in by the clothes of the British people. The white skin of the latter is sufficient to cow down these gutless coolies. If the British have been able to dominate them, it is because the coolies have never raised a voice against domination. If Reggie Hunt looks at every coolie woman with lustful eyes, the coolie women themselves vie with one another to win the attention of the assistant planter. They hunger for money and jewellery. If the planters are cruel, so are the Indian sardars like Buta and Neogi. Shashi Bhushan tries to exact money from the coolies for letting them see Croft-Cooke. The novel is interspersed with such condemnation of the ways of the Indian employees and certainly it lends some objectivity to the novel.

But, in general, Anand's leanings are very clear in the novel and his intrusion is felt very often. Despite his attempts to treat his theme and characters objectively, the fact remains that he has failed to do so. He has not been able to convey his message dramatically and forcefully. Marlene Fisher's appreciation of the novel is acceptable: "*Two Leaves and a Bud* is one of the few creations of Anand's, in which the artist is overpowered by the angry man who is pained by his world."[68] The protests of the angry man mar much of the artistic appeal of the novel. And the saviour figure, Dr Havre, who becomes the instrument to give an outlet to the angry protests fails to emerge as a convincing, true to life character. Anand's discreet choice of an Englishman as his desire-image fails to give an impression of objectivity because of his effort to idealise him. The saviour hero seems to be a personification of selflessness and sacrifice, not a flesh-and-blood figure. His ultimate dismissal from his job and his rejection by Barbara give the novel a pessimistic tinge because it symbolises the defeat of virtue in its fight against vice.

NOTES

1. Margaret Berry, *Mulk Raj Anand: The Man and the Novelist* (Amsterdam: Oriental Press, 1971), 96.
2. R.S. Singh, "From Resentment to Social Protest: Mulk Raj Anand," *Indian Novel in English* (New Delhi: Arnold Heinemann Publishers Pvt. Ltd., 1977), 39.
3. Eliseo Vivas, *D.H. Lawrence: The Failure and the Triumph of Art* (London: Allen and Unwin Ltd., 196l), 11.
4. Margaret Berry, *Mulk Raj Anand: The Man and the Novelist*, 95.

5. *Ibid.*, 73.
6. R.K. Kaushik, "Red Brown and Grey—Ideological Commitment" in Mulk Raj Anand's Novels in *Perspectives on Mulk Raj Anand*, ed. K.K. Sharma (Ghaziabad: Vimal Prakashan, 1978), 17.
7. *Ibid.*
8. Harish Raizada, "Ethics and Aesthetics of Mulk Raj Anand," in *Perspectives on Mulk Raj Anand*, 115.
9. Mulk Raj Anand, "Roots and Flowers: Content and Form" in *Untouchable* and *Kanthapura*, *Littcrit* Vol. 8, No. l (June 1982), 59.
10. *Ibid.*
11. *Ibid.*
12. Mulk Raj Anand, "The Story of My Experiment with a White Lie," *op. cit.*, 18.
13. *Ibid.*, 17.
14. *Ibid.*, 18.
15. Mulk Raj Anand, "Roots and Flowers: Content and Form" in *Untouchable* and *Kanthapura*, *op. cit.*, 51.
16. Saros Cowasjee, *So Many Freedoms* (Delhi: Oxford Uni. Press, 1977), 45.
17. K.N. Sinha, *Mulk Raj Anand* (New Delhi: Kalyani Publishers,1989), 30.
18. Mulk Raj Anand, "The Story of my Experiment with a White Lie," 24.
19. Mulk Raj Anand, *Untouchable* (New Delhi: Arnold-Heinemann Publishers Pvt. Ltd., 1970), 59. All the subsequent references to the novel are taken from this edition.
20. C.D. Narsimhaiah, "Mulk Raj Anand—the Novel of Human Centrality", *The Swan and the Eagle* (Simla: Indian Institute of Advanced Studies, 1969), 111.
21. *Ibid.*
22. P.K. Rajan, *Studies in Mulk Raj Anand* (New Delhi: Abhinav Publications, 1986), 22.
23. *Ibid.*, 54.
24. However, Bakha, unlike Wordsworth, does not have a glimpse of God in his mystic experience. Anand, himself an atheist, would not allow his protagonist to find the presence of the Omnipresent in nature.
25. S.C. Harrex, *The Fire and the Offering*, 51.

26. Paul Verghese, "The Proletarian Humanism of Mulk Raj Anand," *Problems of the Indian Creative Writer in English* (Bombay: Somaiya Publications Pvt. Ltd., 1971), 131.
27. CD. Narsimhaiah, *The Swan and the Eagle,* 111.
28. H.M. Williams, *Indo-Anglian Literature* (1800-1971): *A Survey* (Bombay: Orient Longman, 1976), 39.
29. Mulk Raj Anand in *From Author to Critic: the Letters of Mulk Raj Anand to Saros Cowasjee,* 124.
30. Saros Cowasjee, *So Many Freedoms,* 163.
31. Lindsay, *The Elephant and the Lotus* (Bombay: Kutub Popular, 1965), 31.
32. K.N. Sinha, *Mulk Raj Anand,* 73.
33. *Ibid.,* 75-76.
34. *Ibid.*
35. Mulk Raj Anand, *The Road* (New Delhi: Sterling Publishers Pvt. Ltd., 1984), 6. All the other references to the novel are from this edition.
36. *So Many Freedoms,* 162.
37. Saros Cowasjee, *Coolie: An Assessment* (Delhi: Oxford Uni. Press, 1976), 17.
38. C.D. Narsimhaiah, *The Swan and the Eagle,* 119.
39. Mulk Raj Anand, *Coolie* (New Delhi: Arnold Heinemann Publishers, 1981), 9. All the subsequent references to the text of the novel are from this first Indian edition.
40. James Joyce, *A Portrait of the Artist as a Young Man* (Harmondsworth: Penguin Books Ltd., 1960), 17.
41. In the case of Ratan, the end to smiles does not mean an extinction of life; it means the beginning of life full of troubles.
42. Paul Verghese, "The Proletarian Humanism of Mulk Raj Anand," *op. cit.,* 132.
43. Jack Lindsay, *The Elephant and the Lotus,* 9.
44. M.K. Naik, *Mulk Raj Anand* (New Delhi: Arnold Heinemann India, 1973), 45.
45. H.M. Williams, "Mulk Raj Anand: Realism and Politics," *Studies in Modern Indian Fiction in English* (Calcutta: Writers Workshop, 1973), 27.
46. Saros Cowasjee, *So Many Freedoms,* 128.
47. P.K. Rajan, *Studies in Mulk Raj Anand,* 28.
48. *Ibid.,* 29.

49. S.C. Harrex, *The Fire and the Offering*, 101.
50. Saros Cowasjee, *So Many Freedoms*, 87.
51. Marlene Fisher, *The Wisdom of the Heart*, 46.
52. Quoted by Saros Cowasjee, *So Many Freedoms*, 85.
53. *Two Leaves and a Bud* (New Delhi: Arnold Heinemann Publishers Pvt. Ltd., 1981), l. All the subsequent references to the text of the novel are from this edition.
54. S.C. Harrex, *The Fire and the Offering*, 102.
55. Premila Paul, *The Novels of Mulk Raj Anand: A Thematic Study* (New Delhi: Sterling Publishers Pvt. Ltd., 1983), 37.
56. K.N. Sinha, *Mulk Raj Anand*, 37.
57. Saros Cowasjee, *So Many Freedoms*, 24.
58. Quoted by K.N. Sinha, *Mulk Raj Anand*, 36.
59. *So Many Freedoms*, 85.
60. K.N. Sinha, *Mulk Raj Anand*, 36.
61. *So Many Freedoms*, 92-93.
62. K. Venkata Reddy, "Cruelty of Man to Man: Mulk Raj Anand's *Two Leaves and a Bud*," *Kakatiya Journal of English Studies*, Vol. VIII (1987-88), 56.
63. A phrase used by Matthew Arnold for P.B. Shelley. See Matthew Arnold, "Shelley" in *Essays in Criticism: Second Series by Matthew Arnold*, ed. S.R. Littlewood (London: Macmillan and Co. Ltd., 1964), 147.
64. Harrex, *The Fire and the Offering*, 101.
65. H.M.Williams, *Studies in Modern Indian Fiction in English*, Vol. 1, 37.
66. Premila Paul, *The Novels of Mulk Raj Anand: A Thematic Study*, 37.
67. Quoted by M.K. Naik, Mulk Raj Anand, *op.cit.*, 55.
68. Marlene Fisher, *The Wisdom of the Heart*, 51.

3

PROTAGONISTS AS VICTIMS OF MALE-CHAUVINISM AND FATHER-DOMINATION

Having written the Trilogy, *The Big Heart*, and *Private Life of an Indian Prince*—the novels in which the sufferer and the messiah merge into one person—Anand again chose a victim of social injustice to serve as the protagonist of his novel in *The Old Woman and the Cow* (1960), later on published under the title *Gauri* in 1980. The protagonist, as in *Coolie, Untouchable,* and *Two Leaves and a Bud,* is a weak character who fails to assert herself in the beginning and has to be protected from the unjust practices of society by a stronger and more experienced person. This saviour figure, a counterpart of Mohan in *Coolie,* the poet in *Untouchable,* and Dr de la Havre in *Two Leaves and a Bud,* becomes a mouthpiece to articulate Anand's message. The difference, however, lies in the delineation of the protagonist towards the end of the novel. While Bakha, Munoo, and Gangu fail to support their cause throughout their lives, Gauri overcomes the weakness of her heart and will. With newly gained strength through the notions of female emancipation injected in her mind by Dr Mahindra, she chooses freedom against traditional slavery.

Anand, for the first and the last time, chooses a female character to serve as the protagonist of the novel. He regards this novel as his "offering to the beauty, dignity and devotion of Indian women."[1] The slavish acceptance of the customary male domination by the meek Indian women pains Anand; the pain changes into a protest against male chauvinism and a cry for justice towards the fair sex. The protest and the cry sometimes become unaesthetically strident. Anand again fails to hold back the propagandist in him. The urge to preach overrides his effort to present the situation artistically. The treatment of the life of an Indian woman is, however, realistic. The basic conflict of the novel is between a traditional attitude to man-woman relationship and the modern awareness among women, even men, regarding the need of a change in this relationship. Ali Sardar Jafri, to whom Anand has dedicated his novel, provided much of the inspiration for it. Earlier Anand had been fascinated by the Russian poet, Nekrassov. He acknowledges his debt to the two authors in his dedicatory letter to Jafri: "The story of Gauri has been narrated here from the urge to retell it in my own manner. The spark that lit the fire and has raged in this book came from your heart, many years after Nekrassov had left the smouldering ashes of his epic poem in me."[2]

To deal with the conflict of the traditional and modern attitudes toward life, Anand bases his novel on the Ramayana myth—the myth which has largely guided the husband-wife relationship for a long period in India. But Anand does not employ the popular version of the myth as it is. He very dexterously casts it in the shape of his own ideas which emphasize the need of rejection of the orthodox notion of male dominance. The use of the myth not only synthesizes the past and the present, it underlines the need of improvement in the past experiences. The change is designed to fulfil the intention of the author to call for an awakening among women for their rights. Gauri, a gentle, docile, and submissive girl is married to Panchi, a frustrated orphan who takes out his frustration on his wife who, according to his notions, is completely his possession and whom he can "fold in his arms at night and kick during the day" (11). This is the conjugation of a meek cow to a fiery bull. The beast in Panchi starts asserting itself soon after their marriage. Gauri, with her gentleness and docility, submits to the caprices of her husband.

She accepts all the suffering with devotion like that of Sita although sometimes she feels the strength of Parbati, her namesake and even the annihilating power of Kali, particularly in her relation with her aunt-in-law, Kesaro. The novelty of the novel, however, lies in the deviation from the myth towards the end of the novel. When Gauri is kicked and beaten by Panchi for her stay in the hospital of Dr Mahindra, instead of accepting the beating passively, she leaves her husband's house for ever and goes to work in the hospital of Dr Mahindra. Gauri's choice of the course of liberty against orthodox submission symbolises a spark of revolution among Indian women; it is the victory of modernity over narrow conservatism. The earth does not part to give shelter to the modern Sita. But there is a vast world before her to take shelter in. The transformation of the myth is congruous with the modern attitude toward husband-wife relationship. This skilful merger of the myth and reality, the past and the present, the conservative and the modern makes the novel all the more realistic and appealing. Sinha's appreciation of the use of the "mythic parallel" is true. "The novel," remarks Sinha, "suggests continuous parallels and links between the primitive past and the desolate present and thereby presents the most absorbing image of the human condition."[3]

The transformation of Gauri from a gentle cow to a lady with iron determination is not abrupt or incredible. Anand proceeds to show the traces of Gauri's passive revolution gradually. No doubt, Gauri is a faithful, traditional Indian wife who wants to dedicate herself to the selfless service of her husband but she is not cowed down by the false accusations and the hate compaign of her mother-in-law, Kesaro. Nor does she accept the unfair behaviour of Kesaro with traditional tolerance and patience. Instead, she asserts herself when she tells Panchi: "Patient! Patience—how long can I go on being patient against the nagging of that woman and your shoe beatings on her behalf!" (44-45). Like a confident and courageous woman, she inspires her husband to separate from his cruel aunt and uncle: "Acha, then, separate from them!...I can cook and keep house! Who does all the work here if not

I?" (45). No doubt, she shows much devotion to her husband like a typical loving Hindu wife and does not hit back when physically tortured by him, but she does reveal her resentment through her reticence and long hours of sulking in the dark room. She makes Panchi aware of his guilt through patient taciturnity. Even in a mood to have contact with Panchi, she maintains her dignity by not taking the initiative. The passive assertion is, however, not a struggle for the recognition of her equality with her husband; she merely wants to be accepted and owned. Dieter Riemenschneider's observation is factual and just. The aspiration of Gauri, says the German critic, is "to be accepted as an individual and not for the equal rights of man and woman."[4] She enjoys the occasional moments of conjugal pleasures and does not want anybody to hinder their mutual relations. The pleasure-pain relationship between Panchi and Gauri is very authentically treated by the novelist. Their fights, annoyance, and assertions interspersed by some moments of love-making are true to life. Gauri, like a possessive wife, is not ready to allow Kesaro to take her husband away from her. When the aunt tries to provoke Panchi against Gauri, the latter, very jealously, affirms her right on her husband: "Go out of my house, witch. Get out. You oppressed me enough when I first came as a bride. Until you and your husband turned us out. Now don't come interfering in our lives. If you have no husband, go to some one else, but do not lay hands on my husband!...Go, get out...Evil woman! You want two husbands! Your own for beating you and mine for loving you. Acha, I won't give you my husband! So go!" (95). And to add insult to injury, she catches hold of Kesaro's bun of hair and drags her out of the door. The vociferous assertion belies the epithet "cow" attached to the name of Gauri. We find that she is not unrealistically gentle and tolerant. Nor is such a sudden outburst incredible. The reaction of an oppressed woman is psychologically realistic. Still Anand, to avoid the risk of offending the credulity of the readers, attributes the sudden eruption of strength in Gauri to the appearance of Kali in her. But so far Gauri's fight is not for her liberation or equal rights. Still she tries to win the love of Panchi through devotion and service. She wants to have Mira-like dedication to her "lord and master" (100). When Gauri tells Panchi about her pregnancy, the latter, a coward who like Nur in *Lament on the Death of a Master of Arts* fears the responsibilities as a father, is outraged. Blinded by the rage, he questions the chastity of Gauri and asks her to go to her mother's house. Gauri, like a true Hindu wife, appeals to him not to accuse her of adultery and not to send her back. But when Panchi, not heeding the entreaties of his innocent wife, kicks her, she decides to leave him and save her child against his violence. The reaction again proves that she is capable of taking firm decision to save her dignity. Anand remarks about Gauri's reaction to Panchi's violence: "After he had gone, Gauri raised her head deliberately and wiped her tears. Then suddenly, sobbing intermittently, she got up, determined to protect her womb against any further violence from him. And she began to pack her bundle of things" (103). Such determination after the failure of earnest appeals is well expected and realistic. Moreover, Anand prepares the readers for the following scenes where Gauri reveals great strength—both physical and moral.

In the events that follow Gauri demonstrates great strength of conscience and moral integrity. Her strength lies in her adherence to the virtuous elements in tradition. She does not want anybody to speak against Panchi though the latter has turned her out of his house. She cannot entertain in her mind even a thought of her getting married to anybody else. She strongly protests against the attempts of Amru and Laxmi to marry her off to Seth Jai Ram Das of Hoshiarpur. No reference to the riches and fame of the Seth can allure her. Although she submits to the physical strength of her uncle Amru who compels her to sit on the horse to be carried away to the house of Jai Ram Das, she maintains the moral courage with which she resists all advances of the Seth towards her. All the time she feels herself to be protected by goddess Parbati whom she invokes whenever she is in a crisis. Her stubborn will not only saves her from any assault on her chastity by the Seth but also enables her to resist an attack by Dr Batra in the hospital to which she is removed by Dr Mahindra. Once her mind shows a sign of weakness with the thought that Dr Batra is not an undesirable person. But moral courage smothers the thought before it becomes vivid. She displays admirable mental integrity by nourishing only one desire and that is to go back to her husband. She even wants to walk down to Panchi in the gloomy night. It is the thought of hazards in the forests on the way that hinders the idea. When Dr Mahindra asks her whether she will like to go to Christian Medical Hospital at Ludhiana with Miss Young, her answer is straight and bold: "I want my husband.... I am with child by my husband, and I want to go back to him.... I want to go back home..." (180). Her adherence to tradition is not a proof of her weakness, but a confirmation of her mental strength. Riemenschneider rightly remarks that Gauri's comparison to a cow emphasizes her "gentleness, softness, endurance and obedience"[5] but does not denote any weakness in her character. The comparison, therefore, cannot be extended further.

The transformation of Gauri from a gentle cow into an assertive, self-willed, and awakened woman, which has been gradually taking shape, is complete at the end of the novel. Anand here strikes a dexterous synthesis of tradition and modernity. While advocating awakening among women, he does not obliterate the significance of tradition. Gauri, after her stay in the hospital of Dr Mahindra and her job as a nurse, has cultivated new thinking regarding the man-man and man-woman relationship. She has developed humanistic thinking which has no touch of orthodox religious taboos. She has lost faith in the existence of gods, even God, and has gained a sort of love for humanity. Significantly, she does not invoke even goddess Parbati after her training as a nurse under Dr Mahindra. Under the influence of the latter, she has learnt devotion to work which alone can enable a man to realize his potentiality fully. The warmth and dedication she reveals in her relations with Panchi are a direct result of her shedding away the conservative inhibitions. She believes that gods having died, only a man can heal the wounds of another man. With her healing touch, she is able to strengthen Panchi for some time. The freedom from tabooed, narrow mentality lends an elegance to Gauri's appearance and strength to her movements. Panchi distinctly feels the change that Gauri's short life in the city has wrought in her. He reflects over the change in her character: "No longer was she quite the shy, gentle cow that she had been...when she came as a bride to his home, but there was a power in her limbs of which the glow on her face was the clearest expression, a kind of bewitching light, the reflection of the aliveness of her being. She seemed alert and dignified, her movements full of strength" (252). This strength of will is well revealed both in her acceptance and rejection of Panchi. She strongly faces the censorious remarks of Rakhi; she least bothers about what the villagers will say about her return after a stay in the city; she no longer cares for Kesaro; all her dedication is to her husband and her home. But her dedication does not weaken her against any assault by Panchi. She is ready to give the best of her affection, but she is not ready to accept his brutal behaviour towards her. Her traditional faithfulness to her husband is in conflict with her modern claim of her rights. Her modern defiance wins over her traditional submission when she boldly reacts to Panchi's beating. Very strongly she tells her husband: "Acha if I am a curse upon you, I will go away!...I shall go and work in Dr Mahindra's hospital and have my child there. And I will not come back.... And if you strike me again, I will hit you back" (263). And very bravely she leaves Panchi for ever and goes to work in the town. However, her assertion of strong will is not free from her traditional love for her husband's home. Her steps towards the town are not quick and strong, but hesitant and slow. Her eyes are full of tears and her heart is palpitating. The blend of tradition and modernity is adequately revealed in the last sentence of the novel: "She wiped her tears with the pallav of her saree, lifted her head and walked on, without looking this side and that" (264). Anand has successfully struck a "union of what is imperishable in tradition and what is life-giving in modernity,"[6] remarks M.K. Naik. This synthesis is again obvious in Anand's treatment of the myth of the *Ramayana*. Rejected by her husband, like her counterpart in the Ramayana legend, Gauri does not find shelter in the lap of mother earth. The modern Sita finds a haven in her dedication to work. Like Janki in *The Big Heart*, Gauri throws the inhibitions of tradition overboard and takes a plunge by adopting the course of dedication to work. Like Janki going out to work for social welfare with Puran Singh, Gauri goes to work as a nurse in the company of Dr Mahindra. Both Janki and Gauri reveal a great strength of mind as they choose their course without bothering about the venom which people will surely emit through their tongues and eyes. The rearrangement of the fable, in accordance with the exigencies of the modern age, lends an element of realism to the novel. The heroine emerges as a lifelike character. Marlene Fisher's appreciation of the character of Gauri is without an exaggeration: "Gauri is, moreover, a believable character, not a 'revolutionary woman' but an individual who has convincingly succeeded in becoming human and whole."[7] The development of her character towards wholeness is gradual and convincing.

Anand's psychological insight is revealed not only in his treatment of the character of Gauri, but also in his treatment of Panchi. Though a cause of much of the suffering of Gauri, Panchi himself too suffers much torture. He is not the lion that he is famed to be. Instead, he is a weakling who fails to attain self-control and confidence even when grown up. Every buffet of chance leaves him a faltering, tottering person without any deep moorings. Brought up by Kesaro who feels a kind of Oedipal attachment to him, nourished on the orthodox views, particularly regarding man-woman relationship, and suppressed by adverse circumstances, Panchi has become a young man sans the confidence and enthusiasm of youth. He oscillates between his love for his wife and his allegiance to social, traditional norms. Whenever he starts enjoying his conjugal relations with Gauri, his aunt Kesaro thwarts the continuation of the enjoyment. Either the aunt or one of her allies arouses suspicions in the mind of Panchi against the chastity of Gauri. The weakling very easily submits to suspicion. Such submission ultimately leads to the torture of Gauri at the hands of her husband. In the beginning Gauri, however, puts up with the humiliation and torture after sulking for long hours. She hopes to win Panchi's affection through devotion. But when his beastly behaviour continues, her soul is awakened against such treatment and she starts asserting her strong will and ultimately leaves him for ever. Panchi, with his wavering mind and moral weakness serves as a foil to Gauri who maintains her mental strength though she has to encounter unnerving events. Suffering from a false ego, he fails to face reality in a manly manner. His pride hinders his love for Gauri. He, like Nur in *Lament on the Death of Master of Arts*, is a gutless, spineless figure. His reaction at the news of his wife's pregnancy is quite like that of Nur. He throws aspersions at his wife, but actually he is unable to bear the responsibility of feeding one more member in the family.

Once Gauri actually leaves him, Panchi terribly feels the absence of her soothing presence. He goes to Piplan Kalan to bring his wife back. But when Gauri really comes back to him, he is again torn between his desire for Gauri's loving presence and his suspicion of her chastity, Gauri's warmth, however, strengthens him and he is able to give a befitting treatment to the gossip-mongers, Kesaro and Rakhi. He displays great strength when he wants to save his home from disruption and frankly tells Kesaro: "Go and eat your Masters! Don't come destroying this house again" (284). But the strength again wanes when he has to face the people of the village who are bent upon making him realize that he has made a mistake by accepting Gauri after she has stayed in somebody else's house in Hoshiarpur. He no longer can overpower his weakness and kicks Gauri out of his home. The conflict between his faith in Gauri's purity and his submission to the allegations by the villagers renders him a weak, almost a schizophrenic person. K.N. Sinha rightly judges the personality of Panchi: "Panchi, however, fights his own divided self. He is torn between love and strife; his loyalty to Gauri matched against his allegiance to the villagers."[8] Panchi too, like Gauri, is a tragic character, who, despite his cruelty towards Gauri, evokes our sympathy. This exposure of the weakness of Panchi makes the novel all the more an authentic presentation of life. Marlene Fisher rightly remarks: "The narrative is convincing and effective in part because the sympathy Anand evokes for young Gauri is not at the complete expense of her husband, Panchi. The latter's inability to keep up with his wife in her growth into selfhood is due to his own immaturity, his blind, unquestioning faith in the tradition-bound, orthodox Hindu views governing the relationship between husband and wife, and the pressures of earning a livelihood in a period of drought and famine."[9] Gauri herself understands the psyche of Panchi: "He is not foolish. He is a weak, spoilt creature. Spoilt by Kesaro. He pretended to be a lion among the men of the village. But really he is a coward" (263). His cowardice at grips with his strength makes him a very human and realistic character. Both Gauri and Panchi arouse pity as both of them are the sufferers in their own ways. Jack Lindsay's observation is well based on the textual facts: "Both claim our sympathies as they strive to find happiness and peace in love. But Panchi fails, broken down by the immemorial patterns that now are working only to resist the forces of necessary change, the new relationship of man and woman in trust and equality. Gauri, with far more difficulties to surmount, breaks through. The blind circle is ended. The woman who is banished becomes the woman who herself rejects the narrow world of subjections and fears that enslave Panchi despite his better self."[10]

Anand, however, is not satisfied with only a successful exposure of the plight of women and the weaknesses of men which are a direct result of the restrictions imposed on both husbands and wives by tradition-bound society. He must overtly convey his message through a "wisdom-figure." The reformist zeal dominates his artistic integrity. The novelist is clearly seen intruding upon the world of the novel towards the end. Dr Mahindra is brought in to preach for not only the rights of women but against a number of social and economic factors which have no contextual relevance. The ideas, no doubt, have great contemporary importance but they become really jarring when incorporated into the novel. Anand himself seems to be pouring out his fury from a platform. The six-page diatribe contains Anand's attack on fatalism, immoral greed, the undue servility of Indians, the customs of villagers, and the taboos of religion. The outburst also contains Anand's humanistic philosophy which is based on faith in man and disbelief in the existence of God. Dr Mahindra, like Anand in *The Bubble* and like many existentialists preaches that gods are dead and it is for man to come to terms with his existence. The ideas could win applause of the audience in a political rally. They would have made good contents for an abstract essay. But these speeches of Dr Mahindra do much harm to the novel which otherwise, as says Naik, represents "the high water-mark of Anand's fictional genius."[11] Again, Naik appropriately concludes his criticism of the novel: "*The Old Woman and the Cow* would certainly have been a better book, if Colonel Mahindra had been a man of fewer words."[12] The ridiculous thing, however, is that much of what Dr Mahindra states is beyond the comprehension of his listeners, Laxmi and Adam just as much of what Mahatma Gandhi says is unintelligible to Bakha in *Untouchable*.

Anand, however, seems to be consciously emphasizing the erudition of his saviour hero by making the latter speak against too many social evils. He, like Anand in his confessional novels, criticises arranged marriages. Dr Mahindra, instead of getting outraged at Dr Batra's effort to assault the chastity of Gauri, tries to probe into the psyche of his partner. He traces the cause of Batra's unusual behaviour in his arranged marriage. Refusing to agree with the severe judgement of Nurse Young about Dr Batra's character, he, like a psychiatrist, remarks that "Dr Batra is probably suffering from the usual frustration of our countrymen whose marriages are arranged. And as he cannot get satisfaction from his wife, he seeks this in other women. He may have offended you, but he is to be pitied..." (177). Such psycho-analysis is, however, true to the profession of a doctor. But his ideas about tradition, religion, poverty, *Karma* and government seem to be the articulation of a leader trying to convince the audience of certain things. About the deteriorating economic order he remarks: "I am just saying those Banias who buy and sell, have brought falsity into the life of the village. In the old days, there was often scarcity. But, as no one owned the land, the five elders could give fertile land to whoever complained that his land was fallow. And all the grazing land was in common. And there was milk and butter and whey.... Now, every peasant owns his land and can sell it.... And as he is often in debt to the Seth, he sells out and becomes a labourer in the town factory. And cash has become more valuable than the earth. So there is wretchedness everywhere...your Amru turns crook and you sell your daughter, even as folks elsewhere are selling their daughters!" (224-25). This long speech is followed by Dr Mahindra's condemnation of religion, government, and leaders: "I am blaming your dharma—according to Jwala Prasad you are immoral if you do not pay the interest on debt. To be sure, these hypocrites and the priests are together—Brahmin dogs! In one village the pure, pure Hindus have turned out all untouchables. And this happens in our own Raj. All those white caps. Gone is Gandhi's dharma?" (225). Dr Mahindra continues his diatribe of religion:

> Our Dharma is feeding the Brahmins and paying interest to the Banias. And ill-treating the untouchables. And Vinoba can convert a good man here and a good man there. And some tigers may learn to eat vegetables. But can you tell me of how many sons of ministers have given away their land to the poor at the bidding of Vinoba? And how many have joined him? And how many have become shareholders of the Ram Raj, who have dividends for once following Gandhi and going to jail? They are city folk, brother. They don't understand that our country is still a village.... They make money, as middle men, from bribery while you folks join hands to them.... (225-26)

Further, there are comments on the weak mentality of people about the need to end poverty, about the soul of man, about his disbelief in rebirth. Dr Mahindra now ceases to be a realistic true to life character. He seems to be a superhuman fellow preaching human beings. To Adam Singh and Laxmi he seems to be "a sage who was seated on the terrace under the banyan tree in Piplan Kalan" (226). Adam Singh calls him a "*Karamyogi,*" a saint among a million sinners. His speeches stand out of the main plot of the novel and reveal the novelist's purpose too clearly. Saros Cowasjee, like many other critics, is offended by the presence of Dr Mahindra in the novel whom he considers to be "Anand's most blatant propagandist of a new order."[13] No doubt, his ideas bring a great change in the personality of Gauri. But, as remarks Cowasjee, "...the good he does to Gauri is largely negated by the damage he does to the novel."[14] But for his speeches, the novel would have been an artistic projection of real life of women in Indian villages.

Anand is also guilty of idealizing his saviour character. He has endowed his desire-image with so many virtues that he does not appear to be a real, flesh-and-blood character with human weaknesses. With his great knowledge, patience, courage, medical skill, mercy, psychological insight, conscientiousness, and confidence, he appears to be a product of Anand's own imagination. S.C. Harrex, who admires the novelist's handling of the myth and has a great appreciation for Dr Mahindra's virtues of "Hindu asceticism" combined with the values of a "compassionate heart," criticises Anand for making his saviour hero too virtuous a character. He remarks that "in the portrayal of Mahindra Anand has failed once more to make his intellectual protagonist a figure from real life instead of merely from Anand's private philosophical hemisphere."[15] Not only does Anand make him appear a saintly figure, he makes Gauri remark about him:

> Truly a saint! He has felt the pulse of many half corpses and breathed life into them. He has sensed the root of evil. He says that the peasant has to borrow or starve, if there is no saving and no water. He knows the rates of interest charged by the Birbals of every village. And he knows what scorpions and snakes bite us. And how we lie about like pigs in our own styles. And he says that this must not be. That this is not the Karma of man. He loves people. And he can glimpse the meaning of life. He talked to uncle Adam Singh and my mother. And, I am sure, they have become his disciples. They have

> been freed from the bonds and have become devoted ones (241).

Such description makes him appear as a nearly divine figure. Otherwise, too, at many places, Anand refers to him as a benign dignitary, a god, a saint. He can swallow the poison of bitter words of Dr Batra "almost as God Siva was once known to have done, with the consequence that his throat became blue and his face black" (176). Having brought Gauri to the hospital, he feels he is "responsible for her conscience" (179). He does not want to send Gauri with Miss Young against the former's willingness. He does not want that Gauri should be compelled to adopt Christianity. Dr Mahindra is an embodiment of forgiveness and mercy. He tells Miss Young that he does not believe in revenge. He does not nourish any contempt for Dr Batra despite the latter's misbehaviour. When Dr Batra wants Miss Young to be dismissed, Dr Mahindra, like a fair judge, asserts that Gauri also must be sent away. Still, he wants to send Gauri to wherever she really wishes to go. Such is the confidence of Gauri in the Colonel's mercy that when she is ill-treated by Panchi, she chooses to take shelter in his hospital and deliver her child there. Dr Mahindra has cherished an idea of a model charity hospital which he actually sets up. A character with such virtues could win the admiration of idealists and moralists. But in a work of fiction, he seems to be a lifeless figure—a production of the novelist's idealistic humanistic consciousness.

In this way, we find that *Gauri* is one of the novels in which the presence of the saviour character impairs the otherwise well-conceived and realistically executed plan of action. He is a medium for the novelist to do propaganda for modern, unorthodox attitude towards life. Through Gauri's gradual conversion from a meek girl to an assertive woman, Anand has beautifully revealed the need of struggle among women for their rights. But the direct propagation through an idealized character is against the artistic unfolding of action.

In his novelette *Lament on the Death of a Master of Arts*, Anand again chooses a victim of the social and economic forces prevalent in the contemporary Indian society as his hero, rather as his anti-hero. The protagonist Nur suffers acutely the pangs of poverty, the irony of his unemployment despite his attainment of the degree of Master of Arts, and the taunts that his father and other people shower on him lavishly. The pathetic cry of the negative hero—"Oh, why did you drag me into the dust by making me a Master of Arts?"—which, in fact, is the refrain of this realistic novelette—epitomizes the ironical situation of one who holds a degree of Master of Arts but is worse than a manual labourer when he comes to grips with the realities of life. The futility of education in practical life is adequately substantiated through the plight of Nur who finds himself to be a misfit in the practical world where it is not the academic merit but economic independence which matters the most. He fails to find the job of an officer and cannot do manual labour for fear of being scoffed at by others. Education which otherwise is supposed to lift a man from the dust of ignorance and illiteracy, drags Nur into the dust by rendering him a victim of the ridicule of people, particularly his own father.

As in *Untouchable*, here too, Anand successfully employs the stream of consciousness technique to unveil the feelings and emotions of his protagonist. The technique, however, has been altered a little in accordance with the exigencies of the situation in the context of Indian background. Again, as in *Untouchable*, in this novel too Anand's intention to preach against the inequitable social practices comes to the surface. But the sufferer-saviour relationship differs from that in *Untouchable, Coolie, Two Leaves and a Bud*, and *Gauri*. The novelist does not introduce any celebrated or exalted figure *in propria persona* to occupy the stage and hold the microphone for a long time. Azad is the bosom friend of Nur. Their friendship is, in fact, based on real life. Both Azad and Nur are characters from real life. Azad is actually Krishan Chander Azad [Anand himself] of the autobiographical novels. Nur whom Anand spells as Noor in *Confession of a Lover* and *The Bubble*, as these confessional novels adequately reveal, had been very intimate to Anand. *Confession of a Lover* opens with Anand's experiences in Khalsa College, Amritsar on his first day in the College. Anand was ragged by his senior students and was in miserable condition when Noor had come to his rescue. This had developed a friendship between the two. The confessional novels as well as *Lament on the Death of a Master of Arts* reveal that Azad had been a man of rebellious temperament, an iconoclast, whereas Nur had failed to revolt against patriarchal authority. Azad had found an escape in a foreign country when he felt that his father's cruelty was a hindering block in the way of his free will. On the other hand, Noor's death had been hastened by the opprobrium, which his father so frequently hurled at him. Otherwise both Azad and Nur had been sufferers from the same problem—the problem of domination by elders. Till today Anand abhors the tendency of elders to oppress the free will of youngers. Anand had felt that poetry and philosophy were a way out of the oppressive atmosphere of society which demanded joined-handed submission by the youngers to the logical or illogical dictates of elders. Nur in this novella tells Gama that Azad "awakened me [Nur] to the misery of human condition and made me suffer but he also released all the stifled impulses I had never suspected in myself before.... He initiated me into the mysteries of poetry and philosophy."[16]

But the fact that the sufferer and the saviour have been actually great friends does not save the novel from the fact that the appearance of the spokesman is propagandistic. Although the saviour character enters the world of fiction slyly, his presence is clearly felt once he is there. Moreover, his speeches are not in the form of conversation between two friends; they are speeches by a revolutionary who is trying to awaken people against the cruel social forces. The saviour figure, Azad, appears in the novel stealthily through the memory of Nur. The speeches, as recollected word to word by the protagonist, seem intentionally incorporated to give voice to the author's protest against the social order in which the cash-nexus reigns supreme. That the speeches have been forced into the otherwise realistically executed novel becomes all the more apparent as they are beyond the understanding of the listener, Gama. Moreover, the listener is averse to hear the speeches because of his hostile and jealous feelings towards Azad. Another factor that makes allusions to the speeches of Azad and appears to have been purposely forced is that Nur is able to articulate them with much difficulty because of his frail frame which is the result of his suffering from consumption. But the protest against the evil forces is not as transparent as it is in *Untouchable, Coolie, Two Leaves and a Bud,* and *Gauri.* The curtain of translucence is provided by the fact that the preacher enters the novel in a subtle manner through the mind-process of the protagonist. His appearance through the memory of the protagonist is congruous with the stream-of-consciousness technique.

Anand always had a kind of a abhorrence for the contemporary educational system started by Macaulay. This "bastarised version of English curriculum"[17] imparts only theoretical knowledge and does not guarantee any provision of jobs. The consequence is that when one encounters the realities and claims of worldly life, one is only a helpless creature up against a dark present and a darker future. Anand also has a dig at the teachers in schools and colleges who themselves have no profound knowledge of their subjects. In *The Bubble* Anand clearly states that while in England studying under Prof Hicks for his Ph.D. degree he realized that the education he had received in the college was imperfect and even misguiding. It was in Britain that he was able to understand the essential Hindu philosophy and its relation to western thought. The schools in India are no better than prison-houses where the students fall prey to the whips of the teachers. Most of the teachers are money-grabbers who want to fleece the students by giving them private tuitions. In his *On Education* Anand laments the condition of educational system in India:

> If education is the transmission of life from the living' wrote an independent critic about this debacle, 'then we do not know how to describe the system of teaching that prevails here. It is carrying death from the dead, through the dead, to the dead.[18]

Nur has been a victim of this horrid educational system. He has suffered merciless flogging by his school teacher Kanshi Ram for not taking tuition from him because of the stinginess of his father. He has dedicated himself to his education with only one aim—to secure a government job of an officer which has been the cherished dream of his father. His hard work has won him first class marks and the degree of M.A. But in his case the degree is not a passport to the security of a job. While recollecting his past, Nur is painfully reminded of his desperate efforts to find employment. He has a vivid memory of the hideous experience he had when he appeared in the interview for Forest Service. All his merit was ignored only because he was the son of a confectioner. Nur really feels pained to recollect the fun that the members of the commission poked at him for his being a son of a confectioner. Moreover, the expensive dress and smart appearance were deemed more important than intelligence and knowledge of a candidate. Nur, therefore, had to borrow a suit from his friend for the interview and he rehearsed many times in his borrowed suit before actually appearing for the interview. The absurdity of the selection criterion is obvious in Nur's words: "...jobs were given by the Public Service Commission for smartness, general appearance, the possession of a good pedigree and according to the number of testimonials and recommendations from influential persons that a man may have than for anything else" (42). And Nur was outrightly rejected as he did not have a recommendation from any influential person. Not only for an officer's job by Public Service Commission, but even for a small job in a post office, one's case was hopeless without a recommendation. For a clerical job in the post-office, Nur had to have his father-in-law exert his influence. How difficult it really was to secure even this job is revealed in Anand's words:

> Then, at last, after the exertions of his father-in-law, after the abject crawling of his father with joined hands before that Bhai Bhachanga Singh, Inspector of Post Office, after all the influence brought to bear on the Minister of Education, after all the recommendations, a

> clerkship in the Post Office...One hundred and twenty rupees, and lucky to get it, as fifteen M.A.'s had applied for the same post, and but for the wire-pulling, the favouritism for the Muhammadan and all the other influences, he would never have got it (53-54).

In the context of such corruption, the education of a person is rendered completely futile. And the person who has acquired high qualifications with great labour becomes only a subject of mockery. Deprived of a job opportunity, he is torn between his pride in being educated and his desire to accept any low job. Manual labour is regarded as below his dignity and an office job is not easy to secure. Anand very authentically portrays the plight of a man whose pride in his qualification combines with the fear of being made fun of, to render him a complete misfit in the world of manual work. Nur broods over this mental state:

> "Any kind of manual labour was bad, was low and unworthy. It wasn't respectable to exert one's hands... the only izzat was in Government service.... And it wasn't only that the outside world believed this, the trouble was, if one was honest, that one had begun to believe in the snobbery oneself and was ashamed and embarrassed..." (53).

And this snobbery in conflict with the realization of reality leads to a very disastrous situation. Premila Paul remarks that "the educated man falls between two stools. In short, he becomes a miserable misfit."[19] In the case of Nur, it has left him both physically and mentally very weak; he can only brood, whine and invoke death.

Nur acutely suffers the pangs of poverty. He feels overwhelmed with the obligation of having to depend on the money of his miserly father. Nur's inability to find a proper job has frozen all affection between Nur and his father and even between Nur and his wife, Iqbal. The adversity has hindered the true contact of souls between the husband and the wife. Nur's confectioner father is always cruelly reminding his son that he has spent his hard-earned money on his education. Very mercilessly he rebukes his ailing son that the latter has failed to give a return for the pains he had taken to bring him up and have him educated. One could hardly expect more cruel treatment from a father to his son who is on his death bed than the rebukes of Nur's father:

> You wasted hundreds of rupees of my hard-earned money, and you couldn't even get a job to feed yourself and your wife and child? Why don't you die of shame, and rid me of the responsibility you have imposed on me so long? How long will you go on prolonging the agony of your poor and old grandmother? You have disgraced me and given a bad name to your family! Go to hell and die and be done with it, wretch... (59).

And the helpless Nur can only beg his father's forgiveness. The words "Oh forgive me, father, forgive me...Oh, forgive..." (60) adequately reveal the agony of Nur. The words acquire a particular grimness when we find that this is the last conversation between the father and the son. Nur does rid him of the responsibility a few moments after it. In fact, for the whole of his life he has felt the burden of his dependence on his father's earning. The recollection of the painful days is full of bitterness:

> Then, as the least remaining desire in life, he had wished, between periods of hopelessness and blank despair, and endless, bottomless misery, for the gift of a little job, howsoever insignificant and humiliating, even the job of a peon if it were not in this city, so that he could earn a bread for himself, Iqbal and the child.... But even this last little wish was not to be fulfilled easily.... Only days and unending days, morning, noon and night and the rub of his father's abuse and curses with every morsel of bread and every bite at a bone... (53).

And to add to the misery of the poor, there are the rich snobs who induce inferiority complex among the poor through their airs of superiority. A poor man naturally suffers a feeling of alienation. Nur tells Gama generally about the mental experiences of the poor: "But if you are poor you can't get anywhere, if you can't keep pace with the fashions invented by the rich, they dub you mean and cut you" (32).

Nur laments the adverse effect of poverty on his relations with his wife and child. No doubt, Nur's marriage with Iqbal was not only an arranged one but a forced one, but still Nur feels that he would have been able to have a much more intimate contact with her had his emotions not been curdled by his inability to earn. He had failed to respond to the dedication of his wife with equal affection. In fact, he had made Iqbal a target for wreaking his vengeance against society. Now Nur feels the guilt of his indifference to her. He really feels a prick of conscience for his rigidity. He wails over the gulf that poverty had created between him and his wife: "Poverty had come between him and her, how cruel it had made him to her, how stubbornly aloof and hard and neutral, so that now when he wanted to smile at her, to touch her, he had turned his eyes away, frozen and rigid, too proud and too ashamed to look at her, to yield.... And it was all the world's doing, all..." (51). Thus poverty stultifies even conjugal relations. His behaviour has been quite like that of Panchi towards Gauri. Like Panchi, Nur is not able to take the news of his wife's pregnancy with pleasure and sympathy. Both of them are afraid of the responsibilities of fatherhood and torture their wives at the news. But while Gauri leaves Panchi with a determination to save her womb against Panchi's assaults, Iqbal, like a true traditional wife, sticks to her husband. When Nur sees his little daughter for the first time, he feels like murdering both the mother and the child. Again and again poverty has been responsible for the beastly behaviour of Nur towards Iqbal.

A true humanist, Anand probes into the misery of man. He presents his protagonist struggling helplessly against the oppressive economic forces. Nur fights desperately for existence, but the annihilating forces prove much stronger than an individual who has ultimately to give in. "The novel," says Sinha, "clearly demonstrates that the human condition itself is perilous and that erosion of contours (the fissures of being) is inherent in existence."[20] It goes to the credit of the novelist that the problems of the hero are left unsolved. The conflicts and agonies of Nur are very authentically presented without any resolutions to them. The speeches of Azad present the author's rage against society—"The bitch has no morals. She yields herself to the embraces of any robber, brigand or cheating idiot who has secured for himself the traditional right to a vested interest" (36). Anand has achieved a grand success in portraying a realistic picture of society in a very short space. Anand's suggestion—"The thing is to write—write poetry and try to understand..."—is not an unaesthetic didacticism; it is only an encouragement to try to understand the problems of human life with poetic sensitiveness.

The novel, as we find, is a fine example of the author's profound psychological insight blended with admirable artistic presentation of reality. In a very limited space and with very few characters Anand has very skilfully dealt with the ideas of the futility of life and inevitability of death. The treatment of the grim situation is earnest and realistic. Therefore it seems hard to agree with Premila Paul who remarks: "The radical flaw of the novel is its overdose of sentimentality. Now and then there is the tendency of the pathetic turning into the bathetic due to overtreatment."[21] Nor can we agree with M.K. Naik who finds the novella to be an example of the weaknesses of Anand's art. According to Naik, "Time and again, his compassion for the underdog bowls him over; his indignation at the injustice of traditional practices erupts into hysteria; and he can seldom resist the temptation to squeeze the last tear out of a pathetic situation. His long short story 'Lament on the Death of a Master of Arts' is a glaring example of an unholy alliance of all these weaknesses."[22] The opinion is unjustifiably severe. The novelist does not exaggerate to extract tears of the readers. The tragic but realistic condition of the negative hero evokes a true feeling of compassion. He devotes only two small pages to protest against the cruelties of the world. The saviour suggests no solutions; he only wants people to have a poet's understanding that they may sensitively feel their own miseries and those of others. Anand himself had taken refuge in the world of poetry when he was disillusioned by the evils prevalent in society, particularly in his own family.[23] S.C. Harrex overlooks the significance of the novel in his remark: "Anand's early novels...do contain social observation for its own sake. And Anand was aiming at a composite social picture to which each novel was supposed to contribute a new dimension. Of all the works, probably the fourth—the novella *Lament on the Death of a Master of Arts*—makes the least significant contribution to this picture." One could easily question the truth of such a statement. The novel does present, and very authentically, one of the essential aspects of society—the educational aspect. The contribution of the novel towards the composite social picture is as significant as that of *Untouchable* or *Coolie*. Sinha's appreciation of the novel is well based on the facts: "...an intellectual effort of a high order has gone into the novel's artistry, the design, texture, character, and atmosphere taking on the resplendent quality of true and inimitable vision."[24] One could hardly expect anything more profound and realistic in such a short space and time.

The sufferer-saviour relationship in the novella, we find, differs from that of *Untouchable, Coolie, Two Leaves and a Bud*, and *Gauri*. No doubt, the sufferer and the saviour, as in these novels, are different persons. But they do not hail from divergent worlds. Here we do not have a low-caste or low-class man listening with a sense of adoration, to a man of much higher caste or class of society. Nor is the sufferer an illiterate, innocent person for whom the words of the saviour seem to be those of a superhuman being. The sufferer and the saviour belong to the castes which enjoy almost equal regard in their respective worlds. Both are victims to almost similar problems—the problem of oppression of their free wills by the over-ambitious fathers. But the behaviour character, with his spirit of rebellion and power of assertion refuses to be a puppet in the hands of his father. His vast reading has widened his vision; his love for poetry and philosophy rescue him from oppressive thoughts and inferiority complex. The sufferer, however, has lost all spirit, confidence, strength, and even health because of a sense of failure in the practical world in which what matters is not education but manoeuvers to get adjusted in a job of status is essential. To add to his misery, he is reminded of his failure by not only the words but the looks and behaviour of his father. He wonders at the confidence and boldness of his friend Azad but himself is never allowed to have spirits. He, like Munoo and Gangu, is liberated from his torments by death. However, in the case of Nur, death seems to be neither natural nor accidental. It seems to be hastened by the cruelty of his father.

NOTES

1. See "Publisher's Note," *Gauri* (New Delhi; Arnold-Heinemann Publishers Pvt. Ltd., 1981). All the subsequent references to the text of the novel are from this edition. The novel was first published under the title *The Old Woman and the Cow* in 1960 by Kutub Popular, Bombay.
2. In "Dedicatory Letter to Ali Sardar Jafri" Anand Writes: "The story of Gauri has been narrated here from the urge to retell it in my own manner. The spark that lit the fire and has raged in this book came from your heart, many years after Nekrassov had left the smouldering ashes of his epic poem in me." The 1981 edition of the novel contains this letter.
3. K.N. Sinha, *Mulk Raj Anand*, 73.
4. Dieter Riemenschneider, *An Ideal of Man in the Novels of Mulk Raj Anand* (Bombay: Kutub Popular,1967), 20.
5. *Ibid.*, 17-18.
6. M.K. Naik, *Mulk Raj Anand*, 95.
7. Marlene Fisher, *The Wisdom of the Heart*, 104.
8. K.N. Sinha, *Mulk Raj Anand*, 72.
9. Marlene Fisher, *The Wisdom of the Heart*, 100.
10. Jack Lindsay, *The Elephant and the Lotus*, 29.
11. M.K. Naik, *Mulk Raj Anand*, 95.
12. *Ibid.*
13. *So Many Freedoms*, 159.
14. *Ibid.*
15. S.C. Harrex, *The Fire and the Offering*, 140.
16. *Lament on the Death of a Master of Arts* (New Delhi: Arnold Heinemann Publishers Pvt. Ltd., 1967), 37.
17. Mulk Raj Anand, *Apology for Heroism*, 33.

18. Mulk Raj Anand, *On Education* (Bombay: Hind Kitabs Ltd., 1947), 13.
19. Premila Paul, "Anand's *Lament on the Death of a Master of Arts," A Journal of Indian Writing in English,* Vol. 6, No. 2 (1978), 71.
20. K.N. Sinha, *Mulk Raj Anand,* 45.
21. Premila Paul, "Anand's *Lament on the Death of a Master of Arts," op. cit.,* 70.
22. S.C. Harrex , *The Fire and the Offering,* 105.
23. *The Bubble,* the fourth novel in the series of his autobiographical novels reveals Anand's desire to be a poet because he is sick of the hypocrisy, cunningness, and deceit of the members of his own family.
24. K.N. Sinha, *Mulk Raj Anand,* 45.

4

FROM THE SICKLE TO THE SWORD

In the Trilogy comprising *The Village, Across the Black Waters,* and *The Sword and the Sickle,* the sufferer-saviour relationship varies not only from novel to novel but also in each novel and the fluctuation is so frequent and the relationship so ambiguous that it defies classification. Lal Singh, the protagonist, suffers the pangs of poverty in *The Village* but he, unlike Munoo and Gangu, has a fiery, rebellious spirit. Having a revolutionary attitude, he refuses to fall in with the traditional beliefs of the other members of his family and tries to instigate his passive, listless friends to challenge the authority of the established, irrational shibboleths and taboos. But before he is able to do anything for the alleviation of the suffering peasantry, he falls a victim to the treacherous plan of the village landlord, Harbans Singh. To escape the snare of the landlord, he has himself recruited as a sepoy in the British Indian army. This impulsive action changes the course of his life entirely. In *Across the Black Waters* he loses all individuality as he is only one of a large number of sepoys carrying out the dictates of the British government without questioning the logic of the orders. The novel, no doubt, has some kind characters like Kirpu, Dhanoo, Lachman Singh, and even a few British officers like Captain Owen. But they can only recite wise things and inspire one another; otherwise they are all helpless people fighting a dreadful battle against Germany on behalf of Britain without ever knowing the reason of the war. They are weak, dumb creatures hurled headlong into the fray only because the government pays them eleven rupees a month. As we proceed from *The Village* to *Across the Black Waters*, the theme completely changes and so does the cause of suffering of the protagonist. The scene of action also changes—from India to France. The shift of the scene adds to the war-novel another theme—the theme of east-west encounter. *The Sword and the Sickle* deals with the post-war period in India. Lal singh comes back to India after completing his term of five years as a prisoner of war in Germany. On his return he finds the peasantry seething with the urge to rebel both against the British authority and Indian feudalism. It is in this third novel that the relationship between the suffering and the saviour characters becomes a very complex one. In Nandpur peasants are awakened about their rights and requirements. They are preparing themselves for a rebellion against exploitation by the cruel money-lenders and landlords. Destiny again changes the track of Lalu's life by making him join a group of revolutionaries at Rajgarh. The revolutionaries here are a group of people with varying ideologies and approaches towards the goal of the liberation of landless farmers from the cruel hands of heartless landlords. The peasants here are still passive sufferers. The revolutionaries who organise under the leadership of Kanwar Rampal try to save the suffering and suppressed farmers-turned-labourers. But they fail to achieve anything in reality. These self-styled revolutionaries try to be the saviours, but they are sufferers in their own way. Kanwar Rampal himself is evicted from his estate for incurring the wrath of his younger brother, Kanwar Birpal. Prof Verma is an intellectual fit only for reflecting, brooding, and theorizing. He is incapable of any actual action. He is an arm-chair philosopher. Lal Singh is all the time vague about the real aim of the revolution and is never able to make any resolutions regarding the means to achieve the aim. He is torn between his duty towards his wife Maya and his allegiance to the organization of rebels. Mishra is treacherous and a traitor. Ram Din too fails to plan things properly. Moreover, these revolutionaries are mere parasites who have to depend on Kanwar Rampal even for their pocket-money. Kanwar Rampal, despite his great sacrifice of giving up the allurements of landlordism, fails to identify himself completely with the peasants. His complexes as a rich landlord surface every now and then. Political leaders like Mahatma Gandhi, Jawahar Lal Nehru, and the poet Sarshar are also introduced in the third novel. But they too fail to liberate the peasants from their slavery to their masters. Mahatma Gandhi appears to be a distant, inaccessible leader who wants to impress upon others his ideology of non-violence in a dogmatic manner. His taciturnity and sternness are incompatible with his more humane image in *Untouchable*. The peasants themselves seem to be awakened rebels at some places whereas at others they are still unable to resist the illogical dictates of the feudal lords.

In *The Village* Anand chooses for his hero not a passive slave but an impoverished peasant boy who has received education upto middle class in an English-medium school. His education makes him aware of many of the evil practices prevalent in Indian villages. This awareness dissuades him from complying with the irrational taboos of society and religion. Anand has tried to portray the orthodoxy and backwardness of Indian villages on social, economic, political, and religious levels. In all these spheres Anand condemns the practices which hamper the modern, progressive, untraditional, and scientific attitude toward life. But the condemnation of the evil practices has not been done through long harangues of any saviour figure who appears in the novel only for preaching. No doubt, Hercules Long is introduced to make the villagers realize the need of cleanliness in the village, but Hercules Long, unlike Dr Mahindra in *Gauri* or Dr Havre in *Two Leaves and a Bud* does not indulge in any profound, incomprehensible, and philosophical preaching. The incident of Hercules Long organizing the village boys as scouts with Lalu as their leader emphasizes the fact that Lalu is not a mere passive, spineless character but one who is capable of working practically. Anand makes Hercules Long choose Lalu for organising the boy scouts.

Lalu has much in common with Krishan (Anand himself) in *Morning Face* and *Confession of a Lover*. He articulates many of Anand's own feelings and observations. The other members of the family like his father Nihal Singh, his mother Gujri, and his brothers Sharm Singh and Dyal Singh are counterparts of Krishan's maternal grandfather, grandmother, and uncles.[1] Nihal Singh and Sharm Singh stand for all that is traditional and established. They dislike Lalu's untraditional views. The attitudes of Nihal Singh and Sharm Singh are, in fact, the general attitudes of all the villagers in Nandpur; they, instead, represent the thoughts and feelings of the villagers throughout India. The novel opens with Nihal Singh's condemnation of machines. For him the machine age is "the age of darkness." His remarks about the engine of the train he has traveled by exemplify his regressive attitude: "This machine is like the Devil. How it made my heart jump! Wah Guru! Wah Guru! And the smoke it emits is so bad for the fields, just blights away the harvest, I am glad I have no fields near the railroad. To think of our young corn blasted by the foul smoke and sparks of the stone coal which these injans belch forth day and night, night and day! The age of darkness has come!"[2] And Lalu's answer to such a remark is significant as it forms a prelude to his viewpoint in all the three novels. He tells his father:

> But look how bravely it phuff-phuffs away to the north...I wouldn't mind going to Lahore and Bombay with it. And whatever you say, Bapu, you know you would not like to be carrying all those sacks of grain to Manabad and Sherkot on your back. The bullock-cart drivers stop twenty times, to smoke and to feed the bullocks, and they often get drunk and take two days and a night sometimes. But you can send anything to town in an hour by the goods train (2).

This conversation between the father and the son introduces the major theme of the novel—the conflict between orthodoxy and modernity.

Lalu's dislike for traditional inhibitions is further revealed in his love for individual liberty. He wants to protect his free thinking by resisting the overbearing behaviour of the elders. He does not want to accept all the dictates of the elders without questioning their logic. His resentment against the dominating behaviour of elders is revealed in his remark: "This was the thing.... They were always forbidding you to do this and that, these elders, always curtailing your liberty. Always frustrating your desires. Always frustrating. You couldn't even laugh in their presence. You had to join your hands gravely and say, 'I fall at your feet.' And they were ridiculous fools, ugly, uncouth lumps of flesh, wide-eyed, open-mouthed simpletons, saying prayers and mentioning the name of God all day, even as they lasciviously eyed the young girls passing in the bazaar" (55). Anand himself has always had a contempt for suppression of the freedom of the younger by the elders. "I believe my growth, and that of whole generations of males, has been arrested by father domination,"[3] writes Anand in a personal letter. In *Confession of a Lover* Krishan again and again regrets that the behaviour of elders hampers the free growth of young people. Very frankly he comments on the hypocritical nature of all the elders in his family when he tells Noor: "My father is greedy!.... My mother is stubborn and ignorant and worships her gods all day! My eldest brother Harish takes bribes and goes to Bazaar women! My elder brother Ganesh is insidious and scheming.... I am fed up with their hypocrisy. I am full of hatred and bitterness and anger—when I want to love everyone and learn every thing and grow to master my kismet."[4] His friend Noor too has similar feelings about his family, particularly about his father. Krishan exhorts him to rebel against the domination of oldies and attain freedom."Rebellion and freedom," says Krishan, "Not acceptance and death! It is only through rebellion against everything false that I have written poetry. I want to cast out my fears. Every word must be a gesture of defiance. And I want to embrace the people—even those who are illiterate and down and degraded! Because once we are free, all of us will grow and discover marvelous things!.... We will become a big people! We will make a new life!"[5] In *Lament on the Death of a Master of Arts* Anand reveals how the cruel behaviour of Nur's father leads to the death of the former. Lalu inspires his friends Ghugi, Churanji, and Ghulam to rebel against the overbearing attitude of their fathers just as Krishan advises Noor to defy the authority of his unfeeling father.

With his ardent spirit and rebellious temperament, Lalu wants to introduce reforms in society by making the villagers, particularly the members of his own family, aware of their infirmities. He warns his father and brothers against the dangers of borrowing money from the money-lender. He loses all patience when the money-lender Chaman Lal tries to deceive his father and brother with his treacherous talk. He does not approve of his father's blind faith in Mahant Nandgir. He can very well see the greed, hypocrisy, and lechery of the Mahant. He wonders "why couldn't the family learn better than to waste money on gifts for these charlatans?" (45). He feels disgusted with the self-styled saint who "ate sumptuous food, dressed in yellow silks, smoked charas and drank hemp, and, if reports were true, whored and fornicated" (45). The reports do prove to be true when Mahant Nandgir is caught red-handed with Lalu's sister-in-law, Kesari. With his acute observation Lalu is able to gauge the fundamental character of the deceiving saint who skulks under veil of religion. He warns his father and brother: "There is no elixir of life. And beware of a religious teacher who in greed is so gluttonous that he will suck the blood of the poorest" (24). In the fair, Lalu refuses to be taken in by the fabulous promises made by Lehna Singh to the people whom he wants to allure to be recruited as soldiers in the British Indian army. The promises, for Lalu, are "Too good to be true" (78). He again refuses to be befooled by the quack who is deceiving the poor peasants with his hypnotic advertisement of an elixir of life which could boost their physical power. "The man is a fraud" (76), announces Lalu to the audience.

Lalu has faith neither in the existence of God nor in the validity of age-old customs. He is not a fatalist, but a rationalist. He believes in action, not in contemplation; he does not want to relegate the responsibility of his failures to *Karma* or destiny. With all these sceptical notions, Lalu again appears to be a counterpart of Anand himself [named Krishan Chander Azad] in his autobiographical novels. Lalu challenges the existence of God very fearlessly and refuses to indulge in the ritual of saying prayers. His words reveal his moral courage when he remarks: "If He exists, if He really can punish people for not saying prayers and violating the laws of religion, let him come and strike me dead as I am walking along now.... Where is he? Let him come and strike me dead" (146). This is exactly how Anand himself felt about God after the death of his cousin Kaushalya at the young age of nine. In "why I write?" Anand writes about his atheistic attitude: "I have tended to regard Him, since then, as the enemy of mankind. In fact, from that time my belief in the man with the big beard sitting on top of the sky, determining the fate of everyone, has been shaken more or less completely. And unless I am in the dark, and frightened of ghosts, or in some other danger, or using proverbial speech like 'for God's sake,' I have never invoked the giant Patriarch."[6] In *Morning Face* and *Confession of a Lover* he reiterates his disbelief in the existence of God.

Lalu's revolutionary nature is further revealed in his deviation from religious taboos. The most glaring example of his boldness is his having his hair cut off when he goes to the fair. He has no regard for religious inhibitions. But the cruelty of the fanatics overpowers his rebellious courage. The villagers are shocked to see his hair cut. The punishment they impose is no less than blackening his face and taking him out in a procession on a donkey. The incident unnerves Lalu who feels completely alienated in his own native village. He feels a kind of disdain for life itself. He broods over the cruel behaviour meted out to him: "Oh, I wish I had never been born here if they had to treat me like that!...the abuse...the shouts...the insults...and...oh, how could they...they blackened my face...they put me.... All of them...my own people...oh, how could they...my own father and mother...they used to pet me and love me...my own brothers...that rogue Hardit Singh!...and my own mother, who never slept for nights...Oh! disgraced for ever...beaten and bruised...what can I do?" (98). The incident very well reveals how the rigidity of cruel society can break the will of one who has never wanted to submit to the bondage of customs and taboos. Lalu who had dared to eat in Muslim cook-shops and who had inspired his friends to assert themselves against the domination of their parents feels overpowered by the inflexible, narrow mentality of the traditionalists. His mind is torn between a will to resist on one hand and submission to elders on the other like Bakha's mind torn with a conflict between a desire to hit back and a passive acceptance of his low status after he is disgraced in the temple. Lalu, though more courageous than Bakha, Munoo and Gangu, is, like them, incapable of taking liberties with the norms of society at some stages.

Lalu's boldness despite the treachery of society is again demonstrated in his love for Maya, the daughter of the village landlord. Lalu feels a fascination for the girl while going to the fair in a hay cart. He is bold enough to entertain feelings of love for this daughter of an enemy of their family. But the feelings are completely crushed by the trickery of the landlord who brings a false allegation of theft against Lalu and wants to get rid of the boy with the help of law. Lalu again feels helpless before such cunning and influence of the rich landlord. He has no choice but to save himself by running away. He finds an escape in the British Indian army which he joins on the spur of the moment. The fabulous promises made by the recruiting Havildar Lehna Singh that had seemed "too good to be true" to Lalu in the fair still cannot blind him. But a job in the army seems to be a haven from the inescapable trap of Harbans Singh. And added to it is the allurement that "the money I could earn in the army may help to pay off our debts" (165). His strong will again yields to the power of one who is economically and socially stronger.

But Anand reveals that Lalu and his father, though poor peasants, and weakened by the power of the rich landlord, are not silent sufferers. Though they cannot save themselves and others of their kind, they are not passive sufferers. They do assert their dignity and try to resist the injustice of the landlord. When Harbans Singh comes with the policeman to have Lalu arrested, the reaction of Nihal Singh is that of a respectable, dignified man. The following words prove his self-esteem:

> You touch him and see. You fraud who come to harass honest folk by day and perpetrate your own scandals in the darkness of night. They do not wring the neck of the thief who steals cucumbers, and my sons are honest and even my cattle won't stray into your illgotten fields. It is all a misunderstanding. We have our pride, we have our dignity, and our name is breathed with a prayer and not a curse. You think you will ruin my family both inside and outside the courts, you heartless impostor. You have usurped my land and now, you want to send my son to jail. But you forget that you are dealing with sturdy peasants and not weaklings. Just you touch him! (159-60).

His assertiveness presents a contrast to the servility of the father of Bakha who is ready to accept all assaults on his dignity with hands joined in abject submission. Such assertiveness on Nihal Singh's part is not abrupt or incompatible with his character otherwise. We are told that he has fought bravely against the British on behalf of the *Khalsa.* He takes pride in the fact that he has Rajput blood in him and has served his religion with a sense of sacrifice. When Lalu comes back from the army to see his ailing father, the latter, though on death-bed, has mental strength enough to exhort his son: "Be brave, son. Take courage and don't be a jackal. Go and work with your hands, and be happy, for you are young. And leave me to die if I have to die. Fight your enemies and the enemies of Truth and keep alive the name of your ancestors. Never let it be said of our family that we were cowards in the face of death" (222). He wants to inculcate the spirit of sacrifice in his sons. Sharm Singh too—though Lal Singh disapproves of his orthodoxy—displays courage when he avenges his disgrace by murdering the landlord's son. No doubt, Sharm Singh is hanged for the crime, but at least his reaction to the lechery of the landlord's son is that of a sensitive, brave man who is not ready to pocket any humiliation helplessly. Lal Singh himself faces Harbans Singh fearlessly when the latter comes to have him arrested. With great boldness even at the unnerving moment, he tells Harbans Singh: "Get away, you foul cur, go back home" (161). He escapes the snare of the landlord with great physical and mental strength.

Lal Singh articulates many of the feelings of Anand himself. His escape from the cruelty of Harbans Singh is comparable to Anand's own escape into a foreign land from the clutches of his dominating father. Anand makes his protagonist aware of the evil forces which are bent upon squeezing the poor peasants. So he need not introduce any saviour characters to voice his message. Only Hercules Long is brought into the novel to make the villagers aware of the need of better living conditions for themselves. But Anand's aim seems not to bring home any message to the villagers by Hercules Long. The incident provides Anand with an opportunity to have a dig at the sycophancy of people like Harbans Singh and to bring the simple peasant boys into the limelight by making them scouts who should themselves try for their amelioration. The discomfiture of Hercules Long during his encounter with a cow gives a comic touch to the otherwise sombre tone of the novel. Moreover, the benevolence of the Englishman is a fine introduction to the kindness of some British officials like Captain Owen, an Adjutant in the army.

The novel appears to be fairly free from the propagandistic purpose of the novelist. The message of the novelist is conveyed through the hero-anti hero Lal Singh who suffers all right but does not suffer passively. He does not need a kind person to come to his help or to advise him to rise above the squalor and rigid orthodoxy of the village. He is well conscious of his position in society; he knows what the villagers like him should fight for and against. He tries to resist the greed of the moneylender, the deceit of the Mahant and the intrigues of the landlord. But he is deterred by the poverty of his family and the inheritance of respect for the elders. In him Anand has struck a fine blend of strength and weakness—a true picture of an Indian peasant—both sturdy and infirm. Because the sufferer is aware of what he has to struggle for, Anand does not have to introduce some outside figures to incite the poor peasants to a struggle. The novel, therefore, is free from the element of direct propaganda which mars much of the charm of *Gauri* and *Two Leaves and a Bud*. The novelist retains his integrity as instead of stating his case overtly, he shows it through incidents. Although Lal Singh is not able to do anything practically to save the peasants from the pangs of poverty and the tricks of the landlord and the money-lender, he, at least, is not blind to the evil intentions of these financially powerful exploiters. His awareness forms a prelude to the awareness of other peasants of his village in *The Sword and the Sickle*. The unity of the novel is never impaired by long speeches the kind of which we find in *Untouchable, Coolie, Gauri*, and *Two Leaves and a Bud*. *The Village* lacks a regular plot; still it is a unified whole. The ending of the novel provides a natural, convincing beginning to the next novel of the Trilogy. So although the scene shifts at once from India to France, the shift in the atmosphere does not strike us as unnaturally abrupt.

In *Across the Black Waters* the peasant-turned-sepoy protagonist loses his image as the saviour figure. He no longer is better among the equals as he was in *The Village*; he is a mere sepoy like a large number of other sepoys, mere servants serving the British government for eleven rupees a month which they are given to keep their bodies and souls together. No doubt, there are kind and wise people like Uncle Kirpu, Daddy Dhanoo, Havildar Lachman Singh, and Captain Owen, but they, too, are subordinates to the invisible British authority. They can do nothing except encourage one another with wise homilies. They help one another to the extent to which their own limitations permit them. So they may be termed as good characters or, as Margaret Berry calls them, "wisdom figures." But they may not be regarded as saviour heroes in the sense in which Mahatma Gandhi, the poet Sarshar, Dr Mahindra or Dr Havre are.

The role of Lal Singh changes with the change of theme. The poverty of peasants is sometimes referred to in *Across the Black Waters* because poverty is the cause of the joining of army by many sepoys. But the novel is basically a war novel presenting the futility of war and insanity of governments of even great nations like Britain, France, and Germany. The futility of war becomes all the more glaring in the case of Indian soldiers who have to fight for another government without any nationalistic feelings to goad them to the arena. The most ironical fact is that the soldiers are completely ignorant of the cause of war; they even do not know where they are being taken and against whom they have to fight. The novel is written on an epic scale with the action no less significant than World War I. The bloodshed and destruction in the War are on a large, almost global, scale. The events presented in the novel have world-wide repercussions. The novel opens with Indian troops embarking at Marseilles in France. The imagery that Anand uses to describe the sea and the wind in France is a foreboding of the violent destruction that is to take place in the novel. For instance, Anand remarks:

> ...the black, or rather blue water seemed uncanny, spreading for thousands of miles. It seemed as if God had spat upon the universe and the spittle had become the sea.... The white flecks of the foam on the swell, where wave met wave, seemed like the froth turned out of God's angry mouth. The swish of the air as the ships tore their way across the rough sea seemed like the fury of the Almighty at the sin which the white men had committed in building their powerful engines of the Iron Age.[7]

This beginning of the second novel relates it to the first novel in which Nihal Singh condemns the engine of the train as devilish and the machine age as the age of darkness. In the novel Anand again and again paints the atmosphere of the battlefield as murky and dark. Because the war is presented from the viewpoint of Indian sepoys, Anand chooses Indian mythology to describe the atmosphere of France in which

> the days were the colours of the nights, or only a shade lighter, and the murky, greenish grey sky was the exact colour of the roof of hell which the sages in India spoke about where the souls of the sinners were subjected to the ordeals, first of trailing through the mud of marshes, full of slimy ravenous rats and blood-sucking leeches, then through a forest of tangled bushes and thickets of

> thorns, then to wait in misery, naked and cold and hungry, for the coming of the rain which was to wash them clean of their sins, for the ordeal of fire which was to purge them, and for the final judgement before the throne of Brahma seated in all his glory on a mighty throne surrounded by hosts of angels and fairies (131-32).

The Germans have been called "the hosts of Kali" (152).

The most pitiable thing is that Indian sepoys are brought face to face with the hosts of death without any personal or nationalistic purpose. They fail to know why the governments of so well-developed countries indulge in such destructive activities. They do not know about the place to which they are taken. A few words of encouragement by the British officers, a message of affection by the King of England, and a few claps by the lords of England at the name of Indian soldiers are sufficient to excite these innocent soldiers to be ready to lay down their lives; the hope of a piece of land or a medal of merit is enough to make them survive all troubles and dangers in the battlefield; a meagre salary is adequate to discipline the soldiers and make them faithful servants of the government. For these rewards they are ready to fight till death for those with whom they have no direct contact and against those with whom they have no hostility. The government demands complete submission of the sepoys. Uncle Kirpu's satirical remark reveals the bitter truth: "That [to obey] is the first maxim of the army. But there is another law of army life. No doubts and fears, or suchlike thoughts, shall be allowed to stand between a sepoy and his Destiny. And if you ask what is that Destiny...you will be told it is a medal won for bravery in battle.... And death. That is so all the world over, the same in China, in Japan, on the frontier and in Vilayat" (136-37). To add to the misery of the soldiers, their army is not adequately equipped to face the powerful machine-guns of the Germans. They are provided with bayonets only and are untrained even in the use of these crude weapons. Life in rain-soaked trenches is very miserable. But they have no right to grudge. Any violation of order is likely to result in the sepoy getting shot at and killed. Subedar Suchet Singh kills

Hanumant Singh in cold blood only because the latter refuses to go for a counter-attack as he is suffering from fever. Such strict execution of disciplinary measures has converted the soldiers into mere puppets dancing to the tune of British government. They are "like conscripts, brutalized and willing to fight like trained bulls, but without a will of their own, soulless automations in the execution of the army code, though in the strange dark deep of their natures, unschooled by the Sarkar, there lay the sensitiveness of their own humanity, their hopes, their fears and their doubts" (133). Their sensitiveness is evident in their eagerness to help one another and their reactions to the death of any one of them. The death of Havildar Lachman and Daddy Dhanoo leaves the sensitive sepoys like Kirpu and Lalu utterly shocked. The suicide by Kirpu has a very deep effect on the mind of Lal Singh. But the orders of the government suppress the emotions of the sepoys and overcoming their grief they have to get ready to carry out the army code.

For their dedication to the cause of the British army, the Indian soldiers get no reward except a continuous hope for an award. The most ironical fact is the practice of bestowing posthumous awards. Uncle Kirpu's ridicule of the posthumous award announced for Lachman Singh is, in fact, Anand's own indignation at the absurdity of the practice. "Encouragement is a great thing," says Kirpu, "Promotion is still better and a life pension addressed to Holdar Lachman Singh, Village Pool of Blood, Tehsil Purgatory, District Hell—Wah, don't speak of it!" (208). The promises of land made lavishly during the recruitment of the soldiers are never fulfilled.

Anand lashes not only at the cruel orders of the British officers; he also has a dig at the cruel execution of the orders by the these officers and their Indian sycophants. Anand displays a rare objectivity in his delineation of the characters of British and Indian officers. His prejudices against the British which are apparent in *Coolie* are kept well under control in this novel. If Anand is furious at the cold behaviour of Colonel Green and Major Peacock, he also applauds the kindness of Captain Owen. Unlike most of his countrymen, Captain Owen is not reticent and remote. He, on the other hand, has always a smile, a pat or a word of encouragement for Indian sepoys. He tries to cheer up Khushi Ram telling him that "Civilization also means a sense of humour, you know. Don't let us fall victims to the mere solemnity of civilization..." (215). A British officer condescends to offer a cigarette to Lal Singh. When Lalu, Kirpu, and Khushi Ram are afraid of drinking in the cafe where British and French officers are enjoying their drinks, the latter encourage them with kind words and enjoy their songs. Anand handles with severity the Indian officials like Lok Nath, Suchet Singh, and Subah Singh for their jealous, cruel, and revengeful behaviour towards Indian sepoys. Lok Nath is a heartless brute. He has failed to get promotion in his rank. He takes his peevishness out on his subordinates. Lalu, particularly, is the target of his venom. Subah Singh gets direct promotion through the influence of his father. His pride after the promotion overpowers his friendliness towards Lal Singh, Kirpu and Dhanoo. Now he is completely given to drinking and womanizing. He is an irresponsible lout who is drunk even when he has to go on patrol and who through his lack of responsibility puts the life of others on patrol in danger. The cruelty and jealousy of Lok Nath and Subah Singh compel a conscientious and wise man like Kirpu to commit suicide. Suchet Singh has no consideration for the feelings of others. He refuses to exempt Hanumant from duty even when the latter is suffering from fever. He coldly kills Hanumant when the latter refuses to go for a fight. Anand's firm control over his pet prejudices makes his portrayal of life in trenches authentic and credible.

Anand has revealed the absurdity, futility, and cruelty of war through some convincing episodes. The novel, unlike most of Anand's other novels, is a novel of action. The focus on the protagonist in *The Village* now gives place to concentration on corporate action. Individual life loses its significance in the war. The death of one of the sepoys saddens his friends, but leaves no void in the structure of the army. The friends too have to accept their suffering by subordinating their shock to a sense of duty. Now Anand does not depend on characters to directly narrate the misery of people. He, instead, makes his purpose clear through powerful incidents like the murder of a sepoy for his refusal to fight, the death of a pious and dutiful man like Daddy Dhanoo, the suicide by the wise and friendly Uncle Kirpu. No doubt, Anand has interspersed the novel with remarks on the inhumanity of war and its agents through the mouths of wise and kind characters like Uncle Kirpu, Lachman Singh, Lal Singh, and Captain Owen. But they themselves are bound by their obligations to the British government. They cannot provoke others against the cruel execution of the strict orders of the government; they cannot incite people to revolt against the authorities. They can only cheer up one another whenever something distressing takes place. Because Anand shuns the use of direct narration the novel is free from unaesthetically long harangues the kind of which we find in *Two Leaves and a Bud* and *Gauri*. The novelist here is intent on "showing" rather than "telling." Not that Anand has no message for us, but he has been able to convey his message without the use of manifestly propagandistic device of overstatement. His condemnation of some characters and applause of others again is rather muted and within the limits of credibility.

Along with the theme of war, Anand also touches upon the themes of east-west encounter and the conflict between tradition and modernity. Indian sepoys rooted in Indian culture and habits are brought to France—thousands of miles away from their motherland. The army consists of the Indian and British soldiers who are supported by French allies. The antagonism between India and Britain seems diminishing as they land together in a foreign country. The British officers try to encourage the Indians with kind words. The Indian soldiers give up many of the inhibitions and taboos of the native religion. They derive pleasure from sexual freedom, drinking, and eating beef. The frankness and freedom of French women appeal to them more than the prudish behaviour of women in their own country. A British officer is seen relieving himself, like some Indians, on the ground. The French people are like Indians in hospitality and affection. They give warm welcome to the British Indian troops. The wives and mothers bid tearful farewells to their soldiers. The behaviour of the wife of a French soldier crying hysterically at parting from her husband reminds Lalu of the affection of his mother. The family of Father Carbusier is full of affection. They treat Lal Singh as a member of their family. But the French are much ahead of India so far as cleanliness and advancement are concerned. The farm house of Carbusier is Lalu's old dream come true. The cattle are kept in a very clean place and machines are used for milking the cows. Anand has devoted a very small space to the theme of tradition versus modernity. But he has successfully revealed what India needs to do for its advancement in the age of machine. The theme serves the purpose of uniting the first two novels of the Trilogy. Again, his message is brought home without any loss of artistic integrity. Lalu cherishes the adoption of advanced methods of cultivation and husbandry but his observation does not sound propagandistic in any way.

Across the Black Waters is, thus, a successful novel. There are no saviour figures to overtly state the author's thesis. The urge to propagate seems to be well under control of the artist. Never do we feel the uneasy intrusion of the novelist. The narration of episodes in the war is based on Anand's own experiences in the trenches during Spanish Civil War.[8] The narration, therefore, sounds authentic and truthful. Anand reveals great command over the handling of his material in a suitable style. The tale never seems to go out of his control. K.N. Sinha's opinion that "*Across the Black Waters* lacks the sureness of accomplished art"[9] seems baseless. As a novel of war, it is highly successful. The success owes much to Anand's refraining from propagating through his mouthpieces. Some characters do articulate the authorial purpose but they are not mere spokesmen. Their wisdom is not borrowed but acquired through their own experiences. Their reactions to various incidents form the major action of the novel.

In *The Sword and the Sickle* the protagonist's course is decided unexpectedly. He is no longer on the pay roll of the British government. He comes back from the prisoners-of-war camp in Germany five years after his capture by the German forces during the World War. He is hopeful that he will be amply rewarded by the British authorities for his bravery in the war. He particularly hopes to get a piece of land as a reward. But, to his utter shock, he is demobilized on the flimsy ground that he has happened to listen to some Indian seditionists like Chattopadhyay and Hidayatullah in Germany. Utterly dazed and penniless he returns to his native village where greater shocks are waiting for him. He comes to know about the complete ruin of his family and the auction of their house and lands. All the peasants are suffering from utter poverty in the post-war period. Most of the farmers have now been reduced to landless labourers working in the fields of the feudal lords or serving in factories. But Lalu finds a rebellious spirit instead of the usual abjectness among the peasantry. Lalu who has been fiery and rebellious since childhood feels fascinated by the spark of agitation among poor simple people like his uncle Harnam Singh, his friends Gughi, Santokh, and Ghulam. In a rally organized by these rebels, Lal Singh finds a chance to speak against the injustice of the British government. At the rally he happens to meet Prof Verma. This meeting brings about a drastic change in the role of Lal Singh in society. Prof Verma now belongs to the group of revolutionaries organized by Kanwar Rampal Singh in Rajgarh in the states of Agra and Oudh. Now the sufferer-saviour relationship becomes very complex. Lalu is one of the sufferers but he joins the group of those who want to be the saviours of suffering peasantry. Their intention is to save the landless farmers from the cruel domination of feudal Lords. But these revolutionaries themselves are still vague about their precise purpose and the wherewithal to realize the purpose.

To Lalu's role as a revolutionary is added another role—that of a lover and a husband. At Nandpur, Maya, the daughter of the landlord and the beloved of Lalu, comes back to him. Her husband has died and she, breaking the bondage of strict security in her father's house, is ready to elope with Lal Singh to Rajgarh. Her daring stride is congruous with the general atmosphere of rebellion. Lalu who has suffered much because of the girl does not want to lose her now. The intensity of his passion makes him overcome his annoyance that the girl has been the cause of his family's ruin. At the same time, Lalu finds such elopement to be a way to avenge himself on the landlord. But the action of Lalu is rash and hasty. From the very beginning of their elopement Lalu starts feeling the thoughtlessness of the action as he realizes that the delicate, well-protected, ease-loving Maya may prove to be a hindrance in his revolutionary actions. He starts regretting his step: "Why, oh why, did I encumber myself with a breakable possession like you when I had just succeeded in controlling my own destiny for once?"[10] At Rajgarh he feels torn between his duties towards Maya and his commitment as a revolutionary. Maya does not approve of Lalu's revolutionary and destructive actions till the end of the novel. It is only towards the end that she is ready to face the troubles of living among the poor evicted peasants. She wants to contribute to the revolutionary movement.

Lalu's relations with Maya are in consonance with his character throughout the Trilogy. He is unable to take firm decisions. He decides things on the spur of the moment and then finds it difficult to adhere to his decisions. Lalu himself acknowledges the confusion and doubts in his mind. He broods over his failings attributing them to his lack of conviction. Anand presents the mental state of his protagonist in the remark: "He [Lalu] realized that the reason why he had never been able to control his destiny was because he had been weak and undecided about everything in his own mind. Ever since his youth in the village he had been forced by circumstances to live outside himself, so that he had merely drifted along not knowing what to do...though he found himself clinging tenaciously to himself, he knew that he had no faith in himself; that apart from a nature shaped by stress, he had no character to cling to..." (107). Lalu is never able to overcome this confusion. Iyengar rightly considers this speech to be the revelation of his character. Iyengar regards these words as "the key to Lalu's character, the key too to the understanding of the entire Trilogy."[11] Lalu himself suffering from such mental timidity cannot do much to save the peasantry from their troubles. He himself feels that he has joined the group of revolutionaries to avoid his responsibilities as a son of a wronged family: "Perhaps, he felt, it was this lack of faith in himself that had made him abandon the idea of living his own life and throw himself into this peasant work, a kind of escape from the necessity to face up to himself and the family troubles, the reproaches of the neighbours in Nandpur and the pangs of his own conscience" (107). He does not know what is the actual object of the revolution. He does not have a firm plan in his mind. No doubt, he is enthusiastic, but his enthusiasm is directed to no specific aim. His actions are random and rash. But towards the end of the novel, the conviction of the communist Sarshar puts him on a firm track. In the prison Lalu realizes that the Indians must struggle for a new way of life. They can achieve a new life by their togetherness and dedication. Now the actual target of struggle is clear and so is the approach to achieve the target. He knows that Indians will have to overcome their passions and selfish interests to realize the purpose of revolution. His silent oration in the prison is actually the message of Anand himself: "But it is only after the fight against those who enslave, Comrade, only after the struggle for the new way of life, that we shall rest and sing of the seasons.... Now is the time to learn the ways of struggle, my love, now is the time to live in and through the struggle.... Now is the time to change the world, to fight for life and happiness; now is the time to sing, Comrade, brave songs of the struggle..." (385). But the message is so well ingrained in the text that it does not stand out as a propagandistic speech. It is the thought of one who has suffered much and now wants to relieve the sufferings of others. The news of the birth of a son at the end of the novel is significant. It predicts the continuation of struggle for the upliftment of the poor people. The hope for a new life is revealed through Anand's dexterous use of natural imagery: "Lal Singh lifted his head and saw the new dawn filtering through the doorways with that uncanny milk-white radiance which heralds the coming of a strong sun. The moist smell of the dew blew into the corners of the dormitory, freshening his limbs after the stench, the fatigue and the irritations of the dark night" (386). "The stench, the fatigue and the irritations of the dark night" symbolize the hard period of life that Lalu who, according to Alain Nivanstair, is "Everyman,"[12] has undergone. In *Death of a Hero* Maqbool wants his sister's son to continue the struggle after his death. But the son is still unborn whereas Lalu's son is "alive and kicking" giving a stronger hope of a new life. In Lalu, Anand has struck a nice blend of present confusion and future hope. He is both the sufferer and the saviour—Anand's mouthpiece conveying his message through his own suffering and his attempt to alleviate that suffering.

Another significant character in *The Sword and the Sickle* is Kanwar Rampal Singh, a wealthy feudal lord who shuns a luxurious life and is ready to fight against the rich landlords for the rights of poor people. In the character of Kanwar Rampal Singh, Anand has fused historical facts with an element of imagination. Saros Cowasjee goes in much detail to prove that the Count is modelled on Kanwar Brajesh Singh of Kalakankar in Pratapgarh district. Anand himself stayed with Kanwar Brajesh Singh for some time in 1938. The imaginary town of Rajgarh is actually based on Kalakankar and the Count of Rajgarh has many of the features of the Count of Kalakankar. Anand studied the character of Brajesh Singh from close quarters and brought many of his features in the character of Kanwar Rampal Singh. Like Brajesh Singh, Kanwar Rampal Singh tries to organize the peasants, donates money and shows kindness towards the poor.[13] But Anand does not depend too much on historical accuracy. The ideology of Kanwar Rampal Singh and his idiosyncracies are Anand's own imagination. No doubt, Anand seems to appreciate Kanwar Rampal Singh's initiative in fighting for the cause of the poor peasants. But he does not idealize him much. Anand does not seem to approve of the unplanned actions of the group led by Kanwar Rampal Singh. The members of the revolutionary group stand for different methods of revolution. The Count and Lalu are for a bloody, violent revolution whereas Prof Verma stands for Gandhian non-violent method of bringing about a change.

Ram Din, Gupta, and Mishra do not play any significant roles. There is always a difference of opinions among these revolutionaries. Prof Verma finds himself to be a misfit in this circle of violent revolutionaries and ultimately leaves Rajgarh. Lal Singh keeps loyal to the Count but after the words of Comrade Sarshar he too starts suspecting the Count's capability as a leader. The communist Sarshar condemns the Count for having limited the revolutionary movement to Rajgarh alone rather than integrating it with the general movement of Indian revolutionaries against the British government and feudalism. Sarshar strongly indicts the Count for his behaviour after he has been evicted from the estate at Rajgarh. He does not like the idea of the Count's appealing to the Deputy Commissioner after his eviction by the Court of Wards. Condemning Kanwar Rampal Singh's action, Sarshar remarks:

> Why, of course, it is clear that he should have stuck to his guns. He should have removed to Kisan Nagar and stood by the peasants! But all this is in tune with his past conduct. Playing at Revolution! Setting up a commune! Working in isolation! Exalting himself by deliberately exploiting his position as a feudal patriarch and leading the peasants into the blind alley of spontaneous expression, fooling around and making speeches, fancying himself as some sort of a hero! Why, any fool could have seen that a situation had been reached in these estates when there was clear evidence on all sides of an awakening, and when there were tremendous opportunities for organizing the peasants on a conscious basis of struggle. Instead the peasants are all out for vengeance and destruction rather than struggle! (351).

This criticism of Kanwar Rampal Singh's methods of revolution seems to be Anand's own call for a united movement for freedom. Now Lalu who has been faithful to Kanwar Rampal Singh starts realizing the drawbacks of his approach. He now tends to have faith in Sarshar's plea for joint action against exploitation by the British and their sycophant Indian landlords. Lalu's changing faith is clear in his thoughts after the departure of Sarshar: Certainly slogans were not every thing, as he [Lal

Singh] himself had discovered in his honest moments. But still he had been possessed by a great many strange, inexplicable feelings and urges in his being which he could not control. Therefore he had tended to drown his mind with easy catchwords and phrases. Perhaps, all the members of the Rajgarh group had been ruining the cause through their own weaknesses. The Count certainly liked to hear his own voice, and his talks with his friends had often been mere exhibitions of his own cleverness. And they had all lacked the knowledge of conspiratorial methods and had been too open (357). In the prison too Lalu realizes that the need of the hour was a collective struggle, not an isolated effort.

Anand, in this way, adopts an ambivalent attitude towards the approach to revolution adopted by Kanwar Rampal Singh. He obviously appreciates the Count's sense of sacrifice in giving up landlordism and his effort to awaken the peasantry. He organizes the Kisan Sabha and fights against his own younger brother Birpal Singh. He upholds the cause of the suppressed peasants. He incurs the wrath of the landlord of Nasirabad and his son-in-law Captain Effendi by supporting the evicted and exploited peasants like Sukhua. He organizes the meeting of peasants on the festival of the eclipse. Anand applauds the intentions of the Count but disapproves of his way to realize them. Anand's message is well conveyed through Lal Singh's unuttered words: "For Revolution in a need of togetherness, Comrade, the need to curb malice among men, the need for men to stand together as brothers..." (385). It is the "need of togetherness" which Kanwar Rampal Singh fails to realize. But at least he has been able to encourage the suppressed peasants like Sukhua and Mithu to speak against injustice. This is a great achievement in itself.

As in *Untouchable*, in *The Sword and the Sickle* too Anand is unable to resist the passion of bringing political leaders *in propria persona* in the novel. The two most famous leaders of that period are introduced in the novel. The incident of Pt Nehru's visit to Rajgarh is based on historical facts. The image of Mahatma Gandhi, however, is not that of a leader with unquestionable influence. Both the Mahatma and Pt Nehru fail to achieve much in the emancipation of the poor peasantry. Mahatma Gandhi fails to impress Lal Singh with his ideology. Lal Singh rather dislikes Mahatma Gandhi's dogmatic imposition of the doctrine of non-violence. He says nothing relevant when he is brought amidst the poor peasants and untouchables. To the untouchables also he says only a few words. Unlike in *Untouchable*, he does not expatiate on the problem of untouchability and the ways to cure the evil. He only asks the Harijans to pray with him for the purification of their hearts of the sin of untouchability. He does not speak even a single word for the encouragement of the peasants. The brevity of speech of the Mahatma disappoints the Count, Lal Singh, Prof Verma and the peasants. The frustrated Lal Singh remarks: "He came as an autumn cloud, rained a few blessings and went away" (208). Though otherwise Gandhian in his humanistic ideology, in *The Sword and the Sickle* Anand severly criticises Mahatma Gandhi's stubborn obsession with his ideas of non-violence and the spinning wheel. Prof Verma too, despite his own theory of bloodless revolution, does not approve of Gandhi's slogan of the spinning wheel. According to him, "The Mahatma knows that all the yarn necessary for the needs of the country cannot be provided by hand spinning. So he shuts a corner of his left eye behind his glasses and winks at the factory-wallahs to go ahead with their plans. All that is necessary to cover up the double-dealing in a mystical phrase!..." (212). Although we cannot agree with the charge of "double-dealing" against the Mahatma, his condemnation of machine and support of the spinning wheel certainly seems to be merely an alluring slogan. Anand who has always been for modernity—for the acceptance of machine—really seems to have a sneer for Gandhi's emphasis on the use of the primitive tool. The peasants from Nasirabad fail to develop contacts with Congressmen because of the remoteness of leaders like Mahatma Gandhi. The purpose of their arduous journey is defeated. The only consolation is that Pt Jawahar Lal Nehru, under the influence of the Count, agrees to pay a visit to Rajgarh to see the condition of the peasants.

Pt Jawahar Lal Nehru, though painted in better colours than Mahatma Gandhi, is again unable to practically do anything for the alleviation of the poor, landless, and harassed peasants. No doubt, Pt Nehru is not as remote as Mahatama Gandhi; no doubt, he undertakes an inconvenient journey of two days to remote areas around Pratapgarh; but his hurried departure at the receipt of a telegram from Allahabad renders his visit as futile as was the journey of the aggrieved peasants from Narisabad to Allahabad. Like the brief speech of Mahatma Gandhi, Pt Nehru's visit serves no purpose in the way of the emancipation, or even encouragement, of the poor peasants. The inauguration of the Kisan Sabha is left to the Count and his fellow revolutionaries. The visit of Pt Nehru to Pratapgarh district is based on historical facts as is clear from his *An Autobiography* in which he mentions his visit to this district in June 1920.[14]

The visit, however, does not serve any purpose in the context of the uprising of the poor peasantry against landlordism. It only emphasizes the repressive attempts of the feudal lords like the Nawab of Nasirabad and his son-in-law Captain Effendi to curb all efforts at the revolution by landless farmers. Because of the manoeuvres of the Captain the car of Pt Nehru is punctured during his tour to the countryside. Unlike the other political leaders like Sarshar or the Count, Pt Nehru is not heard discussing any political issues or encouraging the poor farmers. Only his visit makes the peasants more buoyant and enthusiastic. About Lal Singh's feelings during his visit, Anand remarks: "That greater and more enlightened people than himself, who were honoured by every one, should also be devoted to the cause which he espoused, gave him faith" (249). Anand lavishly bestows compliments on Pt Nehru: "Pandit Ji was very very human.... But, apart from his humanity, his casual, free, easy, humorous friendliness, there was obvious in him a sincerity, a breadth of understanding, and the sensitivity and awkwardness of an intellectual" (248). But this elegant leader does nothing practical for the peasants.

Lalu comes into contact with another political personage, the organizer of the Communist Party in Uttar Pradesh, Comrade Sarshar. He advocates Lenin's communism and wants a revolution like that of Russia in India. Anand uses him as a foil to the unplanned, isolated movement of the group of Kanwar Rampal Singh on one hand, and the impression-making, slogan-shouting ways of Gandhi on the other. Margaret Berry considers him to be one of the "wisdom characters" who voice Anand's thoughts and feelings.[15] He wants all individual revolutionary groups to join the national struggle against landlordism and British government. He approves of the revolutionary notions of Kanwar Rampal Singh, but he condemns the latter's approach to achieve the aim. During his first visit to Rajgarh, he doggedly tells the Count:

> I do not doubt the integrity of your ideals. But it is a question of your methods. Anti-Government, anti-landlord, anti-money-lender, anti-religion, anti-Congress, anti-working class, anti-everything—I know that the circle of Kanwar Rampal Singh is out for a little fun. But the situation is serious, Comrade! And unless you can train yourselves and the most promising workers as professional revolutionaries, as members of an India-wide organization, which can provide continuity to the movement, in case of depletion through police arrests, unless you can give the awakening kisans passionate preaching as well as the soundest political education—but what am I talking about? Why unless? You simply must do this (152-53).

The authoritative manner of Sarshar makes the Count feel rebuked like a naughty school boy by a teacher, but he appreciates Sarshar's ideas. During his second appearance in the novel, he severely comments on the Count's ways and tells Lal Singh: "I have no patience with such great men who can't even deign to be in touch with other workers in the cities and imagine they can lead a 'Revolution' all on their own!..." (351-52). He criticizes the terroristic methods of Comrade Razwi. To make his delineation of Sarshar objective and unbiased, Anand makes Lalu disapprove of the commanding tone of Sarshar. Lalu regards his speech to be nothing but "another exaggeration of a too excited, loud and fanatical brain" (353). His obsession with his own notion of revolution seems to be as strong as is Gandhi's apotheosis of the spinning-wheel. He seems to be a prejudiced, unfeeling, and dogmatic advocate of Lenin's philosophy. But Sarshar gives up his stern attitude after some time. It is after his adoption of a modest tone that Lalu is impressed by his philosophy. Now Sarshar's preaching of togetherness brings about a remarkable change in Lal Singh's ideas of revolution. He is so much convinced by Sarshar's notions of a mass movement for freedom that he feels the vagueness, confusion, and doubts in his mind dispelled. Now he very clearly realizes the aim of revolution and the methods to achieve the aim. He makes clear to Lalu that "You just can't pick up a stave, shout a slogan and march forward to Revolution! Why, you will walk right into the arms of the police if you employ such methods! You can't open hostilities against the most organized and deeply entrenched Imperialism with the resources of Kanwar Rampal Singh's gang, having no contacts with circles in other districts, without any systematic and carefully considered plan for organizing, instructing and steeling the workers for a prolonged and stubborn struggle! Comrade Lenin called such primitivism in Russia a 'disease,' in our country it is an epidemic" (355). The clarity of his thoughts leaves a deep imprint on the mind of Lal Singh. It is for the first time that he feels to have been relieved of the burden of doubts and confusion. In the prison Lalu voices Sarshar's ideas in a colloquy with himself: "For Revolution is a need of togetherness, Comrade, the need to curb malice among men, the need for men to stand together as brothers..." (385). Now Lal Singh is aware of the causes of their failure: "We failed because we had not changed, because our habits, ideas, opinions were narrow and contained within the circle of Kisan Nagar. Because neither our leaders nor we ourselves knew what all our other brothers were doing—those brothers who have ended up from the four corners of India in the mills and factories..." (384). Sarshar's preaching enables Lal Singh to step into awareness and maturity shedding away suspicions and illusions. He rises above the narrow-minded Srijut Ladli Prasad Tiwari, the intelligent but theoretical Prof Verma, the benevolent but impractical Count, the humanist but remote Mahatma Gandhi, and the kind but busy Pt Jawahar Lal Nehru. His short stature is juxtaposed with his large mind: "A ridiculous li tle figure of a man, the Comrade seemed to be consumed by the urge to get there, positive and uncompromising and devoted with a demoniac devotion, possessed by some inexplicable quality which raised him above his own diminutive frame, and even above the taller and heftier bodies of others, perhaps a great man, with viscera like everyone else's, but with an inner largeness which gripped one and held one, with which he was hammering himself and others into shape..." (356). As in *Untouchable,* Sarshar provides a ray of hope to the otherwise dismal world of Bakha, in *The Sword and the Sickle* too he illumines the doubt-ridden world of Lal Singh's mind. No doubt, Sarshar indulges in long harangues. But the speeches seem to be a part of the general atmosphere of the novel in which different leaders are busy preaching people for a struggle in their own ways. They seem to lend an authentic touch to the novel dealing with a period of rising revolutionary spirit. The speeches seem to be well fitted in the context of the novel. They do not appear to be forced into the novel with any propagandistic intention.

The Sword and the Sickle, in this way, seems to be an integral part of the Trilogy as it provides an appropriate finale to the action of the previous two novels. The novel makes an authentic study of post-war India when a feeling of nationalism was surging up. As people had come to know that the British were not invincible, they were now ready to fight against them for their freedom. But the struggle had not gained momentum as people were still not able to make up their minds regarding the most appropriate approach to fight. Various political notions were being preached leading to the disillusionment and confusion of the ordinary man. The confusion in the mind of Lal Singh represents the confusion of contemporary Indian society. M.K. Naik's charge that the confusion in the mind of Lal Singh is because of the confusion in the author's mind about how to delineate his character is not tenable.[16] Naik seems to forget the context of the general political atmosphere that Anand tries to present. Nor can we accept the charge that the long speeches are incorporated forcibly to propagate a certain view. The speeches are congruous with the background of political movement in which various leaders preached various ideologies. The Trilogy makes a very convincing study of the transformation of the protagonist's mind from innocence to maturity. Lal Singh, in fact, symbolizes a common man whose mind is split by the pulls of diverse political forces. The confusion ultimately gives place to clarity of vision regarding the struggle in future. Like *Untouchable*, the Trilogy ends on a note of hope. But Bakha passively hopes for the introduction of the flush system or a change in the attitude of people whereas Lalu wants to be an active participant in the fight for the alleviation of the poor, enslaved, exploited Indians, particularly Indian peasants.

In this way, the sufferer-saviour relationship varies from novel to novel in the Trilogy. The change corresponds with the advancement of the suffering hero, Lalu from innocent vigour in the first novel, through hard experiences in the second to matured understanding in the third. The progress of the sufferer, in its own turn, is correspondent with the changing atmosphere in the British-ruled India before and after World War I. Before the war people from middle-class society had started realizing the need of education for their children. Lal Singh has studied upto eighth standard in a school managed by the British. Education has made him conscious of evils prevalent in Indian society, particularly among the uneducated peasants. He, being more awakened than his elder brothers and his friends, has become a revolutionary. His fiery spirit refuses to accept the traditional hypocrisy of the saints, the cunningness of the landlords, and irrational dictates of the elders. But so far he is only a young, fiery boy yet unexposed to the hard realities of life. Because the novel does not deal with incidents of great significance, Lal Singh's rebellious spirit does not encounter hard experiences. The novel is a projection of life in Indian villages in nineteen twenties. Anand presents the life of poor Indian peasants being robbed by cruel landlords. The hero does not want to be victimized by the cruel landlord. But so far he is not strong enough to fight against the powerful, established authority. He, at last, has to run away to escape law which, ironically supports the unfair. But he does not need a leader or an awakened person to exhort him to awaken to the injustice being meted out to him. No saviour hero is, therefore, introduced except Hercules Long who makes Lalu himself the leader of the village boys whom he wants to make scouts.

In *Across the Black Waters* Lalu is no more a rebellious person as in the British-Indian army an unquestioned obedience is demanded from all sepoys. But his contact with wise people like Uncle Kirpu, Daddy Dhanoo and Lachman Singh widens his vision. His exposure to hard experiences of trench war in an unknown land for an unknown cause develops his personality. His life in the Western country France makes his realization of the evils of orthodox Indian society more acute. But he can do nothing for his country because he is now a mere sepoy—an employee of the British government in India. Because all the soldiers, like him, are fighting on behalf of the British government with the purpose of earning money, they are all victims of the cruelty of war. Therefore, no saviour figure is brought in. The futility of war is well revealed through episodes.

In *The Sword and the Sickle*, the peasant-turned-soldier is again brought to his native land. But he is no longer an employee of the British government as he is demobilized. Anand now makes him partake of the revolutionary spirit which sweeps over the whole of post-war India. By making him join a group of self-styled revolutionaries who are ignorant of the ways of revolution, Anand ultimately makes him realize that revolution is possible only with a sense of unity. He is brought into contact with many leaders with diverse political ideologies. But Anand reveals the weaknesses of the political ideology of every revolutionary group. It is only Comrade Sarshar whose viewpoint is based on mature understanding. A hurried meeting with the Comrade makes Lalu understand that a unified and well-organized rebellion is the need of the hour. The Trilogy ends with Lalu's matured understanding. The presence of a number of saviour figures is congruous with the political atmosphere in India after the World War I when nationalistic feeling had spread and there had emerged on Indian political scene various ideologies.

In short, in the Lalu Trilogy Anand handles the sufferer-saviour relationship in a pretty complex manner, putting it to diverse permutations and combinations from the first to the third novel. The second novel of the Trilogy is more of an artistic success largely because of the absence of any saviour character. In the first and the third several saviour characters make their appearance and the suffering hero himself takes up the cudgels on behalf of the sufferers.

NOTES

1. Lal Singh's rebellious temperament, his love for liberty, his abbhorence for orthodoxy etc. are Anand's own ideas as presented in his autobiographical novels. Many of the characters and episodes in *The Village* are taken from the autobiographical novel *Seven Summers.*
2. *The Village* (New Delhi: Arnold Heinemann, 1984), 2. The subsequent references to the novel are from this edition.
3. Mulk Raj Anand, personal letter to me dated May 9, 1990.
4. Mulk Raj Anand, *The Bubble* (New Delhi: Arnold Heinemann Publishers Pvt. Ltd., 1984), 26.
5. *Ibid.*, 28.
6. Mulk Raj Anand, "Why I Write," *op. cit.*, 1.
7. *Across the Black Waters* (New Delhi: Vision Books Pvt. Ltd., 1978). All the subsequent references to the novel are taken from this edition.
8. See Saros Cowasjee, *So Many Freedoms*, 107-08.
9. K.N. Sinha, *Mulk Raj Anand*, 50.
10. *The Sword and the Sickle* (New Delhi: Arnold Heinemann Publishers Pvt. Ltd., 1984), 85. All the subsequent references to the text of the novel are from this edition.
11. K.R. Srinivasa Iyengar, "Mulk Raj Anand," *Indian Writing in English* (New Delhi: Sterling Publishers Pvt. Ltd., 1973), 349.
12. Alain Nivanstair, *The Yoke of Pity: A Study in the Fictional Writings of Mulk Raj Anand* (New Delhi: Arnold Heinemann, 1978), 79.
13. See Saros Cowasjee, *So Many Freedoms*, 115.
14. Jawahar Lal Nehru, *An Autobiography* (1936; rpt. Bombay: Allied Publishers Pvt. Ltd., 1962), 56-57. About his visit to the *Kisans* of

the villages around Pratapgarh, Nehru writes: "Even before my visit to Pratapgarh in June, 1920, I had often passed through villages, stopped there and talked to the peasants. I had seen them in their scores of thousands on the banks of the Ganges during the big *melas.* But somehow I had not fully realized what they were and what they meant to India. Like most of us, I took them for granted. This realisation came to me during these Pratapgarh visits and ever since then my mental picture of India contains this naked hungry mass. Perhaps there was some kind of electricity in the air, perhaps I was in a receptive frame of mind and the pictures I saw and the impressions I gathered were indelibly impressed on my mind" (57).

15. See Margaret Berry, *Mulk Raj Anand: The Man and the Novelist,* 73.
16. See M.K. Naik, *Mulk Raj Anand,* 75.

5

THE GENEROUS AND THE HEROIC

In *The Big Heart* and *Death of a Hero* Anand's protagonists are courageous, fearless, and selfless persons who wage a fight against oppressive forces—one fighting for people of his caste and the other fighting for his nation. Both of them suffer the pangs of oppression—the oppression by the rich capitalistic class in the case of Ananta and by the foreign invaders and Indian traitors in the case of Maqbool Sherwani. *The Big Heart* deals with the pre-Independence era in India when a wave of nationalism was surging up and *Death of a Hero* treats a historical event after Indian independence when Kashmir was invaded by the soldiers of Pakistan in 1947 itself. Ananta has a big heart as he is ready to sacrifice much for the uplift of the unemployed thathiars; Maqbool's heart may be regarded as still bigger as he fights for the national cause against men of his own religion—the "Muslim brethren."[1]

In both the novels the sufferer and the saviour heroes merge into one person. The saviour characters belong to the class of the sufferers themselves. They try to encourage the demoralized, spineless people both through words and their own example. Both of them lay down their lives for the sake of the cause they are fighting for. Maqbool is hanged by the Pakistani invaders and Ananta meets his death at the hands of Ralia—a representative of those whom Ananta is trying to save from starvation. Because the saviours are from among the sufferers, they do not seem to be forced into the novels only to voice the message of the novelist. In *The Big Heart*, Ananta finds a companion in Puran Singh Bhagat but Maqbool dies without any support by his countrymen. Puran Singh Bhagat, like Anand himself, believes in devotion to *Karma*, to one's duty. Again, like Anand, the Bhagat has lost all faith in the benevolence, even the existence, of God. His speeches, no doubt, articulate the thoughts of the novelist but he does not sound to be a mere messenger of the novelist as do Dr Malhotra in *Gauri* and Dr Havre in *Two Leaves and a Bud*. He is more or less like Comrade Sarshar in *The Sword and the Sickle* as both the poet and the Comrade try to unite the sufferers to fight for their cause. Both of them are advocates of togetherness. Because Ananta and Puran Singh share their ideas, the latter does not appear to be only an adviser or a medium to preach. His ideology is the ideology of Ananta himself as both of them have been to far off places and have gathered experience and knowledge. They possess the wisdom of the heart which they intend to communicate to the other sufferers. Maqbool, however, finds no such accomplice. *Death of a Hero*, therefore, is free from long harangues of *The Big Heart*. It is an authentic treatment of a historical figure who dies fighting bravely. Both the novels, however, end on an optimistic note despite the death of the protagonists in both of them. Ananta's work is continued by Puran Singh who encourages Janki to face people bravely and work for the amelioration of society. Maqbool hopes that his sister's son would continue his struggle after his death.

The Big Heart, like *Gauri* and some parts of *The Village* and *The Sword and the Sickle*, presents a conflict between tradition and modernity. The conflict is presented through the rejection and acceptance of machine by different people. Machine symbolizes the modern, scientific advancement and those who accept it as a necessary part of life are the advocates of modern attitudes. But there are others who, like Nihal Singh in *The Village*, regard machines to be the tools of the devil. These people who scorn machines as infernal blood-suckers are regressive, orthodox people. Anand brings to light the evils that have come in the wake of the invention of machines. At the same time he conveys that the evil results of machinery are, to a large extent, the consequences of man's greed and selfishness. It is when the profiteering capitalists turn inconsiderate towards the poor unemployed labourers that the machines become the tools of the devil. The machines then become the agents of widening the gulf between the rich factory owners and the poor labourers. Anand wants a reconciliation between the interests of the capitalists and those of the labourers. The message is conveyed through Ananta, the protagonist who himself is one of the victims of the setting up of a factory. Because the sufferer himself struggles for a solution to the problem of capitalist-labourer war, his actions are more credible and authentic than those of Mohan in *Coolie* and Dr Malhotra in *Gauri*. He does not seem to be a mere instrument to make the message vocal. The author, however, seems to be present in the novel only when Puran Singh indulges in long harangues. But even his speeches are not so overtly propagandistic as are those of Mohan in *Coolie* and Dr Havre in *Two Leaves and a Bud*. Anand's obsessive disdain for rigid casteism again appears in this novel. The theme of industrialisation is interwoven with the theme of caste-complexes. But here there is no political leader like Gandhi in *Untouchable* to rise to the platform and preach against the evil. Here the practice is revealed through characters like Gokul Chand and Murli Dhar. The novel, therefore, is more aesthetically appealing than *Untouchable, Gauri, Coolie, The Road,* and *Two Leaves and a Bud* in which the sufferers and saviours belong to different worlds.

The Big Heart has a compact plot like that of *Untouchable*; the action is confined to a single day in the life of Ananta. The action starts with Ananta's brooding over the nightmare in which he has seen himself chased by the ghastly death itself; it ends with Ananta's actual capture by death. Within the horrible dream and its realization, much is revealed about Ananta's matured understanding of the ways of the world and his desire to find a solution to the problems of those suffering from starvation and unemployment. His efforts to organize the unemployed thathiars like himself fail but his success lies in the fact that he sacrifices himself fighting for the cause. His struggle is to be continued by the poet Puran Singh and Ananta's mistress Janki. Ananta's views are not presented in isolation, but in relation to the views of other leaders like Mahasha Hans Raj and the student Satyapal. The novel follows the pattern of *The Sword and the Sickle*; The political ideas of Comrade Sarshar are made vivid through their comparison and contrast with the ideas of Kanwar Rampal and Srijut Tiwari. While Satyapal, like Kanwar Rampal, believes in spontaneous action, Ananta, like Comrade Sarshar, wants to organise people to fight against their oppressors. Ananta is also comparable to the matured Lai Singh who towards the end of *The Sword and the Sickle* realizes the need of togetherness for waging a fight against the merciless exploiters. *The Sword and the Sickle* ends with the protagonist's awakening to the fact that struggle cannot be successful if launched in isolation. *The Big Heart* begins with the protagonist's matured expression of the same idea. *The Big Heart*, in this way, starts where *The Sword and the Sickle* ends. Ananta very earnestly tries to convince people of the need of organizing into a union, but death puts an end to his efforts. The individual efforts of Ananta end with the end of his life but his struggle continues as the work left unfinished by Ananta is taken up by Puran Singh and Janki.

The conflict between modernity and orthodoxy is presented through a dexterous handling both of the situations and characters. The novel opens with a description of the street Billimaran which represents both tradition and advancement:

> It must be remembered, however, that Billimaran is not a blind alley. Apart from the usual mouth, which even a *cul de sac* keeps open, it has another, which makes it really like a two-headed snake. With one head it looks towards the ancient market, where the beautiful copper, brass, silver and bronze utensils made in the lane are sold by dealers called kaseras, hence called Bazar Kaserian. With the other it wriggles out towards the new Ironmongers' Bazar, where screws and bolts and nails and locks are sold and which merges into the Booksellers'

> mart, the cigarette shops and the post office replete with the spirit of modern times.[2]

The two openings of the street stand for conflicting views of people—the traditional attitudes of some people on the one hand and the acceptance of modern inventions on the other. The clock tower symbolizes the modern scientific age in which most of the actions are governed by time considerations. The temple of goddess Kali and the Golden Temple, on the other side, represent the old and medieval ages. In this setting are placed characters like Ralia and Viroo with their regressive tendencies on one hand and Ananta and Puran Singh with their rational acceptance of scientific progress on the other. The milieu of the novel and its episodes are so congruous with the psyche of its characters that the whole of the novel seems to be a compact, organic whole. The episodes are handled in a convincing manner and the characters are treated without idealization or degradation. The novel richly deserves the applause it received at the hands of critics like K.N. Sinha, M.K. Naik, Saros Cowasjee, S.C. Harrex, and Margaret Berry. The novel, according to Sinha, "is a moving and powerful delineation of passion in its labyrinth, a human drama enacted within the limits of probability."[3] Anand does not encroach the "limits of probability" for the sake of propaganda. S.C. Harrex remarks that "The sociological idea of tragedy which was formulated in *Coolie* and *Two Leaves and a Bud* is taken a stage further in *The Big Heart* in which more appropriate literary measures, particularly use of the dramatic unities, achieve greater dramatic intensity and coherence."[4] C.D. Narsimhaiah, no doubt, observes the weakness of the novel at certain places. But he too makes us mark that "a mature novelist is at work."[5] The community of coppersmiths has been portrayed in a very authentic manner. This authenticity can be attributed to Anand's own birth in the family of coppersmiths. Ananta shares many of Anand's own feelings at the suffering of human beings. The portrayal of Ananta is so well executed that M.K. Naik's remark seems justifiable: "Ananta is perhaps the best realized of Anand's heroes."[6] One of the victims of the setting up of a factory but better than the other victims in wisdom and learning, he makes efforts to organize people for fighting for their cause.

The repercussions of industrialization are obvious in the lives of the coppersmiths who have been rendered jobless. The establishment of the factory has brought with it unnerving poverty and maddening stravation for those who are refused jobs in the factory. When Anand visited India in 1939 he saw that "some of the coppersmiths in Amritsar had adopted machinery, and he had seen that adoption had resulted in conflict and trouble."[7] It is this "conflict and trouble" that Anand tries to reproduce in his novel. The coppersmiths could not stand in competition with the factory owners because now only those utensils were in demand which were made in factories. The wages for piece-work were also reduced by the kaseras. The unemployed thathiars tried to find jobs in the factory but the callousness of Murli Dhar, one of the owners, obstructed their employment. The empty bellies cried for food but there was nobody to listen to the cries. Their life, therefore, became utterly dismal. Anand paints the world of thathiars as bleak and gloomy because "the imagination cannot transform life [in a book like *The Big Heart*] unless the dispersed narrative can build up the mental asylum atmosphere created by evil and greedy men in the pursuit of their self-interest. The hell of the underworld can only be realised in the poetry of nightmares,"[8] wrote Mulk to Saros Cowasjee. He really has succeeded in creating an atmosphere congruous with the dismal state of mind of people like Ralia and Viroo. Marlene Fisher justly remarks that in *The Big Heart* "form and content, character and plot, are inextricable."[9] Even Ananta who hopes for the amelioration of the poor thathiars through a joint crusade against the capitalists, is haunted by a nightmare. The images of death and doom permeate the whole of the novel.

The poverty of the people makes them frustrated—which leads to family scuffles too. Ralia and Gauri are always quarreling because Ralia fails to buy the flour for the family. He drinks and beats her. Anand makes Ralia a representative of all those who are threatened by hunger and who are ill-treated by their landlords. Because of their oppressive poverty, they have lost faith even in the members of their own brotherhood. They refuse to heed the exhortations of Ananta to organize themselves and convince the factory-owners of their demands and requirements. Like Sarshar in *The Sword and the Sickle,* he exhorts the members of his brotherhood: "The Revolution is not yet. And it isn't merely in the shouting. Nor is it in this single battle in Billimaran, brothers. It is only through a great many conflicts between the employers, authorities and the workers, in a whole number of battles which our comrades elsewhere are fighting, that there will come the final overthrow of the bosses. So we must neither be slaves to circumstances nor accept either Fate or unreason, but must rise above them" (209). The coppersmiths fail to understand the rational approach of Ananta towards the problem. They are full of suspicions and jealousies. The fact that Ananta gets work to make a *deg* for the firm of Lal Chand, Khushal Chand makes them jealous towards him. They are easily excited by the vigorous slogans of student Satyapal who incites them for random and reckless action against the capitalists.

The conflict between the unemployed coppersmiths and the bourgeois owners of the factory leads to a contempt for machine among the ignorant coppersmiths. They do not realize that the rich capitalists are responsible for their miseries, not the lifeless machines which are only tools in the hands of their owners. It is the callousness of the owners which makes the poor jobless thathiars think that the setting up of the factory is ominous. They regard machinery as the tools of the devil. They are blind to the fact that "The machine may have demoniac force but man should learn to master their labour-saving public benefactor which is vital for progress."[10] Their fury against the machine is obvious in Ralia's sneer for the machines and those operating the machines: "Yes, machines, machines, machines—phuff, phuff, phuff, grrr...Yes, may I rape the mother of the machines inside there, the machines!...Grrr.... They roar and they spit. They squeak and they squeal! They talk chapper, chapper like Channa.... They are the machines!

Each one of those men there is a machine! That chapper chapper Channa and all those boys working in there are machines" (33). They hate Ananta because of his approval of machine. They call him "machine man." Ignorant and illiterate, they know about Mahatma Gandhi's disapproval of machine and want to follow his ideology. "By Parmeshwar, those boys will be crushed and broken," remarks Viroo about the devilish results of adoption of machinery, "I'll change my name if they do not break under the weight of these machines, as Mahatma Gandhi said they will, all those who trust themselves to the machines" (33). And such is the hatred for machines that "Ultimately, the problem was not so much the machine as men's fears of the machine, their inability to conceive that they might control it."[11] The reasoning of Ananta to accept machine but keep a control on it cannot bring any change in their attitude. Ignited by the zeal of Satyapal, the hatred for machine culminates in Ralia's "Bacchanalia of machine-wrecking."[12] He regards machine as "the Kali of the iron age, the age of machines" (216) and assumes the role of the Destroyer, Shiva, to remove machines from the earth: "This is the Kali Yug, Han, The Kali Yug!...Acha, then, I am the destroyer of this madar-chod age, Shiv!.... Come brothers, I am Shiva" (214). He starts attacking the machines with anarchic violence. Ananta's attempt to moderate the fury of Ralia results in the former's own death.

It is only Ananta who, in the whole of the community of coppersmiths understands the significance and inevitability of machine in the modern world. He too is one of the victims of industrialization but his approach to the problem is rational, unprejudiced, and progressive. Having stayed in Bombay, he has observed the working of trade unions and has realized their importance. He tries to convince the members of his brotherhood that it is not the machine that is to blame for their predicament but the misuse of it by its owners to exploit the poor unemployed workers. He has a liberal, comprehensive approach to the matter. He has a broad view which he tries to offer to his fellow coppersmiths. He believes that "Like the fashionable vilayati bride, we have accepted, we ought to accept the dowry of machines she has brought, and make use of them provided we keep our hearts. Machines do not think or feel, it is the Men who do" (40). The important thing for him is to "keep our hearts." That is why he, like Ratan in *Coolie*, again and again chants: "There is no talk of money, one must have a big heart!" (40). For Ananta, it is not a question whether to accept machine or not; his only concern is how to employ it for the welfare of the whole mankind.

In his attitudes, Ananta is both like and unlike Gandhi. Like Mahatma Gandhi, Ananta is a committed humanist. He wants a bloodless compromise between the capitalists and the labourers. But he is non-Gandhian in his support of the adoption of machine for the progress of the nation. Like Lal Chand, Prof Verma and Kanwar Rampal in *The Sword and the Sickle*, Ananta too is critical of Mahatma Gandhi's rejection of machine.

Ananta's magnanimity is fairly revealed in his reaction to the sufferings of other people. The sight of poor beggars outside the Golden Temple moves his heart. He is unable to bear the sight and cries out "O God, O God, O God" (66). His reaction, as he himself feels, is like that of Gautam Buddha when he saw the misery of Kapilvastu. His heart cries for a solution of the wretchedness of the poor. But he does not pin his hopes on the mercy of God. He rather feels that men may emerge out of their predicament through their joint efforts: "No God, he felt, could make such a world and consign it to such suffering, for if He did so He was not a good God. But that was not the question, and if his friends believed in Fate, he would let them. Only he must convince them that they could not win bread separately but together, and that if they believed in their own manhood and were patient, and held on to each other, he would form a union and help them to come through" (68). Ananta's humanism, like Anand's own, is not based on Vedantic philosophy. Unlike Mahasha Hans Raj, Ananta has no faith in religion and not even in the existence of God. He, like Anand, realizes that man himself has the potential to rise in life. Only he should have faith in his own strength.

Ananta's "big heart" inspires him to share the sorrows of other human beings. He is ready to share whatever he earns with his fellow coppersmiths. When he gets fifteen rupees from the firm of Lal Chand, Khushal Chand, he arranges a feast for all the members of his brotherhood. He tells them: "...if I am richer than you I shall share my money with you, if I am poorer you can spit at me and go your ways" (159). He feels much pained to find that people are without flour and the profiteer Mohkam Chand is not ready to provide it to them. He encourages people to rebel against the hoarder. He clearly tells the policeman: "Your truncheon does not impress me. If you want to control people you must first fill their bellies" (183). When Ananta finds that there is no flour in the house of Ralia, he asks the latter's son, Rhoda, to take flour from his [Ananta's] stepmother. He is ready to distribute among them all the money he gets from Khushal Chand. But the tragedy of Ananta lies in the fact that the members of his brotherhood never appreciate his generosity. With their "small" hearts, they fail to understand Ananta's "big heart." They always suspect his intentions and depricate him as a "machine-man," "a lecher," "a rogue," or "a fornicator." Ananta sacrifices his life in an effort to mitigate Ralia's violent fury. He wants a compromise between the thathiars and the factory owners. But till his death his ideas and ideals are a matter of sneer for his fellow coppersmiths. With his rational attitude and moral strength, Ananta is murdered by Ralia who fails to realize the need of a rational attitude. Ralia represents those who are ignorant as to how to direct their energies and actions towards a reasonable solution of the problem. S.C. Harrex's appreciation of Ananta's doom is just and fair: "This simply is the tragedy of a moral intelligence of the heart—defeated not by its own flawed nature (even though Ananta is aware that he lacks full understanding) but by a diseased victim of society who symbolises humanity's inability to control its environmental fate."[13] But the death of Ananta, though tragic, is not the extinction of his aims and ideals. It provides a powerful finale to the action of the novel; it makes Ananta rise still higher in our esteem because it is the completion of his martyrdom. But the tragic climax does not lead to an end of hope for those for whose sake he wanted to wage a fight. The novel ends on a note of hope. Bhagat Puran Singh hopes that the death of Ananta may achieve what his life has failed to do. He tells Janki: "Perhaps the life of Ananta—I mean the way he lived may be—a greater example for them than any words he could have spoken. Why, they may even recall the things he said to them now that he is dead. For what can be more persuasive than the death of man who loved them?" (229). The ending of the novel seems to be the beginning of the next part of action that its protagonist has been trying for throughout the novel.

Ananta, like Anand himself, believes in "ethics without God." He is a romantic humanist who does not have faith in any religion. All his faith is in the strength and capability of man to free himself from all evil in the world. Even when utterly dejected by the pains of the world, he refuses to look towards heaven and invoke God for help. When Janki asks him to have faith in God, his reaction is an outburst of intolerance of the idea: "O misery of the parched, sighing earth! O agony of damp dwellings on the narrow alleys! ...O put some pity in the souls of these people! Pity, not faith in God!" (171). He reiterates his disbelief in the grace, even existence, of God: "God works in a mysterious way, in such a heartless way that the ominous owl alone has so far taken pains to answer the peasants in the night. God seems to have deserted the world—if ever He were there, helping it along!" (172). He believes that man may change his fate. He believes in *Karma* as preached by the *Gita* and for him action or *Karma* implies a struggle for good against evil: "For, if Arjuna said, 'Live in action,' then he meant us to fight against falsehood in spite of the odds. Only thus can the balance between 'good' and 'evil' be kept in this world" (175). He, however, forgets that it was Krishna, not Arjuna who preached dedication to one's duty. But the significant fact is that Ananta believes in man's own endeavours to uplift themselves. It grieves his heart to find that men try to cause pain to each other. His agonized cry is the cry of a real humanist who finds the suffering of mankind intolerable: "I tell you there is famine in this land. And there are wars raging on the edge of the farthest horizons. And yet my friends here will not stop extracting pain out of each other. Pain, pain, pain—there is such an orgy of suffering in the world! And they torture each other!" (172).

Ananta, with his profound faith in the capacity of man to make himself happy, loses all faith in fate. Saros Cowasjee regards Ananta's inordinate faith in man's strength as a flaw in his character. "Ananta's failure stems partly from his own shortcomings. He believes that man is wholly responsible for his destiny, but the manner of his own death ironically vindicates one of his sacriligious jibes—'God works in a mysterious way.'"[14] No doubt, Ananta's death is sudden and unexpected but we cannot agree with Cowasjee that Ananta's lack of fatalism is a shortcoming of his character. Nor is his faith in man the cause of his failure. He, however, fails in his mission because he lacks the tactics of Satyapal to arouse people. He has the wisdom of the heart but does not know how to impart it to his fellow men.

Ananta's "big heart" dissuades him from falling in with the orthodox taboos and traditions. He is much concerned about the people of his brotherhood but he does not give way to acceptance of its inhibitions. His relations with Janki reveal his free, frank, fearless, and uninhibited mind. He not only advocates but actually practises freedom in love and sex. He cares little for the aspersions of immorality hurled at him by the people of his brotherhood. He feels sorry that at Amritsar he has to neglect Janki because of his distraction towards the cause of unemployed thathiars. His negligence of Janki, however, is not an evidence of his carelessness or irresponsibility, nor does he in any way waver in his love as does Lal Singh in his love for Maya; it, on the contrary, brings to light his earnestness in love; both for his mistress and his fellow-beaings. Like Lal Singh in *The Sword and the Sickle*, Ananta is torn between his duty towards his beloved and the pulls of struggle for mankind. But he is more loving and sincere to his mistress than Lal Singh is to Maya and more dedicated to his cause than his counterpart in *The Sword and the Sickle.* He regrets that he is not able to attend to Janki properly, but he does not regard her as an encumbrance. Janki too has no complaints against him. She herself encourages him to struggle for the cause of thathiars: "...there is no time to lose if these men are to be saved, however unworthy they are" (170). Maya starts living upto the ideals of her husband only towards the end of the novel; Janki, on the other hand, always supports the principles of her lover. K.N. Sinha's comment is well deserved by Janki: "Her frailty has beneath it a reservoir of strength."[15] After the death of Ananta she is ready to undertake the task left incomplete by Ananta. Ananta's own "big heart" is, in this way, coupled with an equally big heart of his beloved. Both of them are endowed with courage to face the challenges of the world and both of them want to fight for the happiness of mankind.

Ananta in almost all of his ideals acticulates Anand's own beliefs. His love for humanity, his lack of faith in God, his faith in man's potential, his espousal of free love, and his modern, scientific approach to the solution of man's problems are the basic traits of Anand's own personality as it is portrayed in his autobiographical novels. Anand finds in his protagonist a medium to voice his own thoughts and feelings. But the achievement of Anand lies in the fact that even while delineating his character subjectively, he can effect complete objectivity. Nowhere does the author seem to be preaching overtly and unaesthetically through the mouth of Ananta. The concealment of intention under the veil of art has been possible because of the merger of the sufferer and the saviour figures into one person. Nowhere do we doubt the author's integrity as an artist because the struggle of Ananta appears to be an authentic reaction of a person who himself is a victim of an evil. His actions and ideas do not seem to be imposed on him; they seem to be the result of the "wisdom of the heart" he has gained through experience. Balaram Gupta's admiration of Ananta's character is not an exaggeration but well based on the text: "Ananta does not seem to be an automaton fabricated to mouth the author's views. There is perfect harmony between what he says and does. If he denounces pain and cruelty, he also acts to remove them from the lives of his fellow-men. His is really a 'big heart', believing in service to mankind and generosity to the poor and the lowly,"[16] His generosity is not imposed on him in an unauthentic manner. They, instead, seem to be the basic traits of his character to which his experiences at Bombay and Ahmedabad have contributed considerably. He, unlike Mahindra in *Gauri* and Dr Havre in *Two Leaves and a Bud,* is not merely a mouthpiece to vocalize the author's intentions from a platform. He is one of the sufferers. His exhortations, therefore, are not sermons from a higher authority but proposals which he himself tries to practise.

Another saviour character in *The Big Heart* is Bhagat Puran Singh. It appears that Anand was not satisfied with showing effectively the predicament of the thathiar brotherhood through the character of Ananta and some convincing episodes. He could not rest with his message conveyed artistically and indirectly. The urge to overtly state his viewpoint is so strong on him that he does bring in a "wisdom figure," the poet Puran Singh. Puran Singh is more learned than Ananta; his travels throughout the world have enriched his knowledge. His ideas are those of a matured, reasonable, and unprejudiced man. But the ideas in the novel, unlike those of illiterate Ananta, are not incorporated into the text properly. They seem to have been forced into the novel only to make Anand's message of modernity and humanism clearer.

Ananta is much fascinated by the maturity of Puran Singh. He appreciates his ideas and feels that he himself lacks the conviction and understanding of the latter. It is only in him that he finds a true friend and companion. Puran Singh tells Ananta: "...if you have the controlling switch in your hand, you can make the machine a slave rather than your master. It is the switch or destruction" (90). He voices Anand's humanistic ideas. He finds dignity in man. He wants that respect and glory should be restored to man:

> I believe in the restoration of man if he is to control machinery at the present time. I believe, in fact, if we can have any religious faith, morality or code at all today,

> it must arise from the reassertion of man's dignity, a pure love for man in all his strength and weakness. Limitless compassion for man. Unbounded love especially for the poor and the down-trodden. So that those who have been left to rot on the dusty roads can be raised and given the izzat which is theirs by the miracle of their birth in this world. Roughnecks and toughnecks in Delhi have uniformly decreed laws and ordinances, detention without trial, mass imprisonment and—oh, the sowing of a harvest of death among the new ripe generations (149).

The ideas are sound and logical. They seem too powerful against the Gandhian philosophy of Hindu Dharam and non-violence advocated by Mahasha Hans Raj and against the half-baked ideas of Satyapal. Puran Singh is not in favour of Gandhian disapproval of machine and tacit support of capitalism. According to him, "Gandhiji always worshipped the kind of truth which was orthodox!...he really accepts private property. The vicious circle of the old order which can never last in India if it has made such a mess of things in the other parts of the world.... Gandhiji may have been innocent, but he certainly never realized the meaning of Revolution for our country and went on believing in an unplanned, individualist, competitive profit making the like of which has thrown these brothers out of their jobs" (150). He, like Ananta, wants a revolution like that of Russia. Socialism, for him, is the solution to the problems of Indian society and economy. He condemns the cutthroat competition in "London, Tokyo or New York" (150) because in such economies a human being is denied the dignity which is his due.

Puran Singh's ideas impress Ananta a lot. Both of them want to unplift human beings and gain for them a dignified position in society. But whereas Ananta is a man of action, Puran Singh is an armchair man of intellect. Ananta is fearless and courageous, Puran Singh is a self-avowed "coward." The Bhagat can make his ideas clear through forceful elocution but he lacks the prowess to execute these ideas. Ananta admonishes him for his over intellectualization of matters:

"The trouble with you learned folk is that you spend so much of your time looking at your own feelings and at the end you are too weak to act" (93). The learned but weak-willed poet is both a companion of and a foil to the illiterate but initiative-loving Ananta. In bringing Ananta and the poet together, Anand has struck an excellent combination of the heart and the head. S.C. Harrex comments on the combination of these virtues: "Ananta embodies those qualities of the heart and the poet those of the head which in combination will create the new Adam of Anand's new society."[17] After the death of Ananta, the poet undertakes to continue the struggle and encourages Janki to shed her fears and work for social welfare.

Both Ananta and Puran Singh voice Anand's own philosophy of classless society. But Ananta's espousal of the ideas does not mar the aesthetic appeal of the novel whereas Puran Singh's harangues clearly reveal the propagandistic attempt of Anand. The novel suffers from only one flaw and that is the indulgence of Anand in direct preaching through Bhagat Puran. M.K. Naik's observation is based on facts: "The only possible flaw in the otherwise well-ordered structure of the novel is once more Anand's penchant for resorting to direct statement, as if he occasionally feels the inadequacy of the fabric of situation and character in externalizing his vision. As at the end of *Untouchable*, here also the Poet holds forth with distressing frequency and at elaborate length on Anand's favourite topics of exploitation, modernity and Humanist faith and the like."[18] Though Naik's charge of Anand's indulgence in direct statement is irrefutable and his comparison of the poet in *Untouchable* and the Bhagat in *The Big Heart* is appropriate, yet the fact remains that the hero in *Untouchable* fails to understand the full implications of the saviour's speech whereas in *The Big Heart* Ananta not only appreciates the ideas of his guide and mentor but also tries to put them into practice. Anand's portrayal of the Bhagat is not that of an unbelievably ideal character. Anand endows him with intellectual depth and vast learning, but he deprives him of strength essential to utilize the learning for practical purposes. Puran Singh himself confesses his weakness and cowardice so far as practical matters are concerned. He is not incredibly virtuous as Dr Mahindra and Dr Havre are.

Anand's obsession with casteism is again in evidence as he weaves the theme of rigidity of caste with the theme of economic problem of unemployment because of capitalism. But he reveals the evil of casteism through situations and episodes, not through the preachings of any saviour hero. He makes clear that many of the social evils are because of the complexes of the victims of those evils themselves. Murli Dhar and Sadanand look down upon the people of their caste after their partnership with Gokul Chand in the setting up of the factory. They want to be regarded as higher than the coppersmiths because they have joined hands with a Kshatriya in the enterprise of the factory. They do not invite Ananta and other members of their brotherhood on the betrothal of Nikka but they are ready to put their turbans at the feet of Gokul Chand. No doubt, Anand has a dig at the false ego of those who want to excommunicate Gokul Chand because he has attended the ceremony at the house of Murli Dhar, but the bigger targets of Anand's ridicule are Murli Dhar and Sadanand who have to bear the brunt of their sneer for their own caste. The discomfiture of the father and the son during the ceremony effectively conveys how caste considerations get indistinguishably entangled with class complexes. It is with the help of powerful situations and befitting characters that Anand hammers his point home. He does not have to depend on any saviour hero to preach his sermon.

The novel, in this way, is a powerful exposure of socio-economic and political problems facing the pre-Independence India. The only flaw in the novel is Anand's resort to occasional direct statements and homilies through the poet. Even then the poet is more lifelike than Dr Havre or Dr Mahindra. He is not incredibly virtuous. He has his own infirmities like the other saviour hero, Ananta. He does not overtly sermonize Ananta or other coppersmiths; he only guides them. Ananta is one of the sufferers but better than them because of the wisdom that experience has imparted to him. Because the sufferer-saviour gap is eliminated in the novel, it makes for a more effective conveyance of the author's message.

The elimination of gap between the suffering and saviour heroes is again found in Anand's historical novel *Death of a Hero*. In this novel, Anand does not try to expose any social or economic evil. For the first and last time he has chosen a real historical figure to serve as the protagonist of a fictional work. Maqbool is a victim of Hindu-Muslim political issue which started before Independence and again erupted after Independence in 1947 itself when the Pakistani invaders tried to usurp much of the territory of Kashmir. Maqbool, though himself a Muslim, refuses to turn a traitor against his country. He tries to save his nation's territory by trying to boost up the morale of many Muslims who had given in to the allurements thrown by the Pakistani "Muslim brethren."

Maqbool, a member of the Kashmir National Conference, is allotted the job of coming back to his native town of Baramula from Srinagar to hearten the demoralized people and rally them to put up resistance against the Pakistani marauders. On the way he comes to know that Baramula is under the control of the Pakistani Muslim bigots who are busy collecting the booty. From his cousin Rahti he comes to know about the atrocities and incendiarism committed by the invaders. The reports by Mahmdoo and Rahti make him aware of the danger which he will be exposed to on his way to Baramula. But he accepts the risk to his life only because he wants to perform his duty. But at Baramula he finds that most of the Indian Muslims have turned traitors. They are siding with the Pakistani bigots. He tries to convince Muratib Ali of the need of resisting the invaders but his efforts go futile. The opportunist Ahmed Shah too has joined hands with the "Muslim Brethren" from Pakistan. Ghulam is a weak, passive character who can be swept off his feet by any powerful wind. He is a sincere friend but a weak person. But Maqbool refuses to give in to the invaders. He is ready to sacrifice his life for the sake of his country. Like Ananta in *The Big Heart*, Maqbool in *Death of a Hero* is a martyr who dies fighting for the cause of his nation. He does not give way to cowardice and opportunism.

He, instead, dies fighting against the fanatics who want Muslim rule in Kashmir.

Though tragic, Maqbool's death, like that of Ananta, does not signalize the end of his struggle after his death. Ananta's struggle is continued by Puran Singh and Janki. Maqbool hopes that Nur's son will fulfil his dreams. The arrival of Indian army in Baramula too indicates the continuation of resistance against the foreign invaders.

In Maqbool, Anand has merged both the sufferer and the saviour hero. Maqbool, like the other people of Baramula is a victim of communal violence perpetrated by the "Muslim Brethren." But unlike Muratib, Ghulam, and many other weaklings, he stoutly tries to save his country from the foreign fanatics. His broad mentality makes him transcend communal interests and fight for the larger, national interests. His question—"Do we believe in Kashmir first, or religion first?"—is a revelation of his patriotic sentiment. He tries to encourage Muratib Ali to fight for the Hindu nation although they have to fight against men of their own religion.

Maqbool is endowed with rare moral courage. He is not intimidated by the straightforward talk of the traitor, Master Ishaq. He is not cowed down by the treacherous behaviour of Ahmed Shah. He boldly faces the punishment pronounced on him though love for life and freedom are the urges of his mind even at the time of death. He does not want to purchase a lease of life at the cost of his patriotism and nationalism. Premila Paul and M.K. Naik are unjustifiably harsh in their judgement of the character of Maqbool. Premila Paul admires his love for his country and lofty idealim but she finds him to be "too passive to be regarded as a hero." According to her, "though the title calls him a hero, he does not grow into any heroic proportions as the novel advances. The panic-stricken Maqbool moves about like a 'sleep-walker' which is rather unbecoming of a hero. As in Joseph Conrad's *Lord Jim,* Anand's hero finds fear an unconquerable emotion. 'Fear is the natural humility of man before ugly reality!...' When Maqbool should be in the fray, he lies ruminating on a hay stack."[19] Regarding his lying in the hay stack, we cannot forget that this is only a way to save his life in the darkness of thc night when there is enemy all around. Safety of one's life is not only a natural instinct but a duty of every soldier and national leader. Exposing himself to the bullets recklessly would have been crazy rather than heroic. His actions also cannot be regarded as those of a "sleep-walker" because he is cautious at every step. He tries his best to gauge the way to rally the people. Premila Paul further charges that Maqbool is not a "Hotspur":

> To pluck bright honour from the pale-fac'd moon, Or dive into the bottom of the deep, where fathom-line could never touch the ground, And pluck up drowned honour by the locks.[20]

The charge is based on the assumption that only people like Hotspur of Shakespeare's *Henry IV, Pt. I* can be regarded as heroic. In that sense none of Anand's protagonists can be considered a hero. Anand's novels are based on the hero-anti hero pattern, as he repeatedly makes clear in his autobiographical novels. Equally unjust is the evaluation by M.K. Naik: "Neither the author nor Maqbool, nor his political mentors for that matter, seem to be quite clear about how he is to go about this business of 'rallying the people.' What we actually find him doing is haranguing friends and members of his own family until he is forced to flee unsuccessfully from his captors. One gets the impression that he is more of a passive victim than an active agent, more acted against than acting."[21] The textual facts substantiate that Maqbool is not "a passive victim" that Naik makes him out to be. The fact that he takes the initiative of coming to tension-torn Baramula, turns down the offer of Khurshid Anwar to join the "Muslim brethren" even at the risk of his life, and proclaims his nationalistic purposes thus incurring the wrath of his father, and makes all-out efforts to save himself from the captors reveals that he is mentally awakened and physically strong. He is not confused regarding his objectives; his misfortune is that before his arrival at Baramula, the town has been captured and the people robbed. They have saved their lives at the cost of patriotic sentiments. The Pakistani raiders are so alert that it is not probable to rally people and encourage them through lectures from a platform. His harangues to his friends are congruous with the atmosphere prevailing. This is the only action we can expect from a man whose own safety is in danger at every step. Any great action in the existing circumstances would have taxed the reader's credulity. M.K. Naik's further allegation that "with the central figure failing to rise above the level of a type, it is futile to expect the minor characters to spring to life. They are either sheep or goats"[22] too seems unfair. Neither is Maqbool merely a type nor are the other characters mere walking-sticks. They may be passive or treacherous but they are true to life. In India religion has been so deeply rooted in the minds of people that it is very likely for them to throw their nationalistic sentiments overboard when they are face to face with religious bias. That Maqbool retains his patriotic flame and gives up communal considerations sharply individuates him. His selfless nationalism is his distinguishing mark. He is indeed a "hero," though of a plebeian sort.

Maqbool has saintly love for mankind and he possesses great moral strength. But his strength is rendered useless by the all-pervading terror of the raiders in Baramula. He is not able to achieve what he is capable of. His faithfulness and sense of sacrifice cannot be called in question. But K.N. Sinha's rhapsodic eulogy is patently excessive. "In a way," Sinha observes, "he resembles Christ in his deathless love, for, like Christ, he is singled out for crucifixion, the cross being his crown."[23] Sinha's comment is based on the death scene of Maqbool. After Maqbool's death, the Indian troops reach Baramula. They reach the spot of Maqbool's hanging and find "the body of Maqbool Sherwani tied to a wooden pole in the stables, with the word 'Kafir' written on the lapel of the shirt.... The body looked almost like a scarecrow, but also like that of Yessuh Messih on the cross" (124). No doubt, Maqbool's sacrifice is great and his love for human beings is admirable. But Christ sacrificed himself for the sake of the whole of mankind whereas Maqbool lays down his life for the sake of his nation. Premila Paul traces some similarities between Jesus Christ and Maqbool, particularly the nature of the sacrifice made by the two. Christ is betrayed by his disciple and Maqbool is betrayed by his friend. Both display admirable fortitude at the time of death. Jesus is dubbed "Inri" which implies "King of Jews" and Maqbool is labelled "Kafir."[24] But the comparison cannot be extended further. Jesus Christ is a divine character with unbounded mercy, forgiveness, and kindness; Maqbool is a human being with human limitations. Christ, through his sacrifice, atones for sins of man and gets him place in heaven whereas Maqbool does not have any faith in the existence or mercy of God.

Maqbool's humanism, like that of Anand himself, has no religious component or reference. Maqbool believes in the innate strength of man and does not turn his eyes heavenward expecting mercy for mankind. He voices Anand's own atheism and love for man's freedom. He has a fiery spirit that wants to rebel against many traditional practices and rituals. Like Lal Singh and Ananta, he disapproves of unquestioned obedience to elders. Like Nur, he despises the ritual of five prayers a day. He has comtempt for the fatalistic attitude of people towards their problems. When his father is cross with him for his disobedience, Maqbool, like Anand in *Confession of a Lover*, retorts: "All the people believe in obedience. We must accept and not rebel. All that happens to us is due to the fate ordained by Allah!... Say five prayers a day, keep the fasts and obey—and die in the process!" (88). He believes in truth, not rituals. He laments the loss of truth in the lives of people: "The trouble is that, in spite of their prayers, they have lost faith—they no longer seek to live by any truth in their lives..." (90). Maqbool's humanistic faith is juxtaposed with the falsehood of ritualistic observance of religious practices by the Pakistani invaders. They indulge in violent bloodshed, rob the innocent people, and hurt the sentiments of others. And the irony is that the cruel war is named "Jehad" or "Holy War" (21). They perpetrate atrocities and spread anarchy in the name of religion. Anand, through the medium of Maqbool, attacks the shallow, false faith which encourages violence.

Maqbool's moral strength and nationalistic sentiments are juxtaposed by the novelist with Ahmed Shah's treachery and fickleness. Ahmed Shah, once a member of the Kashmir

National Conference, is an opportunist and a turn-coat. He gives up all friendship and nationalism; he joins hands with the Pakistani raiders against his own countrymen. He is a selfish, cold-blooded, unfeeling brute who is bent upon having Maqbool murdered. His communal prejudices, egotistic mind, and anarchic behaviour are revealed clearly when he tells Ghulam: "In order to destroy anarchy, we will also resort to anarchy and violence. I believe in reasoning with intelligent men, not with fools!.... I want union with Pakistan...I believe in a central Muslim state, which will be a counter to communism in the north, and to the Bania-Hindu Raj in the South.... And we can connect up with our brethren in the Middle East and revive the glory of ancient Islamic democracy in a world ridden with unbelief!.... The poet Iqbal himself preached this" (72). He is more eager than even the Pakistani leader Khurshid Anwar to have Maqbool executed for his refusal to betray his country. Anand's subtle irony makes Ahmed Shah a more hateful and ridiculous character. Himself he is treachery incarnate and he tells Maqbool, the great patriot: "You are persisting in your treachery and don't realize that a word from Mr Khurshid Anwar and Zaman Khan will finish you off!.... Recant your treacherous stand or I shall have no option but to ask the court to pronounce judgement on you!..." (115). His cruelty is further demonstrated in his order to Zaman Khan: "Lift his corpse and tie it to the pole behind him. And write the word 'Kafir' on his shirt with his own blood. The whole population of Baramula should know that treachery is punishable only with death" (126). The irony becomes stronger when Ahmed Shah, having committed the murder, wants to chant a prayer from the *Koran* and unable to do so, cries out "Allah ho Akbar!" (123). Maqbool's atheism is much more admirable than this brand of faith in God.

Another villainous character in the novel is Master Ishaq. He too turns a traitor because of his fanaticism in religion. In confrontation between nation and religion, he pronounces his faith in the latter—"In religion—in the religion of our Prophet, (may peace be upon his soul), and of our Holy Koran" (21). His bigotry makes him blind to the kindness and brotherhood which the Prophet preached. The brief scene in which he appears is sufficient to reveal his rigidity, fanaticism, and treachery.

Anand is more tolerant towards Muratib Ali, Ghulam, and Begum Jilani. Muratib Ali's factory has been looted and he regrets the loss. He is so demoralized that all efforts of Maqbool to encourage him prove futile. Muratib confesses his cowardice: "I know there will be no peace in our land until we have fought them, Maqbool! I feel sad in my heart.... But we are deserted. Everyone seems to have been cowed down. And I have become a coward!..." (58). He cannot think of principles in the existing dangerous circumstances. His family love further weakens him: "...I cannot deny my mother and my wife anything" (60). But he is not a traitor like Ahmed Shah. He retains a feeling of friendship towards Maqbool and does not want him to be exposed to danger. He is ready to give monetary help to Maqbool so that they may fight against the invaders till help comes from the Government of India. Ghulam too is sincere in friendship though he lacks the guts to revolt against his father. He cannot assert his nationalistic sentiments against his father's domination. But he reveals great courage when he supports Maqbool against the cunning Ahmed Shah. He tells Khurshid Anwar very frankly: "To be sure, I am with my father. But I believe in friendship" (74). His boldness is further revealed in his curt answer to Khurshid: "Maqbool is my guest, as you are, And I would not like to misuse the fact of his visit here to impose a decision on him. Nor to ask him to choose immediately. He need not commit himself. He can think things over and see reason" (75). Although weak before his dominating father, he redeems his image by telling Khurshid: "...you cannot do anything to my guest," and by his blunt reply to Ahmed Shah: "I am saying or doing nothing which is not according to the traditions of Islam. A guest is sacred to me..." (76). Ghulam, in this way, is not a spineless weakling; he is endowed with a sense of filial obedience and sincere friendship.

Begum Jilani and Mahmdoo too win our admiration despite their weaknesses. Begum Jilani has to observe the dictates of her husband. Also she is a fatalist and believes that "The only way...in which this cruelty can be offset is by obedience to destiny. What is written in one's fate will be..." (80). She believes that acceptance of fate brings contentment. She widely differs from Maqbool in her ideas about destiny. But she shows maternal instinct of saving her child from dangers. She lets Maqbool leave her house in her burqah. Mahmdoo too, though afraid of Master Ishaq, stands by Maqbool. He tells Ishaq: "Against murder—one must join even with Shaitan" (22). He is ready to save his guest against the cruel remarks by the Master. He also decides to accompany Maqbool to Baramula. Mahmdoo is a man of reason. He tells Maqbool not to fling himself into danger: "Sire, one does not walk into a burning fire. One allows the flames to die down a little" (17). But when there is the question of friendship he does throw himself into the "burning fire." It is only on being repeatedly asked by Maqbool that he parts company.

The minor characters in the novel are authentically portrayed. They also enable the novelist to reveal the character of the protagonist more vividly. It is through his dialogues with Mahmdoo, Ishaq, Muratib, Khurshid, Ahmed Shah, and his father that Maqbool's ideas and principles come to light. He is not able to talk to Nur because of the paucity of time. But the letter from Maqbool to Nur reveals a lot about the brother-sister relationship. The confidence of Maqbool in his sister and the hope that her son will continue his own unfulfilled task provide a glimmer of hope to the otherwise tragic finale of the novel.

The fact that in *Death of a Hero* Anand has been able to suppress his urge for propaganda is clear as the only saviour figure in the novel is the sufferer himself. He too does not indulge in long harangues. No doubt, he articulates the author's ideology but there is no overt statement of it. The novelist's ideas are incorporated into the novel not forcibly but through the reaction of the sensitive soul of the protagonist to various situations. Maqbool's condemnation of the treachery of Ahmed Shah, his rebellious conversation with Khurshid Anwar and Ishaq, his fiery talk with his father, and his one-sided conversation with Nur through a letter reflect his ideas and the ideas of the author. The absence of any other saviour hero contributes to the aesthetic appeal of the novel.

However, Anand's idealogical (if not downright propagandist) slant assumes insidious ways and becomes manifest in various manners, more or less unconsciously. The very fact that he presents Maqbool who fought against his own co-religionists as a "hero" is symptomatic of his ideological commitment. No Pakistani will ever revere Maqbool as a hero. And no present-day Kashmiri militant either. It is indeed sad that his grave has recently been desecrated by his own townsmen by whom it had been revered for decades. What is of significance to a student of literature is not that in *Death of a Hero* Anand has taken sides (which he always does in almost every novel) but that he has failed to "give fair play all around" (to adopt a Laurentian phrase). All the characters who are on the side of Pakistani marauders and Islam are vilified and those who stand against them are glorified, strictly in proportion to their anti-Pakistan and anti-Islamic sentiments. This is too simplistic. And that is probably the reason why *Death of a Hero* has not risen to the height of some other novels of Anand. It is a work written patently by an Indian. However, we must welcome Anand's dispensing with a saviour figure in this novel. Otherwise we would have been treated to yet another round of boring homilies.

NOTES

1. *Death of a Hero* (New Delhi: Arnold Heinemann Publishers Pvt. Ltd., 1985) 16. All the subsequent references to the novel are taken from this edition.
2. *The Big Heart* (New Delhi: Arnold Heinemann Publishers Pvt. Ltd., 1980), 16-17. The subsequent references to the novel are from this edition.
3. K.N. Sinha, *Mulk Raj Anand*, 57.
4. S.C. Harrex, *The Fire and the Offering*, 124.
5. C.D. Narsimhaiah, *The Swan and the Eagle*, 129.
6. M.K. Naik, *Mulk Raj Anand*, 77.
7. See Marlene Fisher, *The Wisdom of the Heart*, 75.

8. Mulk Raj Anand, *From Author to Critic: The Letters of Mulk Raj Anand to Saros Cowasjee*, 123-24.
9. *The Wisdom of the Heart*, 80.
10. Premila Paul,"Major Themes in the Novels of Mulk Raj Anand" in *Perspectives on Indian Fiction in English*, ed. M.K. Naik (Delhi: Macmillan Company of India Ltd., 1979), 4.
11. *The Wisdom of the Heart*, 76.
12. Alastair Niven, *The Yoke of Pity*, 86.
13. S.C. Harrex, *The Fire and the Offering*, 124.
14. *So Many Freedoms*, 130.
15. K.N. Sinha, *Mulk Raj Anand*, 57.
16. Balarama Gupta, *Mulk Raj Anand: A Study of his Novels in Humanist Perspective*, 76.
17. *The Fire and the Offering*, 127.
18. M.K. Naik, *Mulk Raj Anand*, 85.
19. Paul, *The Novels of Mulk Raj Anand: A Thematic Study*, 72.
20. *Ibid.*
21. M.K. Naik, *Mulk Raj Anand*, 107.
22. *Ibid.*
23. K.N. Sinha, *Mulk Raj Anand*, 76.
24. Premila Paul, *The Novels of Mulk Raj Anand: A Thematic Study*, 72-73.

6

A SCHIZOPHRENIC PRINCE

Anand ventured into a new territory with his *Private Life of an Indian Prince.* His choice now fell not on an untouchable or a coolie for his protagonist; instead, he picked up an Indian prince. Victor Edward George Ashok Kumar—the prince of Sham Pur—is a victim of the post-independence policy of Indian Government to dissolve the princely states. But he is a bigger victim to the tactics of his selfish, greedy, and ruthless mistress. Anand probes into the political and private life of his protagonist. The emphasis, of course, is on the latter aspect. Anand has projected the putrescence and meretri-ciousness of the glittering and gaudy world of the Indian prince in true colours. Because the protagonist in the novel is no less than a prince who claims to be a demi-god, a descendant of Lord Vishnu *via* God Rama, no saviour figure is introduced. The presence of a saviour character would have offended the credibility when the sufferer is a man of high profile. Anand's artistic sense makes him bring into his novel a reporter instead of a saviour. This is the only novel in which the protagonist suffers alone; he has nobody to relieve him from the suffering and he himself is not strong enough to stand against his exploitation.

The suffering prince has his retinue—a personal physician, a private secretary, an aid-de-camp, a political secretary, and a number of attendants who are always at his beck and call. But all of them fail to save their master both from political and personal crises. By virtue of his political authority he stands much above them. All of them are ready to satisfy every whim and caprice of the master to whom they are obliged in one way or another. After the Prince's elopement with Bunti Russel, Dr Shankar observes on the role of the former's associates objectively and critically: "I felt like telling Munshiji how he had been humbugging himself, talking of guarding His Highness against evil influences when he, Captain Partap Singh, the A.D.C., Mr Bool Chand, the political secretary, and myself indulged every whom and fancy of His Highness, in order to curry favour with him, and shut our eyes to what we did not want to see about His Highness, even while we pretended to be so concerned when anything happened to His Highness."[1] And such indulgence is more expected from the "paid servants" (51) of a prince than their efforts to negate the eccentric ideas of their master. In this master-servant relationship, the servants extend their co-operation and help whenever a critical situation arises but they cannot prick the bubble of the King's ego. They can preach sermons, advise him, and apprise him of a situation but they are unable to change his decisions. The absence of the saviour figure, therefore, is according to the demands of the nature of characters.

The absence of the saviour hero is demanded by the period of Indian history in general and the life of Victor is particular with which the novel deals. The action of the novel is set in the background of the very significant historical event of the merger of princely states into the Union of India. All the princes had to sign the instrument of Accession. The protests, the persuasions, and the authority of the princes were of no avail against the iron will of the iron man, Sardar Vallabbhai Patel. Nobody could have saved the Prince from such a situation. And the situation worsened particularly with the people of the state turning rebellious. The other aspect of Victor's problem is his exploitation by his mistress. The aspect is too personal to be dealt with adequately by an outsider. No doubt, the Prince discusses many of his troubles with Dr Hari Shankar, but the latter can at the most warn him against the cunning intrigues of his nymphomaniac mistress. But the manoeuvres of Ganga Dasi and the weakness of the schizophrenic Victor render his guidance useless. Munshi Mithan Lal's religious preachings too become a subject of ridicule with the Prince. Moreover, nobody wants to incur the displeasure of the Prince, with the result that his position goes on degenerating till he becomes completely neurotic. Dr Shankar confesses that "The symptom of his [Victor's] difficulty, of course, was his preoccupation with Gangi. And it had not been possible to remove it, because we had pampered him and made it seem a nice kind of feeling to indulge in under the guise of love, and he had even won sympathy from us in his invalid's privileged position" (291). The "privileged position" is, in fact, two fold. He enjoys the privilege of being an authority over his employees and wins their sympathy for being a weakling who has been left mentally invalid by the ruthless behaviour of his selfish and crafty mistress. In both cases the doctor, the secretary and the A.D.C. fail to save him from his predicament.

The immediate impetus behind the writing of the novel too may be one of the reasons of the absence of the saviour character. Anand might have had the idea of writing a novel on an Indian prince beforehand, but the actual impulse was provided by Anand's personal rejection by his beloved, a hill woman. The shock led to his neurosis. The novel was written at the advice of his Greek dancer nurse who wanted him to write his agony off. The writing that was a therapy to cure a disease required more the true projection of a situation than aiming at ideological propaganda. He, no doubt, touches upon the theme of the administrative deterioration in the state of Sham Pur in particular and all princely states in general, but the concentration lies on the personal tragedy of Prince Victor. Moreover, the princes were already losing their paramountcy; their autocratic administration was giving place to popular governing bodies. At this stage Anand's aim of the exposure of their putrescent lives could not be a reformative or curative one. The reform had already been introduced by Indian Congress Government through curtailment of their powers.

Through the Instrument of Accessation, "the States acceded to the Dominion of India on the three subjects of defence, external affairs and communications,"[2] records V.P. Menon, Secretary to Sardar Vallabbhai Patel. Although the "Accession did not imply any financial liability on the part of the acceding States,"[3] and large privy purses were promised to the princes, the fact remains that these rulers were deprived of much of sovereignty which had been their right for hundreds of years. The corrupting power having been snatched away from the princes, they could no longer trouble their subjects through extortion, exploitation, and injustice. Anand, therefore, curbs his propagandistic instinct in the novel. He does not require a spokesman to condemn the evil of corrupt administration by the princes.

The novel is free from any overt ideological commitment on the part of the novelist. There is no authorial intervention with a purpose to hammer his point home. The novel, therefore, is aesthetically the best by Anand. The life of the prince is very authentically presented. The characters are delineated without any prejudices for or against them. The convincing and captivating episodes enable a reader to have a clear glimpse of the reality that lies under all the glitter of royal families. Anand contrasts the outer shimmer with the inner sordidness. The contrast becomes all the more glaring when people lose all faith in the autocratic set up; they give up their traditional allegiance to the King and fight for their rights. "For I realized," remarks Dr Shankar, "that all this magnificence, the flash and pageantry of the gentry, the polo and the champagne etc., was the decorative outer surface, the appearance, of a crude reality, underneath which all the decencies of life were symbolically or really crushed and ground in the dust" (127-28). The decadent life in the royal court of Sham Pur epitomizes the degeneration of moral values in all the states under princely administration. The author probes into the psyche of both the Prince and the subjects. With rare insights into the psychology of both the corrupt ruler and the awakened ruled, he reveals the process of transition of power from majestic administrators to the common people. Though his treatment of the theme is profound and objective yet the novel has elicited contradictory critical commentary. Cowasjee finds the novel to be "Anand's most impressive work."[4] Jack Lindsay expresses almost a similar opinion: "We feel the conflict of the old and the new in India with an evocative force that marks this book out as a most impressively sustained performance."[5] He goes ahead of Cowasjee to add that "If Anand had written nothing else, his place in the history of the novel would be secure—his place as a profound interpreter of Indian life in a phase of pervasive crisis."[6] On the contrary Balarama Gupta finds Lindsay's comment "too tall a claim to be valid." For him, "the novel is a failure, particularly in so far as there is no close integration between its artistic texture and the author's philosophy of humanism."[7] Naik too finds the novel "hardly a profound interpretation of 'Indian life in a phase of pervasive crisis.'" "It could have been this," remarks Naik, "if it had not been afflicted with the artistic schizophrenia of trying to be at once a case history and a political chronicle."[8] Only a novel with great profundity defies classification and earns such varying opinions. The fact remains that despite a few limitations the novel is the best by Anand.

Private Life of an Indian Prince forms a very authentic portrayal of the schizophrenic Prince and his nymphomaniac beloved. It is "a psychotic odyssey."[9] Anand reveals deep knowledge of the life of Indian princes and an insight into abnormal psychology. The knowledge at both levels may be traced back to Anand's close study of the life of princes when during World War II he served as a tutor to the Prince of Simla. The Prince, like the protagonist of his novel, suffered neurosis and had to find haven in a lunatic asylum.To add to the knowledge of abnormal psychology, there was the novelist's personal suffering from a similar mental state. To provide a sufficient commentary on the working of the protagonist's psyche, Anand adopts the technique of the introduction of a narrator. Very cleverly he makes the narrator the personal physician of the Prince who is privileged to probe into his physical as well as mental ailments. Because Victor confides in him the secrets of his personal and political life, the latter becomes a "friend, guide and philosopher" (30) of the former. Because the private life of the Prince is inseparably interwoven with his political life, the personal physician is able to scrutinize both the aspects of his life. The first person narration gives to the action more of a semblance of reality. In the Author's Note on the novel, Anand remarks about the narrator's role:

> The neutral 'I' of the first person singular has tended, in this book, to become a character in his own right. Most writers know how a character in a novel sometimes takes control and runs away with the story. The author has been content to allow Dr Shankar to take possession of the narrative, as well as become Sancho Panza to the Prince's Don Quixote. Therefore the 'I' in this novel is not to be mistaken for the author, who has reverted to the Indian tradition of anonymity and looks on, like Siva's searing third eye, at the unfolding of this tragi-comedy (24).

Despite Anand's claim of "anonymity," the fact remains that the narrator is Anand himself, the rational part of his split mind whereas Victor represents the irrational, abnormal self of Anand during his neurosis. Anand walks on the pages of the novel safely and without any impression of authorial intrusiveness. Dr Shankar's philosophy is, *mutatis mutandis*, Anand's own as discussed in *Apology for Heroism*. Particularly he expresses Anand's ideas about religion, philosophy, body, soul, and life. He articulates Anand's humanism: "I think that in spite of man's bewilderment and confusion about such questions as to what he is, how he ought to act and where he is going, he is the final fact of the universe. There is nothing higher and more dignified than human existence—" (299). He shares Anand's atheism: "I don't believe that there is any power transcending man, who can decide things for him. Man is responsible for gaining or losing his life" (300). It is through the narrator that Anand projects the eccentricity of Victor both in his administration and his private life. In fact "there is as much of Anand in his Prince as in his narrator, and this partly accounts for the penetrating analysis of the prince's character. Dr Shankar is the rational side of the author analysing the irrational side as seen in the Prince." The relationship between the Prince and Dr Shankar is comparable to that of the two selves of the split personality of Prufrock in Eliot's "Love Song of Alfred J. Prufrock"—the rational self and the passionate self.[10] But unlike other spokesmen of Anand in his novels like *Untouchable, Coolie, Two Leaves and a Bud,* and *Gauri,* Dr Shankar is not a preacher; he is an observer and recorder of the mental state of the Prince. He is a physician and consultant to Victor, but he is not his saviour.

In the novel, the author repeatedly states the actual position of the Doctor and tries to make clear that by virtue of his authority the Prince stands above his physician. The latter can, at the most, advise him according to the demands of the circumstances, but he cannot be his saviour. The Prince, no doubt, confides even the most personal matters in him, but he does not act upon the prescription and advice of the doctor who is a psycho-analyst as well.

Dr Shankar has joined service under the Prince to work off a scholarship he has availed of for the three years of his medical education abroad. He, therefore, is bound to stay in "debt slavery" (125). The colloquy after the Victor-Bunti escapade makes his position clear: "And knowing, as only you do, that His Highness is ill and will behave like this again and again, you should, if only because you have learnt to relish the thought of personal freedom and social justice as elementary needs of your mind and body, not be abject like all the other state subjects, but resign before you get involved any further in the tentacles of that courtesy and affection which the Maharaja seeks to weave round you, with all his all-absorbing ego that knows no bounds" (31). But there is the other voice to remind him of his obligation to the Prince and his duty to his profession: "If you owe the money and cannot pay it off immediately and have accepted the position you are in, it is not easy to get out of it, especially because you still believe that you may be able to help the Maharaja to get well and divert him from the path on which he is travelling. At any rate, it is your duty as a doctor to enable him to regain his confidence in himself, which has been shattered by Ganga

Dasi, and to see him adjust himself to some kind of balanced social behaviour" (31). But the impact of Gangi's sex tactics is so deep that it renders the Prince incorrigible. His sovereignty, moreover, makes him immune to any reformative attempts by any member of his retinue. Dr Shankar, although he enjoys a privileged position among the other employees of victor, again and again feels that he is "the willing slave," "the courtier" who is "cowed down by the refulgent aura of His Highness's prestige, which was always an omnipresent reality to us all" (70). Because of the conciousness of Victor's authority, Dr Shankar fails to save him from the maddening intrigues of Ganga Dasi and the crafty plans of his political adversaries. He keeps pondering over the relationship of Victor with his mistress and his political rivals but the facts become only "rare and precious pieces of information, curios in the museum of knowledge about human affairs that I was building up, to put it in medical terms, an important case history for my files" (122), confesses Dr Hari Shankar. This case history becomes attractive material for narration as Dr Shankar feels that "to expunge the dread, perhaps it would be a good idea to recapitulate and write down my experiences of victor, for in that way I could attempt a conscious apppreciation of my erroneous life. I could find confirmation of my new belief from my memories, the conviction of the preciousness of my integrity that I had let slip through the compromises of the last few years" (353). He also realizes that by losing his integrity, he had not been able to save his master and patient from ultimate neurosis. Instead, while "in the pay of the Maharaja," he was living "only for the gratification of my five senses" (353). The narrator, in this way, is only an observer and recorder of the working of Victor's mind; he is not able to save the Prince from the grim situation of his life. The relief that the Prince gets from his company is that of giving an outlet to his emotions through a discussion of even the most personal aspects of his life. It is only when victor is flung into the lunatic asylum of Pune that he feels free and thinks of leading an instrinsic life. After Dr Shankar's responsibility is transferred to Dr Bhagwat of the lunatic asylum, the former's reaction is not that of sorrow or regret over the fate of the Prince; it is a feeling of relief and freedom from a burden. Now he wants to work for the poor people. He realizes that he has been a coward, a weak-willed character who could not resist the temptation of a comfortable life in the court of the Prince of Sham Pur. He never feels committed to save his patient from his predicament. He can only make the latter aware of certain facts of life. His feelings, observations, statements, and reactions do provide wholeness to the action of the novel; his commentary provides a touch of authenticity to the portrayal of the prince's life; but his presence does not save the protagonist from mental derangement.

The other members of the Prince's retinue, his political secretary, Munshi Mithan Lal and his A.D.C., Captain Pratap Singh also fail to save their Prince. They, instead, worsen the situation by pandering to every whim and fancy of the Prince. Munshi Mithan Lal—"the pedagogic, parsimonious, religious boor" (27)—has to stay in the "thankless job" (21) for money which he requires for the education of his three sons. He is an expert statesman, but he becomes a butt of Victor's jokes. He has picked up some knowledge about the philosophy of celebrities like Emerson, Thoreau, Ruskin, Gandhi, and Bhagwan Krishan. Having committed to memory some of the quotations from scriptures he tries to sober the Prince by quoting them according to the demands of the occasion. But he is not able to change the Prince's mind which, we are told, was "set on other, more pleasant, things than holy men and their wise maxims" (27). When Ganga Dasi elopes with Bool Chand and the Prince is undergoing a spell of profound depression, he comes out with a hackneyed counsel: "Then you must forget her and face your loneliness. Once you face the fact that each man is ultimately alone, you will be able to conquer your lower nature and be free" (266). He warns Victor against carnal passions: "The entrails are the seat of the carnal, animal, lower self, the kama-loka! This carnal ego grows like a cancer at the very roots of life and eats away the soul, destroying the exalted harmony of life, and it causes violent conflicts in the self, which drown all calm and peace with their shrieking and noise" (260-61). But this Vedantist philosophy loses its appeal before the suggestion of Pratap Singh: "Leave the sermons of Mian Mithu alone, Huzoor; We will go to the Hawa Palace and have some fun" (263). Having another woman to fill the gap of Ganga Dasi is a welcome suggestion to get out of the traumatic situation. Mithan Lal helps Victor in having Bool Chand murdered. The impact of the murder makes Victor completely neurotic. He, in this way, is too weak to protest against any desire of the Prince. This gratification of every caprice of the Prince, instead of relieving him, enmeshes him more and more in sensual life. Captain Pratap Singh, with his own lustful and base desires, is always at the disposal of the Prince to arrange girls for him whenever the latter is in a mood of dejection because of the ruthless behaviour of Ganga Dasi. Anand portrays a very ugly picture of the A.D.C.: "Uncouth, lusty, a good boozer, a voracious eater and with nothing in his head except a little white matter under the bun of his long hair." But the uncouth manners are mitigated by "his hearty laugh, his generosity and the prodigal warmth of his uncivilized nature" (33). The tough physique of Pratap Singh comes to the rescue of the Prince when he is manhandled by the washerman of Annandale because of his adulterous relations with the latter's wife. But he feels that he cannot save Victor from the hands of Mr Russel after his escapade with the latter's daughter. Captain Partap Singh feels the pulse of Victor better than Dr Shankar or Mithan Lal. When the doctor and the Munshi philosophize over Victor's situation after Ganga Dasi's elopement with the political secretary, the Captain feels that the solution to Victor's dispondency is that some other girl should be brought to replace Ganga Dasi. While in England, he suggests that June Withers can be suitable for the pleasures of Victor. He helps Victor in arranging a meeting with the girl and winning her over. He colludes with the Prince in having Bool Chand murdered. The Prince confides in him all the secrets of the plot of murder whereas even Dr Shankar is kept out of the planning. But Captain Partap Singh, instead of saving Victor from the traumatic situation, helps in hastening his lunacy. Victor's indulgence in sexual pleasures which the Captain arranges cannot make him forget Ganga Dasi. The feeling of dejection becomes rather keener because of the contrast of other girls with Gangi. The murder of Bool Chand leaves Victor completely distraught. The A.D.C., in this way, shares the vulgarity of the Prince; he tries to cater to the sensual needs of Victor; but he is not able to, nor does he try to, save Victor from disintegration.

Because no saviour characters are introduced and there is no attempt at propaganda, nothing impedes an objective portrayal of the chief characters—Victor and Ganga Dasi. Although the life of the Prince is dismal and that of Ganga Dasi abominable, it is not exaggerated or diminished with a purpose. The history of princely India abounds in examples of the princes who led even more perverted lives. The portrayal of Victor and Gangi is a fine example of Anand's deep knowledge of the material of the novel and profound observation of the working of human psyche. He studies the problems of Prince Ashok Kumar from two aspects—sociological and psychological. The two aspects are so intricately interwoven that they appear to be almost indistinguishable. The one becomes one of the causes behind the other. Sociologically, Victor has inherited absolute sovereignty over his subjects. But power, as usual, has corrupted him socially and personally. Summing up the social life of Victor, Balarama Gupta aptly remarks that he is "an eccentric Indian Prince...wallowing in sloth and sex, squandering the state money, sucking the life-blood of his subjects by inflicting varieties of illegal taxes on them, and stubbornly refusing to merge his state into Indian union after Independence."[11] He has had his childhood spent in his father's zenana and has learnt filthy manners from the court servants. During his boyhood, he has had all his wayward fancies fulfilled. His faulty education at Queen Mary's School, Lahore, at Bishop Cotton, Simla, and Chiefs College, Lahore has only added exhibitionism and posturing to his wilfulness. His depravity is obvious in his marital career. He has snapped all relations with his first two wives; he neglects the third for pleasing his mistress Ganga Dasi. His moral degradation is suitably matched by his mistress's crafty manners.

The problems in Victor's administration of his state start because of his irresistible passion for Ganga Dasi. She has the son of the Tikyali Rani murdered so that her own son should be declared an heir to the Prince. Prince Ashok, blindly devoted to the cunning mistress as he is, fails to see through the greed, selfishness, and cruelty of this seductive woman. The coquettish approach of Ganga Dasi persuades the short sighted Prince to hold a durbar and declare her son the successor to the throne. To start trouble for the Prince, the government refuses to accept the illegitimate son as an heir. Tikyali Rani, Indira, too protests against the declaration. She starts her compaign against the decision by contacting the political department of the government. Already the government is displeased with the maladministration in the state and the grievances of people against exorbitant taxes and extortions, the practices which, again, are resorted to to satisfy the fabulous demands of the greedy mistress who "was the real power behind the throne" (59). The Government, therefore, conducts an enquiry into the matter of the acknowledgement of the illegitimate child as successor. People too start a movement against the unfair administration and form a Praja Mandal which is supported by the Indian National Congress. During the enquiry, the allegations of illegal exactions, deprivations, and oppression are well substantiated. The Government, therefore, imposes certain restraints on the powers and privileges of the Prince. The Prince loses not only a part of his authority, he is also plundered of much property by his scheming mistress. To please her, Victor tries to gratify all her demands and disposes of not only much of his personal property and jewellery, but also a large part of the state property. He, in this way, is impoverished in two ways—in money and in authority.

The Prince is a weakling, a schizophrene who, despite his awareness of the right and the wrong, is not morally strong enough to stand for the right. Physical pleasures so absorb his body and soul that he forgets his administrative duties and rosponsibilities completely. Ho knows about the ignoble past of Ganga Dasi; he knows about her present illegitimate relations with many men; he personally observes her in embrace with Dewan Raghbir Singh and in bed with Kurt Landauer during the hunt; but he cannot give her up. "She is a bitch, but I can't do without her!" (81) confesses Victor to Dr Hari Shankar. That Ganga Dasi possesses him completely is well revealed in the Prince's helpless condition: "The bitch! She comes to me with so many love words, shrieks and hisses that I—well, I like to sleep with her, you see! And she has got me.... I am trapped, I tell you, I am like a rat in a hole!..." (78). Dr Shankar's warning—"she will destroy you emotionally, physically, spiritually. She is an untamed jungli. And she will suck your life-blood and then spit you out. Get rid of her! She is a completely unscrupulous woman" (226)—falls flat on his ears. The seductive power of the harlot is more powerful than the warning by his friends. Even when Ganga Dasi has jilted him to elope with Bool Chand, Victor is not so full of anger against her as he is of desire for reunion with her. He pines for her like a love-lorn romantic: "If only—if only she would come back, I would take her to some enchanted land, to Kashmir, to Southern France, and I would lead her to the sea, or to some rock, where no one could see us, and where everything would be enchanted as in a fairyland, and there I would have her under a blue sky" (261). His regret is not that he ever loved such a fickle-minded and selfish woman; he, instead, repents: "Oh, why was I so thoughtless? Why didn't I give her all that she wanted—houses and land and money and jewellery?..." (261). The idea of renouncing the world and going to Benaras is only a fleeting one. And even this idea is combined with the desire that Gangi should be with him and they should be dedicated to God.

Such is the spell of sexual pleasures which Ganga Dasi provides that Victor is completely oblivious of his administrative responsibilities. He does not realize that people are rising in a "bloodless revolution" (274) against him. Intoxicated by the feeling of inherited kingship, he goes on believing that his people are enjoying the comforts of Ram Raj. He ignorantly feels that he is an ideal ruler: "I too want a state in which the Raja and Praja can live as father and sons. I want to renew in the people the belief that I have their interests at heart...I am not like the other rulers who despise their people!" (115). The irony is that he never thinks of the interests of his people. As a consequence of undue suppression, people have turned revolutionary. The revolutionary spirit is obvious in the reaction of Buta, the professional hunter, to the Prince's rebuke, in the letter of the detenus to Dr Hari Shankar, in the slogan raising against the Prince outside his palace, and the strike by people against firing by the Prince at the rally of the people shouting slogans. The imagery adumbrates the downfall of the Prince which is in the offing: "The sun had gone down and the sky was luminous as though we were going towards the regions of hell, where the blood of victims in the temple of Kali on Siva's hill, and their shrieks, were shooting up to the heavens, for the pink and orange streaks of pain limned the horizon" (128). The sky at the time of sunset, which otherwise presents a feast to the aesthetic eye, seems pain-marred. That the Maharaja has been deprived of much of his authority is obvious from the fact that when he starts from Shimla after his escapade with Bunti Russel, the salute of thirteen guns is reduced to one of seven and at his arrival at Sham Pur, no guns are fired at all. The reduction in salutation is a great humiliation for the Prince. But the greater humiliations at the hands of Ganga Dasi make him forget the shrinking of his political esteem and authority. The actual realization of his downfall comes when he has to sign the Instrument of Accession under the commanding and rigid behaviour of Sardar Patel. After he has come back as a defeated, dethroned monarch, the only consolation for him is that "now I shall be more or less in the same position as Gangi, one of the disinherited! May be, this will bring us closer together" (246). But he is disinherited of his mistress too. His shock is much greater at the loss of Ganga Dasi to his political rival, Bool Chand, than the loss of his sovereignty. He is on the verge of madness. The madness however, is postponed a little by his instant pleasure with June Withers in England. But intense jealousy is not to be suppressed by these momentary pleasures. And he does nothing less than murder Bool Chand, the new paramour of his mistress. The moral and legal repercussions of the crime are sufficient to complete the neurosis to which he has been moving by slow degrees.

Anand's hero, in this way, is a weak-kneed, gutless character. He lacks the confidence, courage, boldness, and initiative of Manohar Malgonkar's protagonist, Prince Hiroji Bedar of Begwad. No doubt, the two princes suffer many similar political and personal troubles, but unlike his counterpart in Anand's novel, Malgonkar's prince has a power of quick decisions and sticks to them. He reveals wonderful fearlessness when he meets his death after he has signed the Instrument of Accession, rather the "Instrument of Destruction,"[12] as the narrator in *The Princes* calls it. Mulk Raj Anand attributes his protagonist's weak will to the circumstances under which he has been brought up. Anand, like a psychiatrist, probes into the mental upbringing of his hero. Prince Ashok Kumar, according to the novelist, is a "hopelessly ill-adjusted personality" (46) because in him there is a confused amalgamation of two civilizations—the values of the feudal order he has inherited and those of the new era in which he is living. Anand presents the clash between these two divergent forces: "The spirits of his dead ancestors were pulling him towards the old virtues, prowess, splendour, firmness, dexterity, generosity, heroism in battle and the other duties of the high-caste, superior, kshatriya prince, while a number of new demons, the fashions of the hour, were pulling him into another direction" (46). The conflict resulted in the irrational, indecisive, weak, and cowardly behaviour of the Prince. Anand's introduction of the Prince prepares the readers for the final fate that he meets. Anand observes "All his scandalous behaviour, therefore, was due to the incongruity of the various strains in him that were trying to unite and become one person, but only made him a kind of montage man, a pathetic creature, a spoilt child" (47). And the behaviour of Victor throughout the novel bears out the introductory sketch of his personality. Still the novel does not give any impression of having been written according to a preconceived plan. That it is a spontaneous expression becomes clear from the fact that the novel "rushed out of me [Anand] in one month"[13] at a suggestion by his nurse.

Anand concentrates on the highly irrational, whimsical, and ignoble behaviour of Prince Ashok Kumar, but the character of the Prince as drawn by Anand does not offend credibility. The presentation of the life of the Maharaja is rather a fine example of restraint on material by the author if we keep in mind the reckless orgies, merry-making, drinking, hunting, womanizing, and feasting in the courts of real Indian princes. For example, it is said that the harem of the Maharaja of Patiala, Bhupinder Singh, consisted of three hundred and fifty women and he had a new religion started for the appeasement of sex-urge. His "Palace of Gaiety" was unmatched for the atmosphere of merry-making.[14] Again, the eccentricity of Victor is much less in comparison with that of the Prince of Junagarh who celebrated the marriage of his bitch Roshnara to the dog Bobby of the Nawab of Mangalore with rare pomp and show. On the occasion, "State holiday was declared for three days and all citizens and visitors numbering about fifty thousand were entertained with all meals, consisting of rich food. The novelty of the entertainment was that food was supplied to all citizens and guests at their residence by special wagons and trucks, three times a day, morning, afternoon and evening, while the rulers and the distinguished guests were entertained more lavishly with sumptuous food and songs by beautiful dancing girls from Baroda, Bombay and Indore."[15] The narration of the ceremony by Diwan Jermany Das is, in fact, a commentary on the impetuosity of the Prince. The behaviour of Victor in the administrative sphere, particularly at the time of signing the Instrument of Accession, again, is without exaggeration by the novelist. Most of the princes ignored state affairs for they were too busy merry-making. About the Maharaja of Patiala, it is said that "his greatest qualification was that he did not interfere in the State administration and occupied his time in merry-making."[16] Regarding the signing of the Instrument, all princes were, naturally, reluctant as it meant giving up authority not withstanding the promises by the government that they would go on enjoying authority and liberty. Maharaja Hanwant Singh of Jodhpur who was persuaded with much difficulty to sign the Instrument whipped out a revolver and threatening V.P. Menon, the Chief Secretary of Sardar Patel, said; "I refuse to accept your dictation." It was only because of the appearance of Lord Mountbatten at that time that the attempt to kill Mr. Menon was foiled.[17] All these instances from history reveal that Anand has shown great restraint. He has not tried to tilt the scales against the eccentric Prince. The portrayal is remarkable for the authenticity which has been a result of the novelist's deep knowledge of psycho-analysis. He analyses the condition of the Prince not merely as a doctor, but also with great sympathy as a fellow human being. That is why we find that "despite the Prince's moral and political corruption the novel's major emphasis lies not in the tyrannical abominations of a Marxian ogre but in the pathetic anguish of a fallen autocrat."[18] The fictional presentation of historical material through psychological treatment makes the novel a grand success.

Anand is more severe in his treatment of his heroine Ganga Dasi—a nymphomaniac, a "consummate concubine," a "non-professional harlot," "a human vampire," and "a viper of a woman." Both Anand and his critics are lavish in showering negative epithets on the woman whose intrigues are a cause of Victor's downfall. But the severity of Anand does not make him waver from the path of authenticity and truthfulness. He not only presents her as "absolute promiscuity" (46) but also traces her past to relate the psyche of the nymphomaniac to the circumstances in which she had her birth and upbringing.

Ganga Dasi has had a past full of variegated sexual experiences. Her past has subjected her to a variety of emotions aroused by her relations with a large number of lovers. Having had an unhappy married life with a Brahmin peon, a drunkard to whom she was sold, she developed attraction for other men. Already being the daughter of a harlot she had acquired the manners of a woman of pleasure. And before she was fourteen, she had been taken by many herdsmen of the village. After marriage too she changed one lover for another without any hesitation. She is a veritable nymphomaniac accepting without resistance the advances of any man who comes to her though she cannot stick to anybody. "The pitfall in the psychology of a nymphomaniac is that she will believe that her next victim will be last," says Dr Shankar, "whereas there is an infinite regress in this business" (194). Her behaviour has its explanation in the peculiar relationship between her father and mother. Her father was a priest and brought fruit and clothes to Gangi. The daughter, therefore, loved the father. But the father suspected Gangi's mother and often beat her ruthlessly. Gangi, therefore, loathed the tyrant in him. Now in every man she finds her father-figure. She is fascinated towards the hero but abhors the tyrant. Her experiences have left her "just a bundle of ill-assorted nerves, impulses and fancies bound up into a knot, as is the peasant woman's bundle, the knot being symbolic of the sharp, instinctive sense of mastery she had of all situations" (75). Victor found in her an appropriate companion because he too was promiscuous and his wife, Indira, was too polished and cultured for his crude manners: "I had behaved badly to my wives, and she had been bad. So I thought that two bad people might make a good pair" (82).

But Ganga Dasi proves to be much worse than the childish, simple, weak-willed, and impetuous Victor. She is a "consummate actress" (78) whose tactics of sex inveigle the Prince so strongly that he feels that "she is bound up with my entrails" (77). He knows about her past love affairs but is inescapably caught in her grip. Such is his fascination for her that he accepts her everytime she has been in bed with somebody else. Her green eyes entice all men, particularly Victor, so strongly that they become blind to the fact that she is using her art of love-making to rob them of their wealth. She attracts a man with her love-words and well trained sex-practices pretending to be a child wanting protection, but once she gets the victim in her grip, she possesses him body and soul. The brief moments of pleasure that Victor has enjoyed in bed with her are sufficient to make her seem indistinguishable from his life. When Victor comes into contact with her, he is so pleased with her love-making that he feels "that someone had come into my life, someone who knew the life of a town like Lahore amidst all these yokels, someone to cling to in the midst of all the artificiality of the state where I was a kind of tin god. To have a private life with someone devoted to you after all the ballyhoo of pomp and splendour! And she was a lovely companion and gave me such assurance. I could work ten times harder because I had a satisfactory personal life" (83). But all this assurance and devotion were a mere pretence to snatch away the money, property, and jewellery from the Prince. Once she has entered into the life of Victor, she dominates him so completely that there cannot be a place for any other woman in his life. She has Victor's wife Indira confined to a lonely place; she has Indira's son murdered so that she may have her own son declared a Tikka. And Victor is under such a spell of her charm that he concedes her wishes and acknowledges her son as his successor even though he is not sure whether the son is his own or is fathered by the Raja Sahib of Badaun with whom she has had an affair before coming into his own life. Such is the hold of Gangi on Victor that when he goes to see Indira and is moved by a feeling of affection for his son, he is "embarrassed that some servant might see him in this tender relation with his child by Indira and report to Gangi" (132). And when Gangi comes to know about his visit to his wife, she turns Victor out of her room at night. She has such a possessive and egoistic nature that "always she strained to be the centre of attraction, the sun towards whom all the sunflowers must turn" (92). It is partly to satisfy her enormous ego that she takes one lover after another.

Ganga Dasi wants Victor, like her other lovers, to cling to her but she herself cannot cling to anybody. She wants all attention from her lover, but herself she is thinking of her other lovers even while making love. She can discard her lover us soon as she finds that he can no longer gratify her greed for wealth. She makes Victor extort money from poor peasants and bestow it on her. She makes him sell public property for the satisfaction of her insatiable desires. But as soon as she finds that he is disinherited of his authority, her green eyes turn to Victor's rival himself because she hopes that Bool Chand will enjoy a good status in the popular government. With her meanness and selfishness, she stands as a foil to Tikyali Rani Indira who, though jilted by Victor for his preference for Gangi, comes to serve her husband in the lunatic asylum. Anand appropriately descirbes her as a "schizoid," "a split personality," at once "sadist and masochist" (143). Anand, like a psychiatrist trying to diagnose the mental ailment of a patient, scrutinizes the problem of Ganga Dasi. He, however, deduces that "since everyman had been a kind of cruel father to her, she loved and hated men in an ambivalence which resulted in the woman's amazonian revenge against man" (143).

Anand's attempt to psycho-analyse the behaviour of Ganga Dasi has a humanistic element in it. He not only gives a statement about her character or merely presents her as a hateful, immoral concubine but is fair enough to cast the blame on the circumstances that have moulded her personality. He tries to probe into the basic cause which can dehumanize a person. Although Ganga Dasi appears more abominable than Victor, Anand is no less fair to his heroine than to his hero. If Gangi is worse in her behaviour, it is so, Anand reveals, because she has suffered more. Dr Premila Paul's charge that "the narrator and the author—both victims of thwarted love—are more concerned with the pathological details of the pathetic hero than with the details of the dazzling heroine"[19] is easily answerable. The fact that the novel deals with both the public and private life of the prince needs the emphasis to be more on the actions of Victor than those of Ganga Dasi who enjoys no public status. Dr Paul's other charge that the reader has very little direct contact with her and that her character is more often described than depicted,[20] too has a clear explanation. It is that Ganga Dasi is not a public figure. Her status is that she is a keep, a mistress—a lady whose chief function is to provide pleasure to her lover in very personal moments. Such a woman cannot be expected to act much publicly. All that this hypnotic but illiterate woman is fit for is to use her sexual attractiveness for acquiring wealth. That too requires more of insidious plans than clearly avowed aims.

Anand, is this way, has been as successful in handling the victims of psychic problems as he has been of treating the victims of social and economic problems. To deprecate the novel merely as a clinical study would be unfair because the novelist has presented a beautiful blend of history, psychology, and fiction. Moreover, his choice of a psychological problem as a subject of his novel is well in keeping with the modern trend in literature. The novel, in fact, is a bigger artistic success than his *Untouchable* or *Coolie* because here there is no saviour character to hold the stage for a long time and impede the progress of the story through long, propagandistic speeches. The narrator, no doubt, at certain places voices Anand's philosophy, but the speeches are well embedded in the dialogues. The narrator himself is weak-willed and timid like the Prince and though a good friend, is not a saviour character. Through skilfully handled episodes, the novelist presents the journey of his protagonist from eccentricity to lunacy. Without exaggeration he presents the failure of his hero in both public and private life. The relationship between the hero and the heroine eludes scrutiny and evades description—the fact in which lies the greatness of literary art of the novelist.

NOTES

1. Mulk Raj Anand, *Private Life of an Indian Prince* (London: Asia Publishing House, 1984), 28-29. All the subsequent references to the text of tho novel are to this edition.
2. V.P.Menon, *The Story of the Integration of the Indian States* (Bombay: Orient Longman Ltd., 1956), 109.
3. *Ibid.*
4. Saros Cowasjee, *So Many Freedoms*, 132.
5. Jack Lindsay, *The Elephant and the Lotus*, 27.
6. *Ibid.*, 27-28.
7. Balarama Gupta, *Mulk Raj Anand: A Study of His Novels in Humanist Perspective*, 87-88.
8. M.K. Naik, *Mulk Raj Anand*, 104-05.
9. S.C. Harrex, *The Fire and the Offering*, 132.
10. *So Many Freedoms*, 141.
11. Balarama Gupta, 82.
12. Manohar Malgonkar, *The Princes* (London: Hamish Hamilton Ltd., 1963), 277.

13. Quoted by Saros Cowasjee, "Mulk Raj Anand: Princes and Proletarians," *The Journal of Commonwealth Literature*, No. 5 (July, 1968), 54.
14. See Diwan Jermany Dass, *Maharaja* (Bombay: Allied Publishers Pvt. Ltd., 1969), 7-11.
15. *Ibid.*, 150.
16. *Ibid.*, 6.
17. V.P. Menon, *op. cit.*, 117.
18. *The Fire and the Offering*, 136.
19. Premila Paul, *The Novels of Mulk Raj Anand: A Thematic Study*, 113.
20. *Ibid.*

CONCLUSION

The foregoing chapters reveal that Anand's choice of characters is determined by the period in which he wrote a particular novel. The introduction or absence of the saviour figures and the relationship between the suffering and saviour heroes depended on the kind of suffering he dealt with in various novels. And the aesthetic appeal of his novels, in its turn, depends on the relationship between the sufferers and the saviours.

Anand appeared on the literary scene with his *Untouchable* (1935) which was followed by *Coolie* (1936) and *Two Leaves and a Bud* (1937). This was the period of British rule when poor Indians were suffering passively under a foreign rule which denied them a life of dignity and respect. The Indians were treated as subhuman beings fit to be enslaved, exploited, and robbed. To make the situation worse, the Indians themselves helped these white-skinned British to develop a superiority complex and keep the natives at a safe distance. They looked at their British masters with awe, wonder, and admiration and behaved like abject, grovelling slaves ready to carry out all orders of the British, whether fair or unfair. To add to the misery of the poverty-stricken Indian labourers, the rich Indians who enjoyed good status joined hands with their foreign rulers to suppress their own countrymen whom fate and chance had denied their favours. The result of the selfishness of these well-fed British and Indian masters was the prevalence of many social and economic evils which added to the social evils like casteism, dowry system, and blind faith in superstitions which Indians had inherited from their ancestors.

It was also a period when reformists like Mahatma Gandhi had started a struggle against both the British rule and social evils. There was an awakening among some educated Indians against the evils prevalent in society. They had started recognizing the need of the uplift of down-trodden compatriots. Mulk Raj Anand, whose long stay in England had not made him oblivious of his Indian brethren, felt the need of asserting the dignity of the weak, helpless, exploited, and suffering humanity whose speech had been choked in their throats by the repressive force of foreign rule. He was much inspired by Mahatma Gandhi's compaign against untouchability. To add to his excitement for the uplift of the poorest in his country, Anand came across Gandhi's exhortation in his magazine *Young India*: "When the self becomes too much with you, try the following recipe: Recall the face of the poorest and most helpless man you have seen, and ask yourself if the step you contemplate is going to be any use to him.... Then you will find yourself and your doubts will melt away."[1] Anand's creative flame which was waiting for ignition, got the spark from the selfless love of Mahatma Gandhi for his people.

He got further inspiration from Maud Gonne who refused to marry W.B. Yeats because she preferred her work for the poor peasants of Ireland to her responsibilities as a wife. Anand's girl friend, Irene, had joined the movement of Maud Gonne. The examples of these ladies gave a new perspective to his vision.[2] He started looking at man as the centre of all philosophy. He lost faith in all non-humanistic and idealistic philosophical theories and pinned all his faith on the human beings. The path was clear before him: "To start life again, in a new home, to reach out to the silent ones, to whom I can give a mouth. I shall go and write my novel about Bakha right from within the untouchable colony, from within its dust and its heat" and he felt his "eyes wide open, my heart full of aching love, my soul gushing forth towards the Bakhas of our country."[3] He wanted to bring in his fiction "the wisdom of heart" while "addressing myself to the naked truth of human life in India."[4] He, therefore, gave up all philosophical theories and dedicated himself to lift human beings from "the labyrinthine depths of degradation" disregarding criticism of those who believed art and life to be entirely different from each other. He never wanted to conform to any aesthetic theory. His aim was to "rescue from the obscure slums of the British Indian cantonement, a man of real flesh and blood, from inside knowledge of the hutments where I [Anand] had lived and played with untouchable children and not a silhouette or profile drawn from above,"[5] "to create in *Coolie* a boy in all his humaneness, as against the fantastic Kim,"[6] to assert the dignity of weakness in a landless labourer.

Apart from Gandhi, Anand also came under the influence of several other thinkers and writers—mostly humanists, romantics, naturalists and Marxians. Like Rousseau—the fountainhead of Romantic thought in Western Europe—Anand developed love for natural man. He wanted to celebrate the beauty and dignity of the natural man because he had been influenced by the novels of Naturalists like Balzac and Zola, humanists like Leo Tolstoy and Dostoevsky, and Romantic humanists like Dickens. Among Indians, he had a great admiration for Tagore's humanistic tendencies in thought and philosophy. Although conscious enough not to make his writings a superficial imitation of any one of these writers, he did bring in his novels an element of humanism. [Anand prefers the term "humanness" to "humanism" to interpret his writings]. His writings are replete with Buddhist compassion because, like the Buddha, he observes "Dukh! Dukh! Dukh!"[7] in the world. In the world torn by demoralising suffering, Anand "expressed his faith in a great renewal of the human spirit which was to embrace, not merely Europe, but Latin America, the West Indies, Africa and Asia—a new and true internationalism. He was the forerunner of protest literatures of the colonial peoples as they threw off their oppressors."[8]

Like Mahatma Gandhi, Anand felt that revolution was the need of the hour—a revolution against foreign authority and indigenous evils. He wanted not only political freedom for even the so-considered lowest sections of society but "basic freedoms"[9] for the full development of human potentiality. His letter to Irene is a proclamation of his aim: "We have to give up the smug pose of lotus eaters, looking at our palms to decipher the times. We have to throw away the faded garlands from the pegs, because they have long lost their fragrance. We have to nourish the flowers of humanity, whom the exalted ones have so far been scaring away from their kitchens, even as they always shooed away the hungry dogs."[10] And he started nourishing "the flowers of humanity"—the despised and degraded human beings—through his novels. He launched a crusade for the oppressed with the Gandhian faith that "the least little untouchable, the darkest dark villager and the most exploited coolie, will come into his own."[11] Anand made an effort to capture in his novels the true psychology of the weak and passive human beings who find their oppressors too mighty for their struggle against them.

Literature with such reformative zeal is not likely to remain objective. Nor does Anand feign objectivity or unconsciousness. He is an avowedly committed artist who uses his art for the exposure of evils with the purpose to awaken people to revolt against them. The authorial intervention is well expected in such novels. Anand manages to enter into his novels through saviour characters like Mahatma Gandhi and the poet Sarshar in *Untouchable,* Dr Prem, Prabha Dyal, Mohan, Ratan, and Sauda in *Coolie,* and Dr Havre in *Two Leaves and a Bud.* These saviour characters retain human feelings in this otherwise corrupt world. They provide a little illumination to the dark world of the suffering protagonists. The 1930s were a period when awakening for one's rights had not extended to the low castes and classes. Only a few educated people had started realizing the need of liberty and equality for all irrespective of their castes and classes. The representatives of this benevolent section got into the novels of Anand in the form of saviour characters who gave voice to the unconscious, dormant desires of weaker humanity.

Most of these saviour figures, because they belong to upper castes or classes of society, fail to identify themselves fully with the poor sufferers. Their speeches stand out as set pieces of exhortations purposely incorporated with a desire to preach. They do not fit well into the main frameworks of the novels. Mahatma Gandhi and the poet in *Untouchable* appear to be speaking from a pulpit to sermonize those who are scarcely able to follow the words of the sermon. Mohan in *Coolie* is too good to be real. He belongs to a well-to-do family and is a graduate. But he is living among the poor coolies to talk them out of their subhuman lives. Sauda presents a charter of demands of the coolies on behalf of the trade union. Such a document clearly reveals the propagandist aim of the author. The kindness of Prabha Dyal and Ratan, on the other hand, is authentically presented. Prabha Dyal is a former coolie who by dint of hard work has become a partner in a factory. He, moreover, has no children. His soft behaviour towards a child, though a poor coolie, is well expected. Ratan is himself a coolie whose experiences in Bombay have enabled him to enlarge his mentality. He has acquired a big heart as he has gathered knowledge and experience. He, like Anand's uncle Pratap of *Seven Summers* and *Morning Face*, exudes a devil-may-care attitude. The co-operation he extends to Munoo in particular and other coolies in general comes naturally from one who has developed love for human beings through his vision of human suffering. Dr Havre in *Two Leaves and a Bud*, like Mohan in *Coolie*, is unbelievably considerate towards the poor Indian coolies. He incurs the wrath of the British masters of tea estates by fighting for the cause of Indian labourers. The pages he writes on the economic conditions of India are sermons of Anand put forcibly into the novel. The villain Reggie Hunt seems to be more authentically presented than Dr Havre, the saviour character. Dr Havre seems to be a lifeless puppet designed in accordance with the propagandistic requirements of the author. It is in these novels that Anand has failed to balance art with propaganda. There are large holes in the framework of the novel giving a clear peep into the aim of the author. They spoil the beauty of the structure and one starts questioning the integrity of the artist *qua* artist.

By the time Anand came to write the Trilogy, that is the late thirties and early forties, awareness of the need of freedom—instead, freedoms—had extended to larger sections of society. It was also the result of widening nationalistic feeling generated by the Gandhian movement for freedom and World War I which shattered the image of the British masters as remote, unapproachable, superhuman, and reticent people. In the War Indian soldiers came closer to the British soldiers and officers and found that they themselves were as good as the British. It encouraged patriotic sentiments in the Indians on the one hand and confidence to fight for their amelioration on the other. Anand, therefore, went to the higher sections of society to pick up his protagonists. Moreover, as Riemenschneider believes, by 1938 Anand had realized that "the all too low status of his former heroes was indeed a handicap which prevented them eventually from shaking off their bondage of slavery and from working out their own destiny."[12] For this he needed a more confident, energetic, sophisticated, and socially advanced character. Lal Singh is "such a figure, as concerned with achieving personal liberty, control over his own destiny, conquest of his own weaknesses, as he is with altering social institutions."[13] Lalu is a fiery and rebellious character who, unlike Bakha, Munoo, and Gangu, is not ready to accept all the unfair practices of the landlords, religious saints and those who happen to be socially and economically superior. He, like Anand himself, is an iconoclast itching to break away from traditions and taboos. He encourages the members of his family and his friends to protest against the cruelty of the established authority.

The action of the Trilogy shifts from a small village of Punjab to the battlefields of France and then to the post-War India where various forces are in action for the freedom—political, social, and economic. With the change in the milieu and period of action the role of the protagonist too changes from that of a fiery rebel to that of a sepoy fighting for his foreign lords and then to that of a frustrated person whose helplessness makes him join a front against the oppressive forces. Anand is discreet enough not to introduce any saviour characters in *The Village* and *Across the Black Waters*—in the first the suffering protagonist himself is awakened enough against the exploiting forces; he does not require anybody to exhort him for a fight and in the second the action makes all sepoys equal, the slavish soldiers ready to do any bidding of the British officers. Hercules Long in *The Village* tries to organize young village boys to improve the living condition in the village. But hardly anything takes place after the speech. And Mr Long too chooses Lal Singh as the leader of the scouts. Whatever message Anand wants to convey, is conveyed through the protagonist himself. In Lal Singh, there is a merger of the sufferer and the saviour characters. Because no outsider is brought to occupy the platform for propaganda, the message of the author remains well concealed in the well thought-out plot of the novel. Because the sufferer himself reacts against the injustice meted out to him and his kind, the reactions appear to be the natural retaliation of one who has suffered and not improvised speeches to advance some ideology. The novel, therefore, remains an aesthetically appealing, authentic study of life in a village in pre-Independence India.

In *Across the Black Waters*, Lal Singh, alongwith other soldiers of British Indian Army reaches the far off lands of France to fight against Germany on behalf of the British government. The soldiers here are treated as soulless machines always at the beck and call of their British masters and having no thoughts, feelings, and moods of their own. Because all the soldiers are rendered helpless slaves, there is nobody to save others from the abyss of despair. Even the turbulent, fiery and revolutionary spirit of Lal Singh is dampened by the stern attitude of the Indian as well as British officers.

Across the Black Waters is more a novel of action than of character. Anand depends more on episodes than on characters to reveal the absurdity and futility of war, especially for those who even do not know the purpose of the war and against whom they have to fight. In the period of crisis, the soldiers of India, no doubt, retain human feelings of sympathy, love, understanding, and kindness. But they cannot exert these emotions to relieve the pain of others because the fear of the officers on the one hand and that of the enemy on the other is always daunting them. Among the Indian soldiers we do have "Daddy Dhanoo, a God fearing Hindu...Uncle Kirpu, who conveys bitter truths of life through his grim and cynical jokes, the brave and courageous Havildar Lachman Singh on whose face always shines a gentle and kind smile, Subedar Major Arbel Singh who threatens to dismiss his son when he learns of his irresponsible behaviour during the patrol party."[14] But keen observations, human compassion, and sense of justice of these soldiers fail to rescue their fellow soldiers from the painful situations created by the arbitrary orders of the British government and their too strict execution by the brutal Indian Officers like Lok Nath and Subah Singh. Uncle Kirpu voices the feelings of Anand but his ironical remarks do not save his friends from pain. What a wise man like him can do to liberate himself from the clutches of the cruel government is to commit suicide.

The Sword and the Sickle deals with the protagonist's trouble-torn life in India five years after World War I when he comes back having completed his term as a prisoner-of-war in Germany. The novel, published in 1942, deals with a period when the freedom movement of Mahatma Gandhi had gathered strength. People disillusioned after the breach of promises made during the War by the British government had started feeling the need of freedom with greater intensity. They also wanted liberty from their exploitation at the hands of bourgeiose feudal lords. Even simple peasants had turned revolutionaries and had joined the double-pronged fight—against the foreign rule and against the native capitalists. In this period of great stir, people adopted different political ideologies. The simple common people joined various factions with various political ideologies. Anand very cleverly introduces leaders with different thoughts in his novel who try to impress upon people (whom Lalu represents) their own political philosophies. They are not saviour characters, but men propagating their own approach to freedom. The objective is one—to fight for liberty and equality—but the methods to achieve the objective are different. There are characters like Kanwar Rampal, Mahatma Gandhi, Pt Jawahar Lal Nehru, Prof Verma, and Comrade Sarshar. Anand brings to light the political ideologies of these leaders but has comments against each of them. Kanwar Rampal believes in sporadic terrorist activities which are not likely to realize the aim of freedom because they are not a part of the larger national movement; Mahatma Gandhi, though a champion of the down-trodden, is a distant, taciturn leader. Although he preaches for a casteless society, he is a tacit advocate of capitalistic order of society. Pt Nehru has humanistic zeal but is too busy to encourage the poor people. He goes away without inaugurating the Kisan Nagar because he has been called back by political urgencies to Allahabad. Prof Verma is too intellectual to be practical. Anand seems to be speaking through Comrade Sarshar whose message of unity and oneness is the actual need of the hour. His approach to struggle for freedom is more convincing than that of all the other leaders. It, no doubt, brings clarity of aim to Lal Singh who so far has remained confused about the aims and methods of the revolutionary group of Kanwar Rampal Singh. But Anand seems to disapprove of the dogmatic and hurried manner in which Sarshar tries to impose his thinking on others. By the end of the novel Lal Singh is a matured personality but the maturity comes through subjection to a series of variegated experiences in India and abroad, not through the efforts of a saviour character.

The absence of an outsider saviour hero is one of the factors behind the marvellous success of the Trilogy. Anand makes his message come home to his suffering protagonist through the interaction of various experiences; he does not preach it from a platform. The result is a well integrated, harmonious and unified group of three novels.

The Trilogy is followed by *The Big Heart* (1944), a novel with a wider humanist perspective and greater artistic maturity. It is a plea for sympathy, sacrifice, and service couched in the artistic mould of a well-planned novel. The novel was published two years after *The Sword and the Sickle.* The protagonist, Ananta, therefore, is endowed with maturity and experience which Lal Singh attained in the end of the Trilogy. *The Big Heart* may be said to begin where *The Sword and the Sickle* ends. Ananta stands for modernity and unity with greater fervour than Lal Singh. Lal Singh's desire of struggle for happiness is Ananta's aim of life and he sacrifies himself waging this struggle. Lalu realizes that "for Revolution is a need of togetherness, Comrade, the need to curb malice among men, the need for men to stand together as brothers..." (*The Sword and the Sickle,* 385) and Ananta exhorts his coppersmith brethren to organize themselves to give force to their demands: "Don't let your sullen hatred simmer in the cauldron of this congested lane on this hot morning. If you have asked Channa whether he can give you jobs and he has said no, then resolve to get together as men. It will make us brothers and make our voice irresistible..." (*The Big Heart,* 29). Lal Singh is full of admiration for the Western adoption of machinery, Ananta's advice to the people of his brotherhood is to accept machinery but not let the owners of machinery enslave them. They should have the controlling switch of the machine in their hands. Ananta's vision of suffering in Bombay and Ahmedabad makes him realize the need of assertion of human dignity. "I know something about the rate at which souls are sold in the markets of Bombay and Ahmedabad" (*The Big Heart,* 28), he tells his friends. It is this knowledge which has given a big heart to him.

A man with such awakening and knowledge need not be sermonized by an outsider. It is he who takes upon himself the task of uniting his fellow men to relieve their and his own suffering. The sufferer and the saviour characters, as in *The Village,* merge in one person, Ananta, who is a representative of all those who are victims of industrialization. Ananta has his friends in Puran Singh and Janki. Puran Singh appreciates Ananta's approach to revolution and Janki is his inspiration. The three of them, says Suryanarayan Murti, represent a combination of three virtues: "It [the novel] is a study of the desire-images of three characters—Puran Singh Bhagat (a progressive poet), Ananta Ram (a young humanist Thatiar), and Janki (a young widow who is Ananta's love)—who represent Anand's ideal Triad: Sympathy and sacrifice and service."[15] Puran Singh, with the help of Janki, intends to continue Ananta's struggle after the death of the latter. Puran Singh voices Anand's message of "limitless compassion for man. Unbounded love especially for the poor and the down-trodden. So that those who have been left to rot on the dusty roads can be raised and given the izzat which is theirs by the miracle of their birth in this world" (*The Big Heart*, 149). The message, however, does not appear as a piece of propaganda. It is, like Comrade Sarshar's speech to Lal Singh, a part of discussion among the leaders with different viewpoints. Janki is a symbol of revolutionary spirit and love for men. The fact that despite her widowhood she is living with Ananta without marriage reveals her unorthodox, rebellious temperament. Her encouragement to Ananta to fight for the cause of the unemployed coppersmiths testifies her love for down-trodden mankind. Anand's message is completely, but not overtly, conveyed through the fight of Ananta, Puran Singh, and Janki for a recognition of human dignity. Their also being themselves among the sufferers makes the novel "Anand's sympathetic depiction in fictional terms of the changing social reality"[16] because the rising of people from among sufferers themselves shows that a revolution is in the offing. The novel becomes a great artistic achievement because Anand is able to suppress his urge to preach overtly through a character forced on the novel with the propagandistic purpose only.

The merger of the sufferer and saviour figures is further found in *Death of a Hero* (1964). Though published in nineteen-sixties, the novel deals with 1947 riots in Kashmir at the time of Pakistan aggression on India after the achievement of Independence. Having fought against the imperialist British for freedom, the Indian people still retained patriotic sentiments and revolutionary zeal. While Ananta in *The Big Heart* keeps planning for a revolution against the oppressors, Maqbool Sherwani actually encounters the enemy and sacrifices his life for the sake of his nation. While Ananta struggles for the rights of men of his own brotherhood, Maqbool fights for a wider cause—the freedom of his state from a foreign power. He goes a step ahead of Ananta in his selflessness and broad mentality because he fights against members of his own religion. Communal and religious considerations are of secondary importance for him when there is a choice between fight for the nation and fight for the religion. He tries to encourage his demoralised friend, Aftab; he feels indignation against the traitrous Ahmed Shah. He knows that by going to Baramula he will be going straight into the trap of death. But a sense of responsibility and chivalry makes him perform his duty of conveying the message that Indian troops would soon be arriving in Baramula. He must save the weakened people of his hometown. He proves to be a true martyr, a true patriot, and a true friend.

Death of a Hero is Anand's plea to the people for discarding narrow religious considerations and communal chauvinism. But here, as in *The Big Heart*, "the author's philosophy is kept subordinate to artistic canons" because Anand cannot be "arraigned of having constructed a hero for the purpose of ventilating his humanist views."[17] Maqbool Sherwani, a victim of communal intolerance of Muslims and treachery of his countrymen like Ahmed Shah, is himself a saviour character too. He, despite danger to his life, fights for the cause of his country. Anand remains within the restrictions of historical facts. He has been able to produce an aesthetically great novel by striking a successful blend of history, imagination, and humanism. Maqbool's doubts, hesitations, and indecisions make him a real human being—not a mere personification of idealism and courage.

Between *The Big Heart* and *Death of a Hero*, there appeared *Private Life of an Indian Prince* (1953), *The Old Woman and the Cow* (1960), and *The Road* (1961). *Private Life* is an authentic study of the decadent princely order in India after Independence. The novel deals with the historical event of the integration of states with the Union of India. But the emphasis lies mainly on the private life of Prince Ashok Kumar of Sham Pur. The private life is indistinguishably interwoven with the political life of the protagonist. Anand, on the one hand, brings to light the splendour and gaudiness of princely life and, on the other, studiously reads the psychology of the Prince who is an egotistical, ignorant, and weak-willed character. This is the only novel in which Anand has been able to keep his propagandist zeal completely restrained. No saviour character is brought in the novel to preach a philosophy; nor is the protagonist bold enough to act as the author's "desire-image." Here, for once, we have a victim without any saviour. The indecisive weakling that the Prince is, he fails to struggle for coming out of his predicament both at the political and personal levels.

Anand employs a new technique to give a clear glimpse of the life of the Prince. He introduces a narrator to provide commentary on the internal as well as external life of the Prince. Anand reveals great ingenuity in his choice of the narrator. His choice falls on the personal physician of the Prince. The doctor, by virtue of his profession and the dignity he enjoys for being intimate to the Prince, is privileged to probe into the mind of his patient as well as read his actions in life. The Prince, with the hope of finding a cure for his oppressive problems, confides all his secrets to the doctor. But Dr Shankar fails to save his patient from neurosis. He himself is weak and cowardly, more particularly because he is a subordinate, an employee of the Prince. He can only philosophize or intellectualize the mental state of the Prince. He observes the catastrophe of Victor "aiding it by his failure to restrain him."[18] For the drowning Victor he becomes "a kind of slippery raft which he had got hold of and to which he tried to hang on for survival," (*Private Life of an Indian Prince*, 257) but the raft fails to take the drowning Prince ashore. Williams observes a meaning in Victor's behaviour towards Dr Shankar in the lunatic asylum: "It is significant that in his madness the Prince displays particular venom against Shankar whom he finally identifies as typical of the sycophants who have surrounded him since birth."[19] The opinion is well confirmed by textual facts; Dr Shankar again and again feels that he was living in the putrescent world of the Prince's court to satisfy his own greed for power and privileges. He, at times, articulates Anand's humanistic philosophy, but not with an aim to propagate it. It is only a reaction to the Prince's fleeting fancy to lead a religious life at Benaras.

Anand has been highly successful in his technique of introducing a narrator. Through the device of the reporter, he has been able to lay bare the souls of a schizophrene and a nymphomaniac. The choice of the subject is in accordance with the increasing interest of modern people in the study of psychic complexities. And the subject does not admit a saviour character. Because the Prince enjoys autocratic power, anybody who is subordinate to him will certainly fail to act as a saviour. The absence of an authorial spokesman contributes to the novel being a successful psychological study.

In *The Old Woman and the Cow* Anand projects the woes of Indian women, another down-trodden section in India. Atrocities of men towards their wives had been in the mind of Anand for a pretty long time. His own escapade to England had been expedited by the fact that his father had beaten his mother for his participation in the pro-Gandhian movement. In *The Big Heart*, Ralia beats his wife. In *Private Life of a Indian Prince*, Gangi's father often beat her mother and Gangi herself had been a victim of the beatings of her husband, Shiv Ram. According to Anand, India is "a land in which this species [wife-beaters] abounds" (*Private Life*, 80). However, it is for the first time that he chooses a woman to serve as the protagonist of a novel. Though the novel was published in 1962—fifteen years after the Independence of India and twelve years after the declaration of equal rights for men and women through the constitution of India, Indian woman was still as ill-treated and as weak as the low-caste and low-class people. Because Anand again takes up a social evil to protest against, he is tempted to propagate his ideas through a spokesman. Because the protagonist is, in the beginning of the novel, unable to assert herself because she is steeped in orthodoxy, there must be somebody to affirm her rights and initiate her into a new, modern life. Dr Mahindra, a replica of Dr Havre of *Two Leaves and a Bud*, is Anand's mouthpiece to give air to his message to women to uplift themselves against male chauvinism of Indian society. Not only does Mahindra preach for women emancipation, his doctrine of salvation "is revealed as an academic platform of progressive educationalism, internationalism, anti-materialism, and socialist economics."[20] All these ideas are so blatantly propagated that Saros Cowasjee indignantly expresses a sweeping, but not exaggerated, opinion: "I can think of no novel of the sixties by a reputable writer which has more overt propaganda than one encounters in the last fifty pages of *The Old Woman and the Cow*."[21] Once again, after *Two Leaves and a Bud*, Anand's artistic talent is negated by his reformative zeal.

The characters of both Gauri and Panchi are better conceived than that of Dr Mahindra. Gauri's transition from innocence to maturity, ignorance to awakening, and from tradition to modernity is gradual and convincing. The tampering with the Sita myth suits the demands of the modern era. The successful handling of the legend with necessary alteration gives the novel relevance in modern times when feministic movements have gathered momentum.

The Road (1961) came out as a conscious effort to substantiate a thesis—to prove to Pt Jawahar Lal Nehru, the then Prime Minister, that untouchability still existed. The novel with a clearly avowed aim is, as would be expected, more propagandistic than literary or artistic. It is, more or less, a repetition of *Untouchable*. The interference of the novelist is clearly felt both in the contrivance of situations and delineation of characters. The reins of imagination are tightly pulled in by an effort to stick to the professed object.

The result of this restrained imagination is that Bhikhu fails to emerge as a lifelike and realistic character like, say, Bakha. He remains only a pale imitation of his counterpart. Dhooli Singh is too idealized to be authentic. He is an embodiment of Anand's humanistic creed. Despite his virtuous deeds, he fails to win our admiration. Like Dr Mahindra and Dr Havre, he is a lifeless puppet dancing to the tune of the author's desire to propagate a thesis. Anand is unable to strike an ideal combination of detachment and attachment which he preaches in his literary essays.

Lament on the Death of a Master of Arts (1967) deals with the mental torment which an unemployed educated person has to undergo. Here Anand "shows man in his confrontation of fate, as forsaken by the goals as well as by other men and women, broken, and decimated by the Machine-Money-War civilization, and illumines his awareness against materiality, dead 'matterliness' and suppression by society."[22] The novel has great relevance in modern times. The sufferer represents inumerable educated people whose failure to settle down in a dignified job makes them a subject of the sneers of society, even their own parents. The novel, written mostly in stream-of-consciousness technique, presents the mind of the protagonist when he is nearing death. The sufferer here cannot be saved by a saviour character because nobody can liberate him from the frustration of a victim of modern civilization. Anand, however, gives a vent to his bitterness through Azad, once a friend of Nur. It is through the memory of the protagonist that the spokesman is brought in. But Azad does not dwell on the problem of education and does not suggest any solutions. He only speaks against the unfair distribution of means in society. The sufferer-saviour relationship is not of audience listening to an inaccessible leader, but of two friends—one weak and the other rebellious. Azad has tried to awaken Nur against the cruelties of society. But Anand does not make Azad exhort his friend directly. Nur himself, while on death-bed, is recalling his past when talking to Gama. Nur himself tells how Azad had given a new direction to his thinking. Though by 1967, people had awakened against injustice, they were still the victims of mental torture caused by frustrated ambitions.

Thus, the presence or absence of the saviour characters, the suffer-saviour relationship, and the kind of suffering Anand chooses to project are, to a large extent, determined by the period of the writing of a particular novel by Anand. And the aesthetic fascination of his novels is maintained or marred by the changing nature of the sufferer-saviour relationship. The novels in which Anand forces an outsider saviour to uplift the too passive sufferers, suffer from the flaw of direct propaganda. In such novels, he fails to achieve a Brahma-like detachment and his intrusive omniscience and self righteousness are irritating and unaesthetic. The novels in which the sufferers themselves are the saviours are fine combinations of spontaneous art and premeditated intention. In these novels, the propagandistic urge is in complete harmony with artistic integrity, and the tale-artist dichotomy all but vanishes. The novels in which the sufferer's travails are depicted without any "saviour grace" to protest against the suffering are artistically grand indeed.

NOTES

1. Mahatma Gandhi, "Talisman," *Little Plays of Mahatma Gandhi*, ed. Mulk Raj Anand (New Delhi: Arnold Publishers, 1991), 8.
2. Mulk Raj Anand, "Letter to Irene," *The Bubble*, 600.
3. Mulk Raj Anand, "A Letter to Father," *The Bubble*, 595.
4. *Author to Critic: The Letters of Mulk Raj Anand to Saros Cowasjee*, 115.
5. Mulk Raj Anand, "Roots and Flowers: Content and Form" in *Untouchable and Kanthapura, op. cit*, 57.
6. *Author to Critic*, 116.
7. Personal Letter to me dated May 9, 1990.
8. Jack Lindsay, "Mulk Raj Anand," *Kakatiya Journal of English Studies*, Vol. II, No. I (1977), 4.
9. *Apology for Heroism*, 202.
10. Mulk Raj Anand, "Letter to Irene," *op. cit.* 604.
11. "Roots and Flowers," 59.
12. Dieter Riemenschneider, "An Ideal of Man in the Novels of Mulk Raj Anand," 10.
13. Margaret Berry, *Mulk Raj Anand: The Man and the Novelist*, 84.
14. Harish Raizada, *The Lotus and the Rose* (Aligarh: Faculty of Arts, A.M.U., 1978), 166.
15. Suryanarayan Murti, "Literature as Soul Search," *Kohinoor in the Crown* (New Delhi: Sterling Publishers Pvt. Ltd., 1987), 100-01.
16. P.K. Rajan, "Patterns of Cultural Orientation in the Approach to Indian Reality," *Mulk Raj Anand*, 91.
17. Balarama Gupta, 80.
18. H.M. Williams, *Studies in Modern Indian Fiction in English*, 45.
19. *Ibid.*, 46.

20. S.C. Harrex, *The Fire and the Offering*, 139.
21. Saros Cowasjee, *So Many Freedoms*, 159.
22. K. Venkata Reddy, *Major Indian Novelists*, 33-34.

SELECT BIBLIOGRAPHY

PRIMARY SOURCES

Novels by Mulk Raj Anand

Across the Black Waters. New Delhi: Vision Books Private Limited, 1978.

The Big Heart. New Delhi: Arnold Heinemann Publishers (India) Pvt. Ltd., 1980.

The Bubble. New Delhi: Arnold Heinemann Publishers Pvt. Ltd., 1984.

Death of a Hero. New Delhi: Arnold Heinemann Publishers Pvt. Ltd., 1985.

Gauri. New Delhi: Arnold Heinemann Publishers Pvt. Ltd., 1981.

Lament on the Death of a Master of Arts. Delhi: Hind Pocket Books Pvt. Ltd., 1967.

Morning Face. New Delhi: Arnold Heinemann Publishers Pvt. Ltd., 1968.

Pilpali Sahib: The Story of a Big Ego in a Small Boy. New Delhi: Arnold Publishers, 1990.

Private Life of an Indian Prince: London: Asia Publishing House, 1986.

Seven Summers. New Delhi: Arnold Heinemann Publishers Pvt. Ltd., 1987.

The Sword and the Sickle. New Delhi: Arnold Heinemann Publishers Pvt. Ltd., 1984.

Two Leaves and a Bud. New Delhi: Arnold Heinemann Publishers Pvt. Ltd., 1981.

Untouchable. New Delhi: Arnold Heinemann Publishers Pvt. Ltd., 1970.

The Village. New Delhi: Arnold Heinemann Publishers Pvt. Ltd., 1984.

Non-Fictional Books by Mulk Raj Anand

Apology for Heroism. New Delhi: Arnold Heinemann Publishers Pvt. Ltd., 1984.

Author to Critic: The Letters of Mulk Raj Anand to Saros Cowasjee. Ed. Saros Cowasjee. Calcutta: Writers Workshop, 1973.

Conversations in Bloomsbury. New Delhi: Arnold Heinemann Publishers Pvt. Ltd., 1981.

The Dancing Foot. Delhi: Publication Division, Ministry of Information and Broadcasting, Govt. of India, 1957.

Hindu View of Art. London: George Allen and Unwin, 1933.

Homage to Tagore. Sangam Publishers, 1946.

Humanism of Jawahar Lal Nehru: Nehru Memorial Lectures. Calcutta: Visva Bharati, 1978.

Is there a Contemporary Indian Civilization? Bombay: Asia Publishing House, 1963.

Lines Written to an Indian Air. Bombay: Nalanda Publications, 1949.

Little Plays of Mahatma Gandhi. New Delhi: Arnold Publishers, 1991.

On Education. Bombay: Hind Kitabs, 1947.

Roots and Flowers. Dharwar: Karnatak University Publication, 1972.

The Third Eye: A Lecture on the Appreciation of Art. Chandigarh: Research Bulletin (Arts) of the University of Punjab, Fine Arts Series No. 1, 1963.

Articles by Mulk Raj Anand

"Art is not Life and Transformation of Nature in Art," *Critical Thought: An Anthology of 20th Century Indian English Essays.* Ed. S.K. Desai and G.N. Devi. New Delhi: Sterling Publishers Pvt. Ltd.

"The Concept of an Asian Mind." *Contemporary Indian Literature,* Vol. IV, No. 10, Oct. 1964.

"Creative Process." *Littcrit*, Vol. 4, No. I, June 1978.

"Gorky's Contribution to the Contemporary World Literature." *Contemporary Indian Literature*, Vol. VIII, No. 22, May 1968.

"How I became a Writer." *Contemporary Indian Literature*, Vol. V, Nos. 11-12, Nov.-Dec. 1965.

"In Praise of Bharata Natyam." *Bharat Natyam: Indian Classical Dance Art*. Bombay: Marg Publications, 1979.

"Intellectuals, the Society and the State." Triveni, Vol. XLII, No. 3, Oct.-Dec. 1973.

"Modernism in Indian and Soviet Literature." *Contemporary Indian Literature*, Vol. V, Issues 11-12, Nov.-Dec. 1965.

"A Note on Henry James and the Art of Fiction in India." *Commonwealth Quarterly*, Vol. 2, No. 7, June 1978.

"A Note on Modern Fiction." *Indian Literature*, Vol. VIII, No. I, 1965.

"Old Myths and New Myths: Recital Versus Novel." *The Banasthali Patrika*, No. 13, July 1969.

"Pigeon Indian: Some Notes on Indian English Writing." *Aspects of Indian Writing in English*. Ed. M.K. Naik. Delhi: Macmillan Co. of India Ltd., 1979.

"Profile to Attia Hosain." *Commonwealth Quarterly*, Vol. 3, No. 9, Dec. 1978.

"Reflections on the Novel." *Commonwealth Literature: Problems of Response*. Ed. C.D. Narsimhaiah. Madras: Macmillan Co. of India Ltd., 1979.

"Reviewing." *Indian Author: Quarterly Journal of Authors Guild of India*, Vol. 5, No. 2, April-June 1980.

"The Rhythms of Indian Life—On Indian English. "*Research and Criticism: Papers Presented to Dr S.P. Adinarayan*. Ed. N. Radhakrishnan. Annamalai University Research Scholars Association, 1975.

"Roots and Flowers: Content and Form in *Untouchable* and *Kanthapura*." *Littcrit*, Vol. 8, No. 1, June 1982.

"Some Reflections on Willam Golding and the Novel Today." *The Indian Literary Review*, Vol. III, No. 1, Jan. 1985.

"Speech." *Soviet Review*, Vol. X, No. 21, March 26, 1968.

"The Story of My Experiment with a White Lie." *Critical Essays on Indian Writing in English*. Ed. M.K. Naik *et al.* Dharwar: Karnatak University Press, 1968.

"Task Before the Writers." *Contemporary Indian Literature*, Vol. II, No. 9, 1963.

"Trends in the Modern Indian Novel."*Journal of Indian Writing in English*, Vol. I, No. I, 1973.

"What Shakespeare Means to Me?" *Contemporary Indian Literature*, Vol. V, May 1965.

"Why I Write?" *Perspectives on Mulk Raj Anand*. Ed. K.K. Sharma. Ghaziabad: Vimal Prakashan, 1978.

Personal letters of Mulk Raj Anand to the author.

SECONDARY SOURCES

Critical Works on Mulk Raj Anand

Mulk Raj Anand: A Home Appraisal. Ed. Atma Ram. Hoshiarpur: Chaarvak Publications, 1988.

Berry, Margaret. *Mulk Raj Anand: The Man and the Novelist*. Amsterdam: Oriental Press, 1971.

Cowasjee, Saros. *So Many Freedoms: A Study of the Major Fiction of Mulk Raj Anand*. New Delhi: Oxford University Press, 1977.

Fisher, Marlene. *The Wisdom of the Heart: A Study of the Works of Mulk Raj Anand*. New Delhi: Sterling Publishers Pvt. Ltd., 1985.

Gupta, Balarama, G.S. *Mulk Raj Anand: A Study of His Novels in Humanist Perspective*. Bareilly: Prakash Book Depot, 1974.

Lindsay, Jack. *The Elephant and the Lotus: A Study of the Novels of Mulk Raj Anand*. Bombay: Kutub Popular, 1965.

Naik, M.K. *Mulk Raj Anand*. Delhi: Arnold Heinemann Publishers Pvt. Ltd., 1973.

Niven, Alastair. *The Yoke of Pity: A Study in the Fictional Writings of Mulk Raj Anand.* New Delhi: Arnold Heinemann Publishers Pvt. Ltd., 1978.

Paul, Premila. *The Novels of Mulk Raj Anand: A Thematic Study.* New Delhi: Sterling Publishers Pvt. Ltd., 1984.

Rajan, P.K. *Studies in Mulk Raj Anand.* New Delhi: Abhinav Publications, 1986.

Mulk Raj Anand: A Home Appraisal. Hoshiarpur: Chaarvak Publications, 1988.

Riemenschneider, Dieter. *An Ideal of Man in the Novels of Mulk Raj Anand.* Bombay: Kutub Popular, 1967.

Sharma, Ambuj Kumar. *The Theme of Exploitation in the Novels of Mulk Raj Anand.* New Delhi: H.K. Publishers and Distributers, 1990.

Perspectives on Mulk Raj Anand. Ed. K.K. Sharma. Ghaziabad: Vimal Prakashan, 1978.

Sinha, Krishna Nandan. *Mulk Raj Anand.* New Delhi: Kalyani Publishers, 1989. The book was first published in 1972 by Twayne Publishers.

Contemporary Indian Literature, Vol. V, Nos. 11-12, Nov.-Dec. 1965. (Special Issue on Mulk Raj Anand).

Kakatiya Journal of English Studies, Vol. II, No. I, 1977. (Special Issue on Mulk Raj Anand).

Other Books, Chapters, and Articles on Mulk Raj Anand

Abidi, S.J.H. *Mulk Raj Anand's Coolie: A Critical Study.* Bareilly: Prakash Book Depot, 1976.

——. *Mulk Raj Anand's Untouchable: A Critical Study.*

Agnihotri, G.N. "Mulk Raj Anand—His Progressive Proletarianism." *Indian Life and Problems in the Novels of Mulk Raj Anand, Raja Rao and R.K. Narayan.* Meerut: Shalabh Book House, 1984.

Agnihotri, H.L. "Gandhian Ethos in Mulk Raj Anand." *Journal of Literature and Aesthetics,* Vol. VIII, No. I, Jan. 1983.

Asnani, Shyam M. "A Critique of Mulk Raj Anand's Literary Creed." *Commonwealth Quarterly,* Vol. 4, No. 13, Dec.

1979. Later on published in *New Dimensions of Indian-English Novel.* Ed. Shyam M. Asnani. Delhi: Doaba House, 1987.

——. "The Indian Princes: Their Portrayal in the Indo-English Novel." *Critical Response to Indian-English Fiction.* Delhi: Mittal Publications, 1985.

——. "Socio-political concerns in the Novels of Dr Mulk Raj Anand." *Triveni,* Vol. XLV, No. I, April-June 1976.

Atma Ram. "Folk Elements in Anand's Novels." *Essays on Indian English Literature.* Aurangabad: Chaarvak Publications, 1988.

Badal, R.K. "Mulk Raj Anand." *Indo Anglian Literature: An Outline.* Bareilly: Prakash Book Depot, 1975.

Bais, H.S.S. "An Endless Search: A Psychoanalytical Study of Ananta in Mulk Raj Anand's *The Big Heart.*" *Indian Fiction in English: Problems and Promises.* Ed. R.S. Pathak. New Delhi: Northern Book Centre, 1990.

Bhatnagar, K.C. "Mulk Raj Anand: Poetic Realism to Protest." *Realism in Major Indo-English Fiction.* Bareilly: Prakash Book Depot, 1980.

Bhattacharya, Binay Krishna. "*Two Leaves and a Bud*: Truth and Fiction." *Kakatiya Journal of English Studies,* Vol. II, No. I, 1977.

Chandra, Suresh. "A Sarvodayee Saint: Mulk Raj Anand." *Culture and Criticism.* Delhi: B.R. Publishing Corporation, 1987.

——. "Social Conscience in the Novels of Mulk Raj Anand." *English Studies in India.* University of Kashmir, April 1985.

Chatterjee, Debjani. "Gandhi's Influence on Anand and his Fiction." *Kakatiya Journal of English Studies,* Vol. II, No. I, 1977.

Chinneswararao, G.J. "Anand's *Private Life of an Indian Prince* and Malgonkar's *The Princes*: A Comparison." *The Journal of Indian Writing in English,* Vol. 4, No. I, Jan. 1976.

Cowasjee, Saros. *Coolie: An Assessment.* Delhi: Oxford Uni. Press, 1976.

——. "Mulk Raj Anand and His Critics." *Banasthali Patrika*, Vol. IV, No. 1, Jan. 1969.

——. "Mulk Raj Anand: Princes and Proletarians." *The Journal of Commonwealth Literature*, No. 5, July 1968.

——. "Mulk Raj Anand: The Fusion of History and Fiction." *Subjects Worthy Fame: Essays on Commonwealth Literature in Honour of H.H. Anniah Gowda*. Ed. L. McLeod. New Delhi: Sterling Publishers Pvt. Ltd., 1989.

——. "Mulk Raj Anand's *Untouchable*: *An Appraisal*." *Indo-English Literature: A Collection of Critical Essays*. Ed. K.K. Sharma. Ghaziabad: Vimal Prakashan, 1977.

Dhawan, R.K. "Mulk Raj Anand: *Coolie*." *Major Indian Novels: An Evaluation*. Ed. N.S. Pradhan. New Delhi: Arnold Hienemann Publishers Pvt. Ltd., 1985.

Dwivedi, S.C. "Existentialism in Anand's *Across the Black Waters*." *Indian Fiction in English: Problems and Promises*. Ed. R.S. Pathak. New Delhi: Northern Book Centre, 1990.

Dutt, Prabhat Kumar."Mulk Raj Anand in Relation to Tagore, Prem Chand and Sarat Chatterji." *Contemporary Indian Literature*, Vol. V, Nos. 11-12, Nov.-Dec. 1965.

Fisher, Marlene."The Art of Self and the Self of Art: Mulk Raj Anand's *Confession of a Lover*." *Explorations in Modern Indo-English Fiction*. Ed. R.K. Dhawan. Chandigarh: Bahri Publications Pvt. Ltd., 1982.

Gupta, Balarama G.S. "The Humanism of Dr Mulk Raj Anand." *Contemporary Indian Literature*, Vol. VIII, No. 3, August 1967.

Harrex, S.C. *The Fire and the Offering*, Vol. I. Calcutta: Writers Workshop, 1977.

Hemenway, Stephen Ignatius. "Pioneers of Indo-Anglian Novel: Mulk Raj Anand." *The Novel of India, Vol. II: Indo-Anglian Novel*. Calcutta: Writers Workshop, 1975.

Iyengar, Srinivasa K.R. "Mulk Raj Anand." *Indian Writing in English*. 1963; rpt. New Delhi: Sterling Publishers Pvt. Ltd., 1983.

Jha, Rama. "Mulk Raj Anand: The Champion of Gandhian Humanism." *Gandhian Thought and Indo-Anglian Novelists.* Delhi: Chanakya Publications, 1983.

Kaushik, R.K. "Red, Brown and Grey—Ideological Commitment in Mulk Raj Anand's Novels." *Perspectives on Mulk Raj Anand.* Ed. K.K. Sharma. Ghaziabad: Vimal Prakashan, 1978.

Kher, Inder Nath. "Mulk Raj Anand: Encounter with Dark Passion." *The Journal of Indian Writing in English,* Vol. II, No. 2, July 1983.

Lindsay, Jack. "Mulk Raj Anand." *Kakatiya journal of English Studies,* Vol. II, No. I, 1977.

"Mulk Raj Anand: A Study." *Contemporary Indian Literature,* Vol. V, Issues 11-16, Nov.-Dec. 1965.

Mathur, O.P. "Two Modern Versions of the Sita Myth: Narayan and Anand." *The Journal of Commonwealth Literature,* Vol. XXI, No. 1, 1986.

Mehta, P.P. "Mulk Raj Anand—the Novelist of the Underdog." *Indo-Anglian Fiction: An Assessment.* Bareilly: Prakash Book Depot, 1968.

Mukherjee, Meenakshi. "Beyond the Village: An Aspect of Mulk Raj Anand." *Critical Essays on Indian Writing in English.* Ed. M.K. Naik *et al.* Dharwar: Karnatak University, 1968.

——. *The Twice Born Fiction.* New Delhi: Arnold Heinemann Publishers Pvt. Ltd., 1971.

Murthy, Laxmana S. "Bakha: An Existential Analysis." *Kakatiya Journal of English Studies,* Vol. II, No. I, 1977.

Murthy Suryanarayan, K.V. *Kohinoor in the Crown: Critical Studies in Indian Engl ish Literature.* New Delhi: Sterling Publishers Pvt. Ltd., 1968.

——. "The Motif of Virtue in Dr Mulk Raj Anand's Novels." *Contemporary Indian Literature,* Vol. VI, Jan. 1966.

Naik, M.K. "The Achievement of Mulk Raj Anand." *Critical Essays on Indian Writing in English.* Ed. M.K. Naik *et al.* Madras: Macmillan Co. of India Ltd., 1972.

——. "Gandhiji and Indian Writing in English." *Critical Essays on Indian Writing in English*. Ed. M.K. Naik *et al.* Madras: Macmillan Co. of India Ltd., 1972.

Narayanan, Gomathi. "The Princes who were Pawns." *The Sahibs and the Natives: A Study of Guilt and Pride in Anglo-Indian and Indo-Anglian Novels.* Delhi: Chanakya Publications, 1986.

Narsimhaiah, C.D. "Mulk Raj Anand—the Novel of Human Centrality." *The Swan and the Eagle.* Simla: Indian Institute of Advanced Studies, 1969.

Nasini Reza Ahmed. "Untouchable: Anand's Language of Compassionate Objectivity." *The Language of Mulk Raj Anand, Raja Rao and R.K. Narayan.* Delhi: Capital Publishing House, 1989.

Niven, Alastair. "The Lalu Trilogy of Mulk Raj Anand." *Kakatiya Journal of English Studies,* Vol. II, No. I, 1977.

Pant, M.C. "Mulk Raj Anand—The Man." *Contemporary Indian Literature,* Vol. V, Issues 11-12, Nov.-Dec. 1965.

Parry, Graham. "Anand, Orwell and War." *Explorations in Modern Indo-English Fiction.* Ed. R.K. Dhawan. Chandigarh: Bahri Publications Pvt. Ltd., 1982.

Paul, Premila "Anand's *Lament on the Death of a Master of Arts*—A Thematic Analysis." *The Journal of Indian Writing in English,* Vol. 6, No. 2, July 1978.

——. "Major Themes in the Novels of Mulk Raj Anand." *Perspectives on Indian Fiction in English.* Ed. M.K. Naik Madras: Macmillan Co. of India Ltd., 1979.

Pontes, Hilda. "Anand's Untouchable: A Classic in Experimentation of Theme and Technique." *Studies in Indian Fiction in English.* Ed. Balarama Gupta. Gulbarga: JIWE Publications, 1987.

——. "Mulk Raj Anand Criticism." Unpublished. The doctoral thesis of Hilda Pontes contains a very comprehensive bibliography of criticism on Anand.

——. "A Select Checklist of Critical Responses to Mulk Raj

Anand's *Untouchable.*" *Journal of Commonwealth Literature,* Vol. XXIII, No. I, 1988.

——. "A Young Rebel's Growing up." *Literary Half-Yearly,* 1987.

Radhakrishan, N. "The Image of Gandhi in Indo-Anglian Novels."

Raizada, Harish."Ethics and Aesthetics of Mulk Raj Anand." *Perspectives on Mulk Raj Anand.* Ed. K.K. Sharma. Ghaziabad: Vimal Prakashan, 1978.

——. "Writers from Northern India: Mulk Raj Anand." *The Lotus and the Rose.* Aligarh: Faculty of Arts, A.M.U., 1978.

Ramamurti, K.S. *Rise of the Indian Novel in English.* New Delhi: Sterling Publishers Pvt. Ltd., 1987.

Reddy, Venkata K. "Anand's *A Master of Arts.*" *The Journal of Indian Writing in English,* Vol. 5, No. 1, July 1977.

——. "Cruelty of Man to Man: Mulk Raj Anand's *Two Leaves and a Bud.*" *Kakatiya Journal of English Studies,* Vol. VIII, 1987-88.

——. "Why don't I Die?: *Coolie.*" *Major Indian Novelists.* New Delhi: Prestige Books, 1990.

Riemenschneider, Dieter. "Alienation in the Novels of Mulk Raj Anand." *Perspectives on Mulk Raj Anand.* Ed. K.K. Sharma. Ghaziabad: Vimal Prakashan, 1978.

——. "Mulk Raj Anand: *Confession of a Lover.*" *Indian Author.* Vol., Jan.-Mar. 1977.

Robertson, R.T. "Untouchable: As an Archetypal Novel." *Kakatiya Journal of English Studies.* Vol. II, No. I, 1977.

Shivpuri, Jagdish. "Mulk Raj Anand's *The Road*: An Interpretation." *Littcrit,* Vol. 12, Nos. 1-2, 1986.

Singh, Mina Surjit. "Female Perspective in the Fiction of Mulk Raj Anand." *Feminism and Recent Fiction in English.* Ed. Sushila Singh. New Delhi: Prestige Books, 1991.

Singh, R.S. "From Resentment to Social Protest: Mulk Raj Anand." *Indian Novel in English.* New Delhi: Arnold Heinemann Publishers Pvt. Ltd., 1977.

Singh, Satyanarain. "Yoke of Pity: The Poet in Anand's Novels." *Kakatiya Journal of English Studies*, Vol. II, No. I, 1977.

Srinath, C.N. "Pariah at Cross-Roads: Image as Symbol of Regeneration in Indian Fiction in English."

Tucker, Martin. "Indian Subcontinent Writers: Mulk Raj Anand." *Modern Commonwealth Literature*. Ed. John H. Ferras and Martin Tucker. New York: Frederick Ungar Publishing Co., 1977.

Varalakshmi, P. "Anand's *Lament on the Death of a Master of Arts*." *The Journal of Indian Writing in English*. Vol. 7, No. 2, July 1979.

Verghese, Paul."The Proletarian Humanism of Mulk Raj Anand." *Problems of the Indian Creative Writer in English*. Bombay: Somaiya Publications Pvt. Ltd., 1971.

——. "Raja Rao, Mulk Raj Anand, Narayan and Others." *Indian Writing Today*, Vol. II, No. 4, Oct.-Dec.1968.

Williams, H.M. "The Doomed Hero." *Three Contemporary Novelists*. Ed. R.K. Dhawan. New Delhi: Classicial Publishing Co., 1985.

——. *Indo-Anglian Literature* 1800-1970: *A Survey*. Bombay: Orient Longman Ltd., 1976.

——. "Mulk Raj Anand: Realism and Politics." *Studies in Modern Indian Fiction in English*, Vol. I. Calcutta: Writers Workshop, 1973.

Zaheer, Sajjad. "Mulk Raj Anand." *Contemporary Indian Literature*, Vol. V, Nos. 11-12, Nov.-Dec. 1965.

General

Allen, Walter. *The English Novel: A Short Critical History*. Harmondsworth: Penguin Books Ltd., 1954.

Allott, Miriam. *Novelists on the Novel*, 1959; rpt. London: Routledge and Kegan Paul, 1977.

Arnold, Matthew. *Essays in Criticism*. Ed. S.R. Littlewood. London: Macmillan and Co. Ltd., 1964.

Booth, Wayne C. *Rhetoric of Fiction.* Chicago: Chicago Uni. Press, 1964.

Dass, Jermani Diwan. *Maharaja.* Bombay: Allied Publishers Pvt. Ltd., 1969.

Harvey, W.J. *Character and the Novel.* New York: Cornell University Press, 1965.

Indian Journal of American Studies (Special Issue on Survey of Theory), Vol. 18, No. I, Winter 1988. Hyderabad: American Studies Research Centre, 1988.

Joyce, James. *A Portrait of the Artist as a Young Man.* Harmondsworth: Penguin Books Ltd., 1960.

Lodge, David. *20th Century Literary Criticism.* London: Longman Group Ltd., 1971.

Malgonkar, Manohar. *The Princes.* London: Hamish Hamilton Ltd., 1963.

Menon, V.P. *The Story of the Integration of the Indian States.* Bombay: Orient Longman Ltd., 1956.

Murdoch, Iris. "Against Dryness." *Encounter*, 1961. First published by Philip Henderson, *The Novel Today.* London: The Bodley Head, 1936.

Nehru, Jawahar Lal. *An Autobiography.* Bombay: Allied Publishers Pvt. Ltd., 1962.

Sartre, Jean Paul. *Existentialism and Humanism.* Translation and Introduction by Philip Mairet. London: Methuen and Co. Ltd., 1948.

Selden, Raman. *The Theory of Criticism: From Plato to the Present: A Reader.* London: Longman Group (UK) Ltd., 1988.

Watt, Inn. *The Rise of the Novel: Studies in Defoe, Richardson and Fielding.* 1957; rpt. Harmondsworth: Penguin Books Ltd., 1979.

Wellek, Rene and Austin Warren. *Theory of Literature.* New York: Penguin Books Ltd., 1986.

INDEX